THE SCOTTISH ENLIGHTENMENT & EARLY VICTORIAN ENGLISH SOCIETY

ANAND C. CHITNIS

CROOM HELM
London ● Sydney ● Dover, New Hampshire

©1986 Anand C. Chitnis
Croom Helm Ltd, Provident House, Burrell Row,
Beckenham, Kent BR3 1AT
Croom Helm Australia Pty Ltd, Suite 4, 6th Floor,
64-76 Kippax Street, Surry Hills, NSW 2010, Australia

British Library Cataloguing in Publication Data
Chitnis, Anand C.
   The Scottish Enlightenment and early Victorian
English society.
   1. Scotland—Intellectual life—18th century
   2. England—Social conditions—19th century
   I. Title
   941.107   DA812

ISBN 0-85664-580-X

Croom Helm, 51 Washington Street, Dover,
New Hampshire 03820, USA

Library of Congress Cataloging in Publication Data
Chitnis, Anand C.
   The Scottish enlightenment and early Victorian
English Society.

   Bibliography: p.
   Includes index.
   1. Scotland—Intellectual life.   2. Philosophy,
Scottish—18th century.   3. Enlightenment.
I. Title.
DA812.C485   1986   941.1   85-22379
ISBN 0-87664-580-X

Printed and bound in Great Britain by
Biddles Ltd, Guildford and King's Lynn

CONTENTS

For Bernice

PREFACE

The present study is concerned to delineate certain ideas of the so-called Scottish Enlightenment and the education that purveyed them; it considers, too, those who taught and received that learning and how it was taken to England where, through the mediation of individuals, it contributed to familiar and unfamiliar areas of historical development. The concentration is on social thought and medical practice, high Whig politics and political economy as well as the professional experience and socio-cultural significance of Scottish-trained physicians.

The book partly results from the assistance of the then Social Science Research Council, who awarded me a grant from 1974 to 1976 to study 'The Scottish Enlightenment and the Evolution of Victorian Society', and of the University of Stirling who awarded me study-leave in the autumn of 1979. I am also indebted to Professor R.H. Campbell for the time he gave so generously to reading and commenting on various versions of chapters; to Dr David Bebbington; to Mrs Carolyn Rowlinson and various of her colleagues in the University of Stirling Library; to Miss Margaret Hendry for a high degree of both tolerance and efficiency in processing the words of my manuscript; and to the librarians who have kindly permitted me to quote from documents in their keeping.

1 THE SCOTTISH ENLIGHTENMENT: THE TEACHING AND THE PROFESSORS

I

The phrase 'Scotch knowledge' was used in the spring of 1809 by the future prime minister, Lord John Russell, in a letter to his father, the Duke of Bedford, from the Iberian Peninsula whence he had been sent after leaving school in the company of Lord and Lady Holland. He was replying to the suggestion that on his return he should study in Edinburgh:

> I do not know what you will think best for me afterwards; but the thing I should most dislike, and, I think, least profit by, would be an endeavour to acquire Scotch knowledge in a Scotch town. Political economy may surely be studied in England. As for metaphysics, I cannot even understand the word.[1]

This apparent denigration of 'Scotch knowledge' on the part of an immature youth who had been to Spain and Portugal but who still thought British civilisation ended north of Woburn, partly indicates what was considered the distinctive content of Scottish university education. Those of a wider outlook would also have specified medicine and its auxiliary sciences as Scottish specialities since at Edinburgh medicine was the university's leading pedagogic sector. Political economy, moral philosophy, medicine and allied subjects constituted distinctive areas of teaching imparted to students at Scottish universities in the later eighteenth and early nineteenth centuries.

During the eighteenth century, Scotland had participated in the European-wide movement known as the Enlightenment. Scottish philosophers, scientists and doctors made distinguished and often original contributions to their respective fields of interest. This essay argues that an appreciation of eighteenth-century Scottish writing and teaching on particular aspects of man and society, its permeation of the arts syllabus in Scottish universities, and of Scotland's professional approach to medical education at the time, highlights a neglected but significant dimension of areas of English history in the first half of the nineteenth century. The dimension is significant because of the sub-

1

sequent activities of students who had been exposed to the distinctive education.

II

In their concern for man and society, writers of the Scottish Enlightenments displayed an historical approach. Most philosophers accepted that human society had passed through four sequential phases, characterised by their economic base, the primitive, the pastoral, the agrarian and the commercial. Two noted Scottish literati, Adam Smith and John Millar, summarised this historical and economic analysis — Smith in his lectures on justice, and Millar in his *Origin of the Distinction of Ranks*. First, Smith:

> The four stages of society are hunting, pasturage, farming, and commerce. If a number of persons were shipwrecked on a desert island their first sustenance would be from the fruits which the soil naturally produced, and the wild beasts which they could kill. As these could not at all times be sufficient, they came at last to tame some of the wild beasts that they might always have them at hand. In process of time even these would not be sufficient; and as they saw the earth naturally produce considerable quantities of vegetables of its own accord they would think of cultivating it so that it might produce more of them. Hence agriculture . . . The age of commerce naturally succeeds that of agriculture. As men could not confine themselves to one species of labour, they would naturally exchange the surplus of their own commodity for that of another of which they stood in need.

Then his pupil, Millar:

> [Man's] first efforts are naturally calculated to increase the means of subsistence, by catching or ensnaring wild animals, or by gathering the spontaneous fruits of the earth; and the experience acquired in the exercise of these employments, is apt, successively, to point out the methods of taming and rearing cattle, and of cultivating the ground. According as men have been successful in these great improvements, and find less difficulty in the attainment of bare necessaries, their prospects are gradually enlarged, their appetites and desires are more and more awakened and called forth in pursuit

of the several conveniences of life; and the various branches of manufacture, together with commerce, its inseparable attendant, and with science and literature, the natural offspring of ease and affluence, are introduced, and brought to maturity.[2]

As society became more settled, when cattle were herded or crops cultivated, certain social features became apparent. The most important feature of society was the possession and influence of property. Whether by fortune or by industry, inequalities of property-ownership would arise among individuals and lead to the dependence, as servants or employees, of other members of society upon property-owners. Inequalities of property-ownership also led to distinctions of dignity, rank and power between individuals. Millar discerned that

> The poor are naturally dependent upon the rich, from whom they derive their subsistence; and, according to the accidental differences of wealth possessed by individuals, a subordination of ranks is gradually introduced, and different degrees of power and authority are assumed without opposition, by particular persons or bestowed upon them by the general voice of society.[3]

Possessors of property could also transmit relationships of dependence to their heirs and thus perpetuate distinctions and dependence in subsequent generations:

> As the superior fortune which is . . . acquired by a single person is apt to remain with his posterity, it creates a train of dependence in those who have been connected with the possessor; and the influence which it occasions is gradually augmented, and transmitted from one generation to another.[4]

It was also clear from the historical approach of the Scottish Enlightenment that the political arrangements of society would be at their least sophisticated in the primitive phase and become increasingly elaborate as society advanced in wealth and possessions. The philosophers pointed to property as the principal source of political authority: 'Till there be property there can be no government', wrote Adam Smith, 'the very end of which is to secure wealth, and to defend the rich from the poor.' John Millar's view was:

> From the acquisition of landed possessions, which by their nature

are less capable than moveables of being defended by the vigilance and personal prowess of the possessor, the necessity of the public interposition, and of public regulations for the security of property, must have been more universally felt.[5]

The historian, William Robertson, followed the dictum, 'upon discovering in what state property was at any particular period, we may determine with precision what was the degree of power possessed by the King or by the nobility at that juncture.' Once government was established the property-owners proceeded to frame law: 'where the idea of private property is incomplete, and no criminal jurisdiction is established, there is hardly any function of internal government to exercise.'[6] As Smith so succinctly expressed it:

> Civil government, so far as it is instituted for the security of property, is in reality instituted for the defence of the rich against the poor, or of those who have some property against those who have none at all.[7]

The ownership of property, with its accompanying political significance, was subject to fluctuation between and within each economic phase. Millar exemplified the development in his discussion of the lesser barons and their place in Parliament which declined in the 11th year of Edward I's reign: 'In consequence of the progressive alienation and division of landed property their personal influence was continually sinking, while that of the mercantile people was rising in the same proportion'.[8] David Hume perceived that in the commercial phase authority and consideration were drawn to the 'middling rank of men': 'They covet equal laws, which may secure their property, and preserve them from monarchical, as well as aristocratical tyranny.'[9] In Millar's view, superior wealth dominated the commercial phase: a landed gentleman could dissipate his fortune on the luxuries and refinements now available without proportionately adding to his income:

> His estate therefore, being more and more incumbered with debts, is at length alienated, and brought into the possession of the frugal and industrious merchant, who, by success in trade, has been enabled to buy it, and who is desirous of obtaining that rank and consequence which landed property is capable of bestowing. The posterity, however, of this new proprietor, having adopted the manners of the landed gentry, are again led, in a few generations, to squander their

estate, with a heedless extravagance equal to the parsimony and activity by which it was acquired.

Consequently,

opulent families are quickly reduced to indigence; and their place is supplied by professional people from lower orders; who by the purchase of land, endeavour to procure that distinction which was the end of their labours.[10]

Two remaining points of interest in the social philosophy of the Scottish Enlightenment merit consideration here: the relationship between human circumstances and social institutions and the division of labour. As is clear from the last example, writers of the Scottish Enlightenment were keen to show the evolution of society, how the institutions of society adapted to the changing social and economic circumstances of mankind. No one was clearer on the subject than John Millar. It could not be imagined, he asserted,

that a government can be so contrived as, for ages, to remain equally suited to a nation whose condition and circumstances are perpetually changing. As the husbandman varies his mode of culture and management, according to the meliorations of the soil, and to the alterations in the state of his farm, or of the markets, the legislator must accommodate his regulations to the progressive changes in the condition of the people for whom they are intended, to their progress in manufactures and commerce, their increase in opulence and their advances in luxury or in refinement.

Millar gave instances from history, the Wittenagemote in the Anglo-Saxon era, for instance, whose constitution and procedure were altered at least partly by progressive changes in the state of property and the circumstances of the people, and the charters of the reigns of William I to Edward I. While these charters were not intended to confer liberties on the common people, such liberties were eventually secured by the peasantry and others of low rank as a result of their industry so that they were admitted to the same privileges as had been claimed by men of independent fortunes:

The limitations of arbitrary power, which had been calculated chiefly to promote the interest of the nobles, were thus, by a change of circumstances, rendered equally advantageous to the whole community as if they had originally proceeded from the most exalted spirit of patriotism.[11]

As for the division of labour, discussions of the subject are commonplace in the writers of the Scottish Enlightenment, especially Smith and Millar but also Adam Ferguson. One feature of the sequential phases was an increase of wealth, and one of the ways in which wealth was increased was by the way in which labour was organised. The writers diagnosed that division of labour posed problems for which they proposed solutions. They agreed that the benefits were obvious – greater volume of production, better quality products, greater profits. The system did, however, operate against the social spirit that was natural to man – 'society is made to consist of parts, of which none is animated with the spirit of society itself,' wrote Adam Ferguson.[12] Smith agreed:

> [Man's] dexterity at his own trade seems . . . to be acquired at the expence of his intellectual, social and martial virtues. But in every improved and civilized society this is the state into which the labouring poor, that is the great body of the people, must necessarily fall unless government take some pains to prevent it.[13]

In addition, trades in an advanced society were reduced to simple operations which could be performed by young children, thus removing them from parental authority and encouraging their mob unruliness.[14] For Millar, the mechanics and labourers, who were the most numerous persons in a commercial nation, would be cut off from information, and as their superiors advanced in knowledge, they would become 'involved in a thicker cloud of ignorance and prejudice'. They then were in danger of being duped by their superiors and of being degraded.[15]

Smith had indicated that a government should take some pains to prevent these evils. It was commonly agreed by Smith and Millar that there should be established schools and seminaries of education modelled on different lines from those hitherto available to higher social ranks. For Millar, '[i]t is plainly the interest of the higher ranks to assist in cultivating the minds of the common people, and in restoring to them that knowledge which they may be said to have sacrificed to the general prosperity.' It was also important to make them 'sober and industrious, honest and faithful, affectionate and conscientious in their domestic concerns, peaceable in their manners, and averse from riot and disorder'. Such habits must be taught because to keep the common people in ignorance was absurd, abhorrent and provided only temporary security.[16]

The concentration here has been on selected but important points in the social philosophy of the Scottish Enlightenment. They are selected because they provide intellectual background, because they are relevant to social and political debates in the early nineteenth century, and because key participants in the debates would have been familiar with the arguments rehearsed here, and their familiarity would have enhanced the contribution they were able to make.

III

In their concern for medicine, practitioners in the era of the Scottish Enlightenment displayed a concern for the ancillary sciences, a systematic curriculum and practical care, all of which led to a professional education. Medicine may be viewed as an organised and specialised response to that social instinct in man that had underlain the analysis of the philosophers. The principal seat of development was Edinburgh, where social, economic and political promptings caused the establishment of an elaborate medical school before any other British city. In eighteenth-century London, for example, apprenticeship, walking the wards, and attendance at private medical schools were the means of medical and surgical training, and the teachers invariably came from Edinburgh, Leyden or Paris. Adam Smith once observed of the state of medicine in the south that

> The great success of quacks in England has been altogether owing to the real quackery of the regular physicians. Our regular physicians in Scotland have little quackery, and no quack accordingly has even made his fortune among us.[17]

Scotland conformed to the pattern that prevailed throughout Europe, except for England, of associating medical education with universities as in Edinburgh and, later, Glasgow.

Prior to the eighteenth century, no such education was available even in Scotland. Aspiring doctors travelled to such continental universities as Leyden, Utrecht, Rheims and Angers in order to qualify, and aspiring surgeons served apprenticeships. Increasingly those who had studied in the Netherlands felt the need to establish in Edinburgh the kind of medical school that existed in Leyden, not least because of the chaotic state of Scottish medical practice. They had to confront and gradually overcome the opposition of several interests who felt that the establishment of a college of physicians in particular would infringe their rights. The entrenched opposition of Edinburgh surgeons, with power deriving from their position as an incorporated trade of the city, was pre-eminent: they feared the introduction of a medical hierarchy in which they would be the underlings.

Dutch inspiration was boosted after 1688 when Presbyterian chaplains to the new king, William III, were given key posts at Edinburgh and Glasgow universities, managed to secure funds for their institutions, and sought to model them on Dutch lines. Furthermore, from the early eighteenth century, the Edinburgh town council, the university's patron, began to feel certain pressing economic needs. The city had lost status and trade after the union of the Crowns, but lost even more with the union of Parliaments. Students abroad were additionally felt to be a serious drain on the country's finances, though the Nine Years' War and the War of Spanish Succession served to deter them from continental travel and accentuated the need for educational facilities at home. The combination of the Monro family, who themselves studied in Leyden and who sought to establish a similar school in their native land, and George Drummond, the Edinburgh politician who saw in the university, the medical school and several other projects the required stimulus to the city's economic fortunes and to the union, was more than sufficient to found in Edinburgh a competently-staffed medical school, with a hospital for clinical education, that duly detained Scottish students at home and became a magnet for Englishmen and for others from overseas.[18]

In Glasgow a different situation prevailed because the faculty of physicians and surgeons did not see the educational functions of a university as complementary to their task of licensing, and because the city had no need to boost or supplement its economic life for most of the eighteenth century. Hence, the university medical school developed more slowly than that of Edinburgh, and did not achieve distinction until well into the nineteenth century. Adam Smith, whose own fame has redounded to Glasgow's credit, remarked in 1785: '[I] have no hesitation to recommend the University of Edinburgh in preference to any other. It is at present better provided in Professors than any other Society of the kind that I ever knew; and it is likely soon to be still better provided than at present.'[19]

Intellectually, Scotland had early taken to heart the scientific lessons of Isaac Newton. St Andrews, Edinburgh and Aberdeen all appointed Newtonians as Professors of Mathematics between 1668 and 1725. The Newtonian approach to science, the concern for observation and experiment, had its impact on medicine and the sciences auxiliary to medicine. Scottish medical men undertook research in a wide variety of fields: there was the work of the first Alexander Monro (1697-1767) in anatomy, osteology, lymphatics, neurology and embryology; that of Robert Whytt, Professor of Physiology at Edinburgh 1747-66, in reflex actions, hysteria and tuberculous meningitis; and that of the second Alexander Munro (1733-1817) in nervous physiology and comparative anatomy. In the ancillary sciences, Edinburgh had from the 1670s realised the importance of botany to medicine and had provided a series of botanical gardens. From about the mid-eighteenth century, Glasgow and then Edinburgh witnessed the chemical research of William Cullen (1710-90) and Joseph Black (1728-99). Cullen contributed to the pathology of the nervous system and was led by his work here into the study of heat and cold. Black discovered carbon dioxide in the course of seeking a means to dissolve stones in the bladder, and was stimulated by Cullen into discovering latent and specific heats. The preoccupation with the science of heat contributed not only to James Watt's improvements to the steam-engine, but also to the theory of the earth propounded by Black's close friend, James Hutton. Hutton's theory, more than any other, caused special interest in geology and earth science in Edinburgh from the 1780s to the 1820s.[20]

The result of the practical and intellectual groundwork of the early to mid-eighteenth century was the large-scale development of medicine as a university discipline in Edinburgh and Glasgow. In Edinburgh, nine Chairs associated with medicine were founded between 1705 and 1807 — anatomy (1705), chemistry (1713), midwifery (1726), natural history (1767), materia medica (1768), surgery (1777), clinical surgery (1803), military surgery (1806) and medical jurisprudence (1807). All were occupied by professors with an MD degree, with the exception of the foundation professor of natural history. The Edinburgh faculty of medicine was formally established in 1726. A similar but more modest pattern appeared at Glasgow: a Chair of Medicine was founded in 1713, a lectureship then a Chair of Anatomy in 1720, the celebrated lectureship in chemistry held by Cullen and Black in 1747, a lectureship in materia medica (1765), a lectureship in midwifery (1790), a Chair of Natural History (1807), two Regius Chairs of Surgery and Midwifery (1815) and two Regius Chairs of Botany and Chemistry (1817 and 1818).

It was in 1767 that Edinburgh first enacted solemn statutes for the conferring of medical degrees which, with only slight modifications on eight occasions, lasted until 1833. The statutes required the completion in Edinburgh or another university of a course of six months' study in each of anatomy, surgery, chemistry, botany, materia medica and pharmacy, the theory and practice of medicine, and of clinical medicine in the Royal Infirmary. Midwifery was added to the list in 1825 as was three months' study each of two subjects chosen from practical anatomy, natural history, medical jurisprudence, clinical surgery and military surgery. In 1783, the students' course of study was fixed at three years in length including at least one year in Edinburgh so 'that the professors may be acquainted with their character, conduct, and diligence in prosecuting their studies'. In 1825, the course of study was lengthened by a year for all students without specific experience.

The prescribed examinations were all to be conducted in Latin and to be rigorous. Until 1811, the first examination, conducted privately in a professor's house, covered all branches of medicine, anatomy, surgery, chemistry, botany, materia medica and pharmacy, theory of medicine and practice of medicine, each professor posing questions to him in order. The candidate was also required to submit a thesis to one of the professors who revised it and subjected it to the consideration of the medical faculty. There then followed an examination in the university library on points not touched in the first examination, the candidate had to explain and illustrate in writing an aphorism of Hippocrates and to answer and comment on a medical question. The cases of two patients were given to the candidate with questions: he was required to illustrate the cases in writing and give a proper solution to each question. Upon a report of the medical faculty on these proceedings and the faculty's approbation of the candidate, the dissertation was published and had to be defended in the common hall of the university against the professors appointed to impugn it. It was not at all unknown for candidates to be remitted to their studies and for a considerable proportion of successful candidates to attend the colleges of medicine several years beyond graduation. No person was admitted as a candidate for a medical degree unless he had attended the clinical lectures.[21]

Despite the appearances conveyed by the regulations, there must be doubt if the view of Adam Smith, expressed to William Cullen in 1774, was any less applicable later. He noted that

Your examination in Edinburgh, I have all reason to believe, is as serious, and perhaps more so than that of any other University in Europe. But when a student has resided a few years among you, has behaved dutifully to all his Professors, and has attended regularly all their lectures, when he comes to his examination, I suspect you are disposed to be as good-natured as other people.[22]

While the requirement of an MD thesis could often be the basis of future research for a graduate, the emphasis on practice was a special feature of medical education in Edinburgh. Such practice took three forms: the use of botanical gardens and museums for teaching purposes, clinical education and the experience given to students in a variety of institutions associated with public health. Botany was more important than chemistry to eighteenth-century medicine because contemporary practice was remedial rather than preventive. Throughout the eighteenth century successive professors were concerned to broaden the university's collection of plants and to use them, along with diagrams and experiments, to illustrate the rival botanical systems, the natural system and Linnaean classification. John Hope, Professor of Botany and Materia Medica (1760-86) encouraged students' interest in plants by awarding an annual gold medal for the best herbarium. The Professors of Materia Medica were also concerned to collect appropriate pharmaceutical apparatus and materia medica to permit demonstrations before the students, and a museum was formed. From 1748, clinical medical lectures were inaugurated on the Leyden model by John Rutherford: he sought to examine patients thoroughly in the sight of students, gave a history of the pertinent disease, indicated its causes and suggested a prognosis. He indicated a cure and how he would cope with the development of new symptoms. Rutherford never claimed to be infallible but he did hope to train students in accurate observations and descriptions of disease.[23]

In time, clinical education became the hallmark of Edinburgh medicine. It was normally taught by four professors in rotation, each taking charge of the clinical wards of the Royal Infirmary for three months every second year, so that the students could be shown a variety of practice. (The academic session was about six months long.) The objectives, as spelled out by Rutherford, remained the same even when the system was well established, with the emphasis on accurate and continual observation. The teaching of clinical surgery, which began privately in Edinburgh in 1786 and was not raised to the status of a Chair until 1803, was not taught on a rota basis but left to one man on the grounds that surgery was a skill to be taught and that the emphasis should be on teaching rather than on involving in the scheme all the practising surgeons of the Infirmary.

The range of experience given to Edinburgh medical students in various institutions was wide, including as it did obstetrics, and work in public dispensaries, and mental and fever hospitals. In the 1760s, one ward of the Infirmary was set aside for up to six maternity cases, and greater numbers of students were given experience of delivering babies. Consequently, in 1792, Alexander Hamilton, Professor of Midwifery 1780-1800, opened a lying-in hospital to satisfy both needs. By 1824, his successor, his son James, had opened a lying-in institution to assist poor married women to have their babies at home because poverty was most acutely felt when a child was due. By means of the institution, such women found a doctor or midwife on hand, as well as appropriate medicines, bed linen and other necessaries. Between 1790 and 1815 the obstetrician John Towers established a lying-in hospital in Glasgow which, though maintained largely at his own expense, he used both for teaching and medical purposes.

Andrew Duncan, Senior, Professor of Physiology, had founded a dispensary in the old town of Edinburgh in 1776. He viewed it as a medical teaching centre which provided different opportunities from the Infirmary. By the 1790s, the dispensary was used as a means of encouraging vaccination against smallpox: pauper children were visited in their homes and inoculation was free. In 1801 a vaccine institution was established in the city and within five years, smallpox was reckoned a rare occurrence even among the poor. The dispensary in the new town was founded in 1815 to attend to those of the poor who were sick, diseased or pregnant, and to give free vaccination to children. It was used especially by expectant mothers since the lying-in institution was not founded until 1824, but in general it provided for the many everyday medical needs of the poorer sections of the community. It made possible visits to patients' homes, and the professors involved in the work of the dispensary insisted on students attending their practice. One physician even divided up the poorer areas of Edinburgh among his students. Another, William Pulteney Alison, Professor of Physiology and Dean of Edinburgh's medical faculty, used his experiences in the new town dispensary for his *Observations on the Management of the Poor in Scotland and its Effects on the Health of the Great Towns* (1840), which attracted the detailed attention of both Edwin Chadwick and Friedrich Engels. Knowledge and experience of public health work was introduced and developed by means of Edinburgh dispensaries.

Two specialised areas may additionally be mentioned. From 1819, a surgical professor, John Thomson, began to lecture on diseases of the eye and, in 1824, he founded an eye dispensary. The other specialised area was mental health: one of the country's leading advocates of enlightened treatment was Andrew Duncan, Senior, who gave his name to the hospital in Edinburgh that bears his name. From 1792 until its foundation in 1807, Duncan called for the erection of a public mental hospital, being moved by the death of the young Scottish poet, Robert Fergusson, who, once removed from his home suffering from delirious mania, could only be placed in the city bedlam. Mental diseases were taught by Alison in his physiology course, not least because he appreciated that many Edinburgh students left to become physicians in mental hospitals. The concern for psychiatry was not confined to the medicals: for example, Dugald Stewart, Professor of Moral Philosophy at Edinburgh (1785-1810), wrote of abnormal psychology in his *Elements of the Philosophy of the Human Mind*, and his interest in the field was known to medical students.

Over a period of about 100 years, a thoroughgoing medical education was established in the Scottish capital during the era of the Enlightenment. The emphasis of that professional education was on effective practical experience and on public health.[24] Social medicine accompanied social philosophy in the university curriculum.

IV

The writings of the philosophers, effective teaching by several professors of arts and medical subjects in the era c. 1780-1820, and the learning acquired by those who sat at those professors' feet, enabled 'Scotch knowledge' to be disseminated in the first half of the nineteenth century. John Millar alone of the major writers taught until his death in 1801 and conveyed a personal impression in addition to that conveyed by his works to his students and to others who came into contact with him. Prior to any consideration of the professors who acted as intermediaries between the concerns of the Scottish Enlightenment and the nineteenth century, some observations require to be made about their impact. It is clear that the hierarchical nature of the medical profession and the authority and confidence that comes with experience conferred an aura on the professors. Consequently, professors of medicine and surgery were often idolised by their students and cults could easily arise.[25]

In arts subjects there are instances of the same phenomenon: here the

Scottish students were often very young and, therefore, impressionable. The content of philosophic teaching must often have gone over their heads and all the students remembered was the manner in which it was delivered. In law, neither of these factors is so true: the professors were not engaged in an area that made them susceptible of worship and the students were not juveniles. Millar, however, was preaching a political message that appealed to idealistic young men in troubled times. The older generation in Scotland, the establishment – whether nobility, gentry, the judges or Kirk leaders – all rallied round the principle of the Royal Prerogative in the face of French revolutionaries, so that the Tory grip on Scotland, manifest especially in Edinburgh, was tight. As in all such eras, certain sections of the universities were suspect: particular professors were reported to the courts for allegedly seditious statements made *ex tempore* in lectures, and students were likewise hauled before university authorities for espousing dangerously liberal causes in their societies' debates. As a later commentator was to discern, '[i]n vain did the exacting spirit of conformity to the tenets in vogue brood over Scotland, while session after session, to fresh relays of eager and delighted listeners, John Millar's eloquence fixed deeply in their minds the principles of free constitutional government.'[26]

So, the hierarchical nature of the medical profession, the impressionable age of some arts students and the cogent teaching of youth, frustrated by the conservatism of their elders and their times, may all contribute to an explanation of the commonplace, fulsome tributes that were paid to some teachers in the last years of the Scottish Enlightenment. It is as well to remember the parallel between the lecture and the sermon, both important features of separate but vital Scottish social institutions that were remembered for their impact. They redounded to the credit (or discredit) of the professor or preacher. What exists is a significant body of tributes to particular teachers. The tributes take numerous forms – poetry, memoirs, reviews, letters, dedications, to list but a few – all testifying to the enormous impact made on their auditors by philosophical, scientific, legal and medical professors, an impact that lingered on well into the adult life of the auditors. While some of the tributes can be laid at the door of nostalgia in advancing years, this is by no means true of all of them.

Three teachers of non-medical subjects stand out: Millar, Dugald Stewart and John Playfair. James Lorimer, Professor of Public Law at Edinburgh University between 1862 and 1890 and a Scottish university reformer in the later nineteenth century, described the trio as 'so instrumental in moulding the modes of thought of the society' to which they belonged, and as 'such powerful agents in determining the subsequent current of affairs'.[27] As can be apprised from Lorimer, the three shared a number of common distinctions, one of the most important of which was political Whiggery.

Like a number of eighteenth-century Scottish literati, John Millar was a son of the manse, but of a well-to-do background. His family had long owned and lived in a country house near Blantyre, where he himself was brought up by a paternal uncle; he later inherited the house and he was always to be found there from mid-May to early November. He only ever visited London twice for short visits in 1774 and 1792. His mother's first cousin was William Cullen, a central contributor to the scientific achievements of the Scottish Enlightenment. Millar went to school in Hamilton and then to Glasgow University on the assumption that he too, would enter the ministry, but he was not attracted by Divinity as much as by the prelections of Adam Smith whose lectures he first attended in 1751, and by the philosophic discussions and the library of Lord Kames in whose house he was living in the late 1750s while tutoring Kames' son. He practised briefly at the Edinburgh bar in 1759 and dedicated his bar examination *disputatio* to Kames, being called in 1760. Kames was instrumental in his being allowed to plead at the age of 25 in the Inner House of the Court of Session before the full assembled court of fifteen judges, and it was in Kames' house that he came to know the philosopher David Hume. He so impressed Hume that later Hume sent his eponymous nephew (Baron Hume of Scottish legal fame) to study under Millar.

Kames and Smith were also his principal supporters for the Glasgow Chair of Civil Law, which he secured in 1761 and held until his death from pleurisy 40 years later. A university career rather than a more uncertain one at the bar became necessary following his marriage, late in 1759, and his subsequent fathering of thirteen children. The numbers enrolled in his classes rose too, from five in 1761 to 40 in the latter part of the century. His subject was vast, comprehending all that was not canon law, namely Roman law, jurisprudence, government and Scots law, covered by over 250 lectures in all in an academic year. His lectures on government, 46 of them, were meant for those who wanted a broad arts course, one that purveyed information and fostered the virtues of good citizenry. High Whigs from England and Scotland valued these lectures, particularly for the sound political education they provided.

Thomas Campbell, the poet, has left a physical description of Millar:

there was an air of the high-bred gentleman about [him] that you saw nowhere else. . . . He was a fine muscular man, somewhat above the middle size, with a square chest and shapely bust, a prominent chin, grey eyes that were unmatched in expression, and a head that would have become a Roman senator. He was said to be a capital fencer; and to look at his light elastic step, when he was turned of sixty, disposed you to credit the report. But the glory was to see his intellectual gladiatorship, when he would slay or pink into convulsions some offensive political antagonist. He spoke no mincing affectation of English pronounciation; but his Scots-English was as different from vulgar Scotch, as that of St James's from St Giles. Lastly he had a playfulness in his countenance and conversation that was graceful from its never going to excess.[28]

Millar lectured extemporaneously, his manner was naturally animated and he possessed a delicate facility for being able to perceive when his auditors had fully understood him. Francis Jeffrey, lawyer, politician and reviewer, wrote two articles on Millar in the *Edinburgh Review* in which he vividly recreated the professor's lecturing style:

it is to little purpose, indeed, to make harangues to young men from a velvet gown and an elbow chair. Their teacher must *talk* to them, after a certain age, if he wishes to do them any good. He must put them on a level with himself, and associate them in some measure in his inquiries. He must talk to them, too, in a good degree as they talk to each other. He must work with them, as well as for them; and instead of appalling them with the splendour of his attainments, he must encourage them, by shewing how easily they may be made, and with what facility the notions which they throw out in common conversation, may be improved into solid arguments, and pursued to valuable conclusions. Mr Millar is the only public lecturer we have known, who seems to have been fully aware of those facts; and, by attending to them, he certainly delivered a series of most instructive lectures in a more attractive and engaging manner than any other teacher we have heard of; commanding the attention of all descriptions of hearers, at the same time that he convinced their understandings; and not only putting them in possession of knowledge, but making it familiar and serviceable to them. . . . No individual, indeed, ever did more to break down the old and unfortunate distinction between the wisdom of the academician and the wisdom of the man of the world: and as most of the topics which fell under his discussion, were of a kind that did not lose their interest beyond the walls of a college, so the views which he took of them, and the language in which they were conveyed, were completely adapted to the actual condition of society; and prepared those to whom they had been made familiar, to maintain and express them with precision, without running the least risk of an imputation or pedantry or ignorance. ... [A] professor thus [laid] aside the shield of academic stateliness, and not only to expose his thoughts in the undress of extemporaneous expression, but to exhibit them, without any of the advantages of imposing or authoritative pretences, on the fair level of equal discussion, and with no other recommendations, but those of superior expediency or reason.[29]

Millar was known for bringing even the dryest of subjects alive to his students. Elsewhere, Jeffrey asserted that it was from Millar's books, which contained the substance of his professorial prelections, that Millar's students derived their earliest notions of politics:

He passes from the general speculations of philosophy to the peculiar doctrines of his party, without altering his manner, or seeming to expect a different reception; and delivers the most questionable of his opinions with the same coolness and confidence that distinguishes his statement of the most obvious and indisputable truths. In this way, he avoids the violence and exaggeration that is apt to be engendered in the management of an avowed controversy; and maintains a certain dignity of discussion, that is lost either by bristling suddenly up to repel an antagonist, or by trying to mollify him with elaborate and ineffectual apologies.[30]

Millar was also known for breaking down timidity in students, encouraging them to form a circle around him after his lecture, debating with them the ideas he had just canvassed, correcting misapprehensions, elaborating further, clarifying or repeating anything that had not been adequately grasped: Jeffrey doubted much 'if any teacher of youth has exposed himself to equal hazards, since the days of Socrates and Plato'.[31] Additionally, as was commonplace among Scottish professors, he took student lodgers into his house. There he encouraged their juvenile pursuits and amusements not only because the young men were inclined to them but also to assess the pupils themselves, since his domestic instruction was additional to that undertaken in his classroom. The boarders were charged high fees, which inevitably meant they were well connected but not necessarily unable young men. If their connection or ability later led them to office or a position of influence, 'his proud independence of mind made him rather decline, than cultivate [their] friendship'.[32]

As for Millar's political views, it has already been intimated that he was a Whig, but of a decided sort. It is well appreciated now that the key political question in Millar's time was that of Royal Prerogative, and Millar's view was to accept and maintain that limited form of monarchy established by the Revolution of 1688-89 with its implicit constitutional balance between legislature and executive. Hence, he was a Foxite Whig but one who made original contributions in the context of his times: for instance, he argued that capitalist economic development had extended executive power in that it had led to a range of instruments (armed forces, excise agents, tax collectors) necessary to defend and advance trade and raise revenue, that were subject only to executive authority. He was also original in his attack on traditional Whig myths of ancient liberties and in his alternative proposition that the evolution of commercial society had led to the development of political liberty.[33] Education would counter the mob characteristics of the populace and protect society from that threat to liberty just as limiting Royal Prerogative and asserting the pre-eminence of the Commons would protect society from the arbitrary dominance of monarch and executive.

In the memoir which his professorial colleague George Jardine read at the Literary Society of Glasgow shortly after his death, Jardine observed:

> However much we may have differed from him on these subjects; respecting his zeal and good intentions, there can be . . . but one opinion. No little ideas of private interest, no narrow views of advantage or emolument, sunk him to the level of party politicians; but, fair, resolute, and decided, he was, from first to last, the enlightened and manly defender of what he conceived to be the rights and liberties of mankind.[34]

Unlike Dugald Stewart, for example, he always refused any honours or sinecures offered him by government administrations. When he died, he left several chapters of an unfinished treatise 'on the present and actual state of the British Government which, if ever published, would have been a trenchant comment on the politics of his day to add to the two works of philosophical history that alone can be attributed to him with certainty.[35] A specific instance of his views can be drawn from Glasgow University business in 1798: the Faculty voted £300 to aid British defences in the French wars at a time of national economic difficulty. Millar was opposed to the vote on three counts: first, he believed that the money had not been given to the university for such purposes but for the payment of salaries and for other university expenditure; second, he believed that if donations of this nature were made, there would necessarily be a reduction in the responsibility of those who ought to be contributing to the war effort by way of taxation; thirdly, he believed that the donation was illegal because Parliament did not permit the alienation of university funds.[36]

Other specific instances of his commitment are to be seen in contemporary issues beyond the walls of the college. In difficult political conditions he espoused, as has been noted, the cause of liberty — liberty controlled by government and by law, which were the means of assuring order and stability. If liberty were ever restrained by the controlling mechanisms of society, then the mechanisms were at fault and were to be corrected. Millar was wary of enlarging the functions of government as that strengthened the executive in its relations with the legislature and led to an increase in the royal prerogative. He perceived that royal power had increased since 1688 whereas he wanted to assert the pre-eminence of the Commons. In the 1790s, he linked this increase in monarchical power in England with the support Pitt and his successors gave to the European monarchies: both were means of aiding the abetting designing kings.

Millar has been portrayed as a Jacobin sympathiser, a common smear experienced by Foxites in his time. In fact, he viewed Jacobinism as a perversion of the just causes of the French Revolution and as a real obstacle to reform in Britain. In 1791, with his professorial colleague, Thomas Reid, he shared the chair of the Friends of Liberty meeting in Glasgow. In 1793, he was suspected of purveying revolutionary ideas to his students, yet the Chancellor of Glasgow University at the time was no less than Edmund Burke who knew Millar to be a moderate influence, and to whom Millar protested that his sole objective was a limited monarchy.

On the question of war, Millar saw that it was connected intimately with the issue of parliamentary reform. The war was an attempt to protect the British constitution by suppressing demands at home in the face of revolution in a neighbouring country. The interference in French affairs was unprovoked and the excesses of the Revolution, such as the Terror and the hunger, were caused not by the French, but by the warmongering nations. Parliamentary reform would prevent such an irresponsible foreign policy; the present foreign policy was an instance of the exercise of Royal Prerogative; judges that were meting out justice to political protesters were appointed by or in the pay of the Crown; the circumscription of opinion did not harmonise with the development of commerce and industry, and the general economic progress of the era could only be continued if the people were protected from excessive interference from the head of state; and finally Millar wanted a decrease of national expenditure, which had been boosted by the war, because if it was high, it increased the power of the Crown. Such were the political views of Millar, and it can be readily seen how they were shaped by his social and historical theories as recounted earlier.[37]

Virtually contemporaneous with Millar, but practising the art of professorial pedagogy on the east coast, was Dugald Stewart. In Lorimer's words, 'he was the centre in Edinburgh circles of all what was distinguished in literature, science, or intellect, while as a public lecturer he was, and has remained, without a rival'.[38] Eloquent was an ascription commonly applied to Stewart and he himself recognised the power of eloquence. He wrote to a friend in 1783 after attending a Commons debate that '[a]s yet I have seen nothing which has made such an impression on my mind as the Eloquence of Mr Pitt.' It is an appropriate juxtaposition, therefore, to recall immediately the letter of James Mill, father of John Stuart Mill and close associate of Jeremy Bentham, who wrote to a friend of his in 1821: 'I have heard Pitt and Fox deliver some of their most admired speeches but I have never heard anything nearly so eloquent as some of the lectures of Professor Stewart.'[39] Mill was not at all alone; Henry Cockburn, a noted nineteenth-century Scottish judge, whose *Memorials of his Time* (1856) evoke so well the atmosphere and history of Edinburgh in the late eighteenth and early nineteenth centuries, wrote of Stewart's lectures being for him, 'like the opening of the heavens', and even that 'there was eloquence in his very spitting' (an asthmatic tendency caused Stewart to clear this throat often while lecturing). Elsewhere, Cockburn noted that there had never been 'any difference of opinion with respect to his unsurpassed excellence as a moral teacher. He was one of the greatest of didactic orators . . . He was the great inspirer of young men.'[40]

Mill and Cockburn were both taught by Stewart; other young men he taught were inspired to write odes. Alexander Campbell, the musician and author, drew a comparison in his ode between Plato and 'my *Scotian Plato*' and wished

The feeling heart oh could I please
(with such effect, and so much ease,)
As thou my loved Preceptor, Friend,
Canst point out man's *chief good and end.*[41]

Lord John Russell went to Stewart's retirement home in the summer
of 1812 and addressed him as follows:

To nearer worlds the source of life and light,
To further orbs a guide amid the night
Each sun, effulgent, fills its radiant throne,
Gilds other systems, and preserved its own;
Thus we mark Stewart on his fame reclined,
Enlighten all the Universe of Mind;
To some for wonder, some for joy appear;
Admired when distant, and beloved when near'
'Twas he gave laws to fancy, grace to thought,
Taught Virtue's laws, and practised what he taught.[42]

Professorial colleagues were likewise impressed, though their zeal was
more tempered and conventionally expressed. In 1779 Andrew Dalzel,
Professor of Greek at Edinburgh, wrote to Sir Robert Liston, the diplo-
mat, that Stewart was 'making a wonderful figure' as Adam Ferguson's
substitute in the Chair of Moral Philosophy, and that the 'great fluency
and distinctions with which he speaks, and the extent of his knowledge
upon the different subjects of the course are amazing. . . . The students
even like him better than Ferguson.'

Well-known authors of the day amplified the eulogies. Robert
Heron, a biographer of Robert Burns, wrote in 1792 of 'Mr Stewart,
whose eloquence, dignified, pathetic, winning, soothing, animating,
irresistibly interesting, continues to allure our Youth to the study of
Morals; — whatever the profession to which they are destined, — or
although they be destined to no profession at all.' Sir Archibald Alison,
the historian, remembered attending Stewart's lectures in the professor's last session before retirement:

Simple in his manners, unostentatious in his habits, but ardent in his
enthusiasm, Mr Stewart warmed in the professor's chair into a glow
of eloquence which, combined with the beautiful quotations in
prose and verse interspersed in his lectures, entranced his hearers and

produced an indelible impression on the mind.

Macvey Napier, later editor of the *Edinburgh Review*, wrote in the *Quarterly* not long after Stewart's retirement, that '[a] s a Lecturer, he has been long regarded as the chief ornament of a university, not a little celebrated for the eminence of its professors.'[43]

Stewart was a classic eighteenth-century philosopher, polymathie in his learning and in his capacities. He was born in 1753 and was to die in 1828. His father had been a Professor of Mathematics at Edinburgh, he studied at Edinburgh High School, Edinburgh and Glasgow Universities and his first inclination was to be an Episcopal minister. He was diverted from that course as a result of his interest in Thomas Reid's so-called commonsense philosophy. He also considered joining the East India Company's Corps of Engineers. He was familiar not merely with mathematics and moral philosophy but also geology and natural history, sciences that developed rapidly in eighteenth-century Scotland. At the age of 19, he was substituting for his father in the university's mathematics classes. In 1775, he was appointed conjunct professor of mathematics and he also took over, in 1778, the moral philosophy classes when Adam Ferguson was appointed Secretary to the Commissioners sent to negotiate with the rebel American colonists. That year he also lectured on astronomy. By the early 1780s, mathematics teaching was beginning to pall and in 1785 he transferred to the Moral Philosophy Chair in which he was to make his reputation. He held the Chair till the end of the 1809 session during which his son George died, an event which desolated him. But his appointment in 1785 did not end his forays into other disciplines. In 1787-88 he took over the duties of the Natural Philosophy Chair during John Robison's illness ('[I] am just now employed in premeditating two Lectures – the one on the Air-Pump, and the other on the Immortality of the Soul');[44] he also supplied one winter for the Professor of Greek, and he wrote a work on Sanscrit. At the turn of the century, he began to offer a third class in moral philosophy devoted to political economy. Edinburgh and Glasgow Universities offered the first public teaching of the subject in the kingdom, and in Edinburgh they were given by the first expositor of the writings of Adam Smith, Dugald Stewart.

Stewart wrote extensively: his collected works run to some eleven large volumes. He had a talent not so much for original thought, but for expounding and popularising the work of other philosophers, a talent which also found ample outlet in his teaching. His principal philosophical works were three volumes of *Elements of the Philosophy of the Human Mind*, two volumes of *Philosophy of the Active and Moral Powers of Man*, and a volume on *Philosophical Essays.* He also wrote for the *Encyclopaedia Britannica* a *Dissertation exhibiting the Progress of Metaphysical, Ethical and Political Philosophy since the revival of Letters in Europe*, and for the Royal Society of Edinburgh three memoirs of distinguished members — Adam Smith, William Robertson and Thomas Reid. Two volumes of his political economy lectures, including his lectures on government, also appeared in his *Collected Works.* He made clear to his students the principal characteristics of the philosophy of the Scottish Enlightenment: he was steeped in philosophic history, in the lessons of Bacon, Locke and Newton, in the contribution to social analysis of Adam Smith, and in the psychological philosophy of Reid especially, without adding hugely to any of them. His lasting impact was thus as a lecturer: it was Dugald Stewart that his auditors remembered, not the Smith or Reid whose work he exhaled. As will be seen later, however, it was Stewart representing the Scottish tradition who was commonly invoked on major public issues of the day in the opening decades of Victoria's century.

Stewart's politics were openly Whig in the contentious decade of the 1790s during which he taught a number of young men, both aristocrats and commoners, who were to become prominent Whig politicians in the first half of the nineteenth century. Two judges of the Court of Session upbraided him in 1794 for allegedly revolutionary tendencies in his writings, which he stoutly defended. Like other British Whigs, Stewart had at first welcomed the French Revolution. He visited France not infrequently, spending the summers of 1788 and 1789 in that country. On 27 August 1789 he wrote from Paris to Archibald Alison, the historian, describing 'the wonderful Revolution which has taken place here within these two days'. In 1793, he responded to Alison's request that he be godfather to his newly-born son:

> I don't know what duties your [Episcopal] Church imposes on a godfather, but I promise to do all I can to make him a Philosopher and an Economist; and I engage, as soon as he beguns to snuff . . . to make him a present of a very handsome box which I received lately with the *Rights of Man* inscribed on the lid.[45]

Then in 1794, a Lord of Session, Alexander Abercromby, read Section VIII of Stewart's *Elements of the Philosophy of the Human Mind* entitled 'The Use and Abuse of General Principles in Politics'[46] which he interpreted as an attack on established institutions. Abercromby reported his allegation to his fellow judge, William Craig, who proceeded to write to Stewart in the following terms:

> That even allowing the principles in that chapter, however erroneous, to have been written with the most innocent intention at that time, that after the massacres in France, and the dreadful actings such principles had produced, and after the consequences of them had been expressed in such horrible and bloody characters, it could not only not be innocent to maintain those opinions but that that conduct could not be innocent which did not disavow them. . . . the *triumphs of philosophy and reason*, daily exhibited in France, ought to have satisfied every thinking and every virtuous man of the danger of unhinging established institutions, even though such institutions should appear, when considered abstractly in the closet, to be less perfect than the theories of speculative and ingenious men.

Stewart was asked to retract his views.

The professor replied to Craig on 20 February 1794, denying that he was pernicious: 'no reference has been made to my opinions (so far as I have been able to learn) by any of the inflammatory writers of the times.' He denied that he approved of the French philosophers in general, with their supposed tendency to corrupt morals, indeed, 'I opposed them with zeal, at a time when the profession of scepticism was not quite so unfashionable as it is at present.' He denied that he was encouraging revolution since he 'was aware of the mischiefs to be apprehended from the spirit of innovation, and from sudden changes in established institutions'. Indeed, he always concluded his moral philosophy course by showing 'the peculiar excellencies' of the English constitution, 'of which I have always enlarged upon in the warmest and most enthusiastic of terms'. He concluded:

> Of the utility of my labours as an instructor of youth, it does not become me to judge, but I may be allowed to say, that I have long enjoyed, and that I continue to enjoy, every testimony of approbation which the public can give.[47]

Stewart became a victim of his times. As Henry Cockburn perceived:

> Yet we had wonderfully few proper Jacobins; . . . There were plenty of people who were called Jacobins; because this soon became the common nickname which was given, not only to those who had

admired the dawn of the French liberation, but to those who were
known to have any taste for internal reform of our own.

And he continued, 'Stewart, in particular, though too spotless and too
retired to be openly denounced, was an object of great secret alarm.'[48]
In 1805, he was in the forefront of a campaign to resist an attempt by
the Tory and moderate Edinburgh Presbytery to foist one of their own
number on the university as Professor of Mathematics against the lay-
man, John Leslie, who near fatally had quoted Hume approvingly on
causation in a footnote of one of his books. The campaign involved him
in a pamphlet war and in much clerical and other denunciation. Some
time after, his wife was to be found writing to an old friend that he
would find Stewart much the same as he left him:

> His few hairs are indeed gray, and perhaps the sad history of the
> world for the last twenty years may have made his manner more
> serious and reserved in company than it was when you knew him,
> but it is only in company.[49]

After 1790, Stewart always read his lectures from a script rather than
extempore from notes so as to minimise the political risks he ran. In
his political economy lectures he was especially careful:

> I shall also pass over, without examination, another project of
> taxation, which has been lately carried into effect in Great Britain,
> — I mean the *tax upon income*, as I am always unwilling to touch
> upon any questions which are connected with the political discus-
> sions of the times.[50]

Stewart's political economy lectures were heavily influenced by the
philosophy of his predecessors as literati in the Scottish Enlightenment,
who asserted the primacy of the economic base of a society in any
explanation of its property-holding, government and law. His first
objective in teaching the subject arose from his belief that the correct
implementation of the principles of political economy would promote
human happiness. Political economy, he observed,

> may be extended to all those speculations which have for their
> object the happiness and improvement of Political Society, or, in
> other words, which have for their object the great and ultimate *ends*
> from which Political regulations derive all their value; and to which

Wealth and *Population* themselves are to be regarded as only subordinate and instrumental.

A second objective Stewart proclaimed was the definition of the occasions and limits of state interference:

> one of the most important [objects of political economy] is the solution of that problem which Mr Burke has pronounced to be one of the finest in legislation: 'to ascertain what the State ought to take upon itself to direct by the public wisdom, and what it ought to leave, with as little interference as possible, to individual discretion'. The mischievous consequences that may result from the tendency of mistaken notions on this point, to produce an undue multiplication of the objects of law, must be evident to every person who has the slightest acquaintance with Mr Smith's political disquisitions.

And elsewhere he noted:

> the great and leading object of [Smith's] speculations is to illustrate the provision made by nature in the principles of the human mind, and in the circumstances of man's external situation, for a gradual and progressive augmentation in the means of national wealth; and to demonstrate, that the most effectual plan for advancing a people to greatness, is to maintain that order of things which nature has pointed out, by allowing every man, as long as he observes the rules of justice, to pursue his own interest in his own way, and to bring both his industry and his capital into the freest competition with those of his fellow-citizens.

A third objective was 'to enlighten those who are destined for the functions of government, and to enlighten public opinion in respect of their conduct'.[5]

An average of 49 students attended the lectures and they were given in the difficult first decade of the nineteenth century when the French economists (and Adam Smith consequentially) were believed to have been responsible for the excesses of the French Revolution. He covered the general principles of population, the theory of national wealth, including free trade and the circulation of money, regulations affecting the poor, and plans for the education of the lower orders. In his biography of Smith, Stewart wrote of the atmosphere in which he found himself teaching:

The doctrine of Free Trade was itself represented as of a revolutionary tendency; and some who had formerly prided themselves on their intimacy with Mr Smith, and on their zeal for the propagation of his liberal system, began to call in question the expediency of subjecting to the disputations of philosophers, the arcana of State Policy, and the unfathomable wisdom of feudal ages.[52]

Stewart was well connected with Whigs south of the border: he was known in the political houses of Bowood and Holland House, he had a number of prominent Whig heirs lodge with him while they studied in Edinburgh, and other prominent Whigs of less noble birth acquired their earliest political, social and economic knowledge in his nursery. Stewart's firm links with the Bowood circle were forged by his intimacy with Sir Samuel Romilly, the English jurist, who had himself been introduced there in the 1780s. Philosophers of the circle included Joseph Priestley and especially Etienne Dumont, to whom Romilly wrote after a visit to Edinburgh in 1793: 'the person whom I most saw and lived with at Edinburgh, was our friend Mr Dugald Stewart, whom the more I know, the more I esteem for the qualities of his heart, and the more I admire and respect for his knowledge and his talents.'[53] The intimacy between Stewart and Romilly was such that one of his executors, John Whishaw, travelled to consult Stewart about the publication of Romilly's papers and relied heavily on Stewart's judgement of what should be published.[54] Bowood, the country house in Wiltshire of William, Earl of Shelburne, was a centre of Whig reforming ideas. Shelburne enthused over Enlightenment ideas and plans for the reform of government after a visit to France in 1771 and determined to patronise radical thinkers and writers so that they and men of government could work in harness.

By 1782, when Shelburne became First Lord of the Treasury, he had gathered around him a formidable brains trust in the Bowood circle, most of whom were members of the Constitutional Information Society, and before whom Jeremy Bentham's *Introduction to the Principles of Morals and Legislation* had been read in 1781. The schemes to extend reform of the civil list, to overhaul accounting and taxation, to reorganise the Treasury, Navy Board and other government departments with the aim of greater administrative efficiency on which Shelburne embarked, had all been canvassed originally at Bowood. After Shelburne left public life in 1783 he went again to

France and recruited Etienne Dumont as his assistant; and it was at Bowood that Bentham met Dumont. Throughout the 1780s, Bowood was an important political centre where intellectuals of the day congregated — and the intellectuals came from the Scottish as well as the Whig, humanitarian, Unitarian, utilitarian and Benthamite schools.[55] It is not surprising, therefore, that Shelburne (now Marquess of Lansdowne) was to send his heir, Henry Petty, to study under Stewart at Edinburgh in 1796-97, where he met other young men of lower birth but greater talent.

Just as Stewart visited Bowood, so is he known to have visited Holland House too. In the winter of 1799, the dinner books show him to have been a frequent guest.[56] Holland and Stewart corresponded and fed each other information on their mutual interests.[57] The Hollands were related to the Lansdownes and their home succeeded Bowood as the premier early nineteenth-century focus of Whig politicians and intellectuals. The Edinburgh reviewers and other students of Stewart's were known to make Holland House their place of resort.[58] The Whigs acknowledged their debt to Stewart when in 1806 they created for him the sinecure of the writership of the *Edinburgh Gazette*, with a salary of £300 a year and emoluments from the sale of the paper.

John Playfair (1748-1819) was Stewart's closest colleague, and was once described by him as the Scotsman who resembled d'Alembert so nearly.[59] For all his misgivings when the idea was first put to him, Lord John Russell went to lodge with Playfair when he studied at Edinburgh and found him 'one of the best and the noblest, the most upright, the most benevolent, and the most liberal of all philosophers'.[60] Playfair was born at Benvie, near Dundee, and his father was the minister of Liff and Benvie. He went to St Andrews University to study for the Kirk, and it was while he was there that his ability in the mathematical sciences became apparent. While still a student, he substituted for the ailing Professor of Natural Philosophy, William Wilkie. When aged only 18, he submitted himself to an eleven-day trial as a candidate for the St Andrews Chair of Mathematics, coming third in a field of five. Upon leaving the university, he spent some time in Edinburgh before being called to his father's livings. In his spare time, he continued to prosecute his studies in the physical sciences and he made the acquaintance of a number of influential men such as Nevil Maskelyne, the Astronomer-Royal. In 1782, he resigned his livings to become tutor to Robert and Ronald Ferguson of Raith, in Fife. The post gave him the opportunity to reside in Edinburgh and to visit London. Maskelyne introduced him to the scientific milieu of the capital.

In 1785, Playfair was appointed Professor of Mathematics at Edinburgh. He wrote prolifically on a wide range of topics and in a variety of forms, including his papers to the Royal Society of Edinburgh, his biographical memoir of Dugald Stewart's father, and his works on barometrical measurements, Indian astronomy and porisms. He wrote textbooks for his classes, a common source of assured professorial income at the time, and from which he profited when he transferred to a second Chair in 1805, that of Natural Philosophy. He was a Fellow of the Royal Society and secretary of the Royal Society of Edinburgh, and he travelled widely in pursuit of his many interests. After 1802, he contributed some 60 articles before his death to the *Edinburgh Review*. Most were concerned with mathematics, natural philosophy and geology, but he was interested, too, in military and naval tactics, university education and travelogues.

His major contribution was in the way he made the interested British public familiar with the discoveries of continental mathematicians and natural philosophers, to show how they had developed the ideas of Newton, how they adopted the algebraic notation of Leibniz, extended and systematised calculus and made progress in algebra, geometry and trigonometry: Laplace, Euler, d'Alembert, Lagrange, Clairaut and others all had their work first drawn to the attention of the British through the publicising work of Playfair, and their innovations were covered in the curricula of the areas he taught. He criticised Oxford and Cambridge Universities for their ignorance of the latest research in the physical sciences.

He was also the principal advocate of the geological theories of a fellow Scot, James Hutton. He published his *Illustrations of the Huttonian Theory of the Earth* in 1802, and wrote many articles in the *Edinburgh Review* championing the Huttonian cause. In addition, he travelled widely to European mountain ranges to test the theory and wrote about the results of his journeys.

He was a popular university teacher and was admired by his students and his lodgers. He was a well-known figure in the social circles of Edinburgh, not least for his philandering. An Edinburgh student later wrote that he was 'rather inclined to look upon Playfair's loves with indulgence. The *literati* [sic] in our English Universities (none of whom are fit to keep the door of his lecture-room) are in general such bears about women, that one is rather pleased with the contrary extreme. However, it must be comical enough.' When, after Playfair had courted a certain West Indian heiress, Mrs Apreece, she married Sir Humphry Davy in 1812, the same student commented that 'the widow's choice has given chemistry a most undue triumph over the exact sciences.'[61] An active Whig, Playfair fought a number of campaigns with Stewart — none more successfully than that which sought to ensure that Edinburgh University would not be 'priest-ridden' or parochial, namely the championing of John Leslie in 1805 as Playfair's successor in the Chair of Mathematics.

The medical lectures had a fascination and a power that were no less than those of Millar, Stewart and Playfair. Francis Jeffrey told the Royal Commission of 1826 and 1830 which investigated the Scottish universities that the value of the medical lectures:

> resides in their authors, themselves masters of their arts, who, by their genius and talents and industry, and scientific discoveries and zeal, acquired a mastery over the minds of the pupils, which elicited whatever zeal, and enthusiasm, and talents they possessed, and thus riveted in their minds what was propounded to them.[62]

The power and influence of the medical professors lay in the nature and traditions of a hierarchical profession and also in the effective communication of practical methods, successive professors taking the trouble to spell out their teaching objectives and/or to assemble equipment to assist them in their task. The results of their endeavours were the comprehensive medical school, as in Edinburgh, that was described earlier and which depended on individual efforts of professors.

V

Part of the corpus of knowledge pursued by the literati of the Enlightenment in Scotland was concerned with a dynamic analysis of history, economics and society; another part was concerned with medicine. Both concerns informed and invigorated university education in Scotland, especially in Edinburgh and Glasgow, in the later eighteenth and early nineteenth centuries. Some of the leading lights of the movement were still living; there were others, with gifts of teaching and the talent to exploit particular aspects of the educational system; together they sought to transmit the concerns of the Scottish Enlightenment to the generation of students frequenting the Scottish universities of that era. It is, therefore, to those students that this essay now turns, to examine those who were there to absorb 'Scotch knowledge', how they did so, and the relationships they established while at Scottish universities among themselves and with their professors who have, thus far, been the main concern.

Notes

1. Lord John Russell to the Duke of Bedford, 27 April 1809, quoted in Spencer Walpole, *The Life of Lord John Russell*, 2 vols., 2nd edn (Longman, 1889), I, p. 43.

2. Adam Smith, *Lectures on Jurisprudence*, ed. R.L. Meek, D.D. Raphael and P.G. Stein (Clarendon Press, 1978), p. 459; John Millar, 'The Origin of the Distinction of Ranks', in William C. Lehmann, *John Millar of Glasgow 1735-1801: His Life and Thought and his Contributions to Sociological Analysis* (Cambridge University Press, 1960), p. 176. Adam Smith (1723-90) is best known for his authorship of *The Theory of Moral Sentiments* (1759) and *An Inquiry into the Nature and Causes of the Wealth of Nations* (1776). His principal academic posts were Professor of Logic (1751-52) and of Moral Philosophy (1752-63) at Glasgow University. John Millar (1735-1801) was a student of Smith's at Glasgow in the early 1750s, qualified for the Scottish bar in 1760, and was Professor of Civil Law at Glasgow University, 1761-1801. An active Whig, his principal works were *The Origin of the Distinction of Ranks* (1771) and *An Historical View of the English Government* (1786). He is discussed more fully below.

3. John Millar, *An Historical View of the English Government from the Settlement of the Saxons in Britain to the Revolution in 1688*, 4 vols. (London, 1803), I, p. 127.

4. Millar, 'Ranks', in Lehmann, p. 204.

5. Smith, *Lectures on Jurisprudence*, p. 404; and Millar, *Historical View*, I, pp. 76-7.

6. William Robertson, *Works*, 12 vols. (London, 1812), IV, pp. 265-6, and *The Works of Wm. Robertson, D.D.*, 8 vols. (Oxford, 1825), VI, p. 372. William Robertson (1721-93) was minister of Gladsmuir, East Lothian (1743-59), minister of Greyfriars Kirk, Edinburgh (1759-62), a Moderator of the General Assembly of the Church of Scotland (1766-80)and Principal of Edinburgh University (1762-93). Among his works are *History of Scotland* (1759), *History of the Reign of Charles V* (1769) and *History of America* (1777). He was Historiographer-Royal for Scotland from 1763.

7. Adam Smith, *An Inquiry into the Nature and Causes of the Wealth of Nations*, ed. R.H. Campbell, A.S. Skinner and W.B. Todd, 2 vols. (Clarendon Press, 1975), II, p. 715.

8. Millar, *Historical View*, II, p. 222.

9. David Hume, *Essays, Moral, Political and Literary*, ed. T.H. Green and T.H. Grose, 2 vols. (London, Longmans, Green 1874), I, pp. 306-7. David Hume (1711-76), was one of the eighteenth century's leading philosophers and the author of *Treatise of Human Nature* (1738), *Essays* (1742), *Enquiry concerning Human Understanding* (1748), *History of England* (1754-1761), *Natural History of Religion* (1759), *Dialogues* (posthumously 1779) and many other works.

10. Millar, 'Ranks' p. 291, and *Historical View*, IV, p. 130. See also *Historical View*, III, pp. 105-7. The following passage which opens Book II, Chapter VII of Benjamin Disraeli's *Sybil*, first published in 1845 is, perhaps, of some interest when set beside Millar's historical observation on social mobility:

In a commercial country like England, every half century develops some new and vast source of public wealth, which brings into national notice a new and powerful class. A couple of centuries ago, a Turkey Merchant was the creator of wealth; the West Indian Planter followed him. In the middle of the last century appeared the Nabob. These characters in their zenith in turn merged in the land, and became English aristocrats; while, the Levant decaying, the West Indies exhausted, and Hindoostan plundered, the breeds died away, and now exist only in our English comedies, from Wycharly and Congreve to Cumberland and Morton. The expenditure of the revolutionary war produced the Loanmonger, who succeeded the Nabob; and the application of science to industry developed the Manufacturer, who in turn aspires to be 'large-acred'; a better security for the preponderance of the landed interest than any corn-law, fixed or fluctuating.

11. Millar, *Historical View*, IV, p. 78, I, p. 358, and II, p. 81.

12. Adam Ferguson, *An Essay on the History of Civil Society 1767*, ed. Duncan Forbes (Edinburgh University Press, 1966), p. 218. Adam Ferguson (1723-1816) was a chaplain to the Black Watch in the '45, Hume's successor as Keeper of the Advocates' Library (1757), and Professor of Natural Philosophy (1759), Moral Philosophy (1764), and of Mathematics (1785) at the University of Edinburgh, though he effectively retired in 1785 and in 1778, was secretary to the abortive Carlisle Commission that negotiated with the rebellious American colonists. His principal works are *An Essay on the History of Civil Society* (1767), *Institutes of Moral Philosophy* (1772), *History of the Progress and Termination of the Roman Republic* (1783) and *Principles of Moral and Political Science* (1792).

13. Smith, *Wealth of Nations*, II, p.782; see also Millar, *Historical View*, IV, p.146.

14. Smith, *Lectures on Jurisprudence*, p. 540.

15. Millar, 'Ranks', pp. 381-2.

16. Millar, *Historical View*, IV, pp. 158-9.

17. Adam Smith to William Cullen, 20 September 1774, Letter 143 in *The Correspondence of Adam Smith*, ed. E.C. Mossner and I.S. Ross (Clarendon Press, 1977), pp. 86-97.

18. See my 'Provost Drummond and the Origins of Edinburgh Medicine', in *The Origins and Nature of the Scottish Enlightenment*, ed. R.H. Campbell and A.S. Skinner (John Donald, 1982), pp. 86-97.

19. Adam Smith to Dr James Menteath, 22 February 1785, Letter 243 in *The Correspondence of Adam Smith*, p. 280.

20. Anand Chitnis, *The Scottish Enlightenment: A Social History* (Croom Helm, 1976), pp. 128-30, 163-73. See also Roy Porter, *The Making of Geology: Earth Science in Britain 1660-1815* (Cambridge University Press, 1977), esp. pp. 149-56, and Chapter 8.

21. 'Extract from the Statutes of the University of Edinburgh, respecting the conferring of degrees in Medicine, produced by Principal Robertson, approved of by the Senatus Academicus, and ordered to be published. 8 December 1783', *Evidence, Oral and Documentary, taken and received by the Commissioners appointed by His Majesty George IV. July 23d. 1826; and re-appointed by His Majesty William IV., October 12th, 1830; for visiting the UNIVERSITIES OF SCOTLAND*, 4 vols. (HMSO, 1837), Vol. I, *University of Edinburgh*, p. 137. Hereafter *Edinburgh Evidence*.

22. Adam Smith to William Cullen, 20 September 1774, Letter 143 in *The Correspondence of Adam Smith*, p. 176.

23. D.B. Horn, *A Short History of the University of Edinburgh 1556-1889* (Edinburgh University Press, 1967), p. 56.

24. The last five paragraphs summarise information and sources given in Anand C. Chitnis, *The Edinburgh Professoriate 1790-1826 and the University's*

Contribution to Nineteenth Century British Society, unpublished PhD dissertation (University of Edinburgh, 1968), pp. 301-6, 310-17.

25. The instance of Brunonianism demonstrates the ease with which medical 'systems' could gain ground among students, but it is not a good example of hero-worship since it represented for the students a revolt against the beliefs of the medical establishment. John Brown (1735-88) attributed disease to a state of excessive or inconsiderable excitability of the tissues, and he preached stimulation or soothing as appropriate. The very simplicity and facileness of the 'system' appealed to students and debates consumed the Royal Medical Society in the 1780s. Brown's ideas spread at least as far as Mexico. The atmosphere of Edinburgh medical circles at the time of the impact of Brunonianism is described in *Memories of the Life of the Rt. Hon. Sir James Mackintosh*, ed. R.J. Mackintosh, 2 vols. (London, 1835), I, pp. 23-6.

26. James Lorimer, 'Letters and Discoveries of Sir Charles Bell', *Edinburgh Review*, CXXXV (1872), p. 406.

27. Ibid.

28. Quoted in Lehmann, pp. 30-1.

29. Francis Jeffrey, 'Craig's *Life of Millar*', *Edinburgh Reivew*, IX (1806), pp. 86-7.

30. Francis Jeffrey, 'Millar's View of the English Government', *Edinburgh Review*, III (1803), p. 159.

31. Jeffrey, *Edinburgh Review*, IX, p. 88.

32. Ibid., IX, p. 89.

33. Ibid., III, pp. 158-9; and Michael Ignatieff, 'John Millar and Individualism', *Wealth and Virtue: The Shaping of Political Economy in the Scottish Enlightenment*, ed. Istvan Hont and Michael Ignatieff (Cambridge University Press, 1983), pp. 324, 326.

34. Quoted in Jeffrey, 'Craig's *Life of Millar*', Edinburgh Revue, IX, p. 91.

35. Ibid.

36. Lehmann, p. 51.

37. I have drawn freely for my account of Millar's political views from Lehmann, p. 64-76, which assumed that Millar wrote the *Letters of Crito*, published between May and September 1796 in the *Scots Chronicle*, and which constitute an attack on Pitt's war policies; and which less justifiably assumed that he also wrote the *Letters of Sydney on the Inequality of Property* which followed the *Letters of Crito*. A more recent assessment of Millar, in the light of 'fitful and contradictory reincarnations' which have sought to claim him as the pioneer of the materialist interpretation of history, as the father of mainstream sociology, as a Smithian 'scientific' Whig or as 'the social scientist of the radical petty bourgeoisie in the transient heyday of petty commodity production', is Michael Ignatieff, 'John Millar and individualism', *Wealth and Virtue*, pp. 317-32 (Parts I-III).

38. *Edinburgh Review*, CXXXV, p. 407.

39. Dugald Stewart to William Robertson, advocate, Douai, 4 June 1783, N[ational] L[ibrary] of S[cotland], ms. 3943, f. 150; James Mill to Macvey Napier, 10 July 1831, *Selections from the Correspondence of Macvey Napier*, ed. Macvey Napier (London, 1877), p. 30.

40. Henry Cockburn, *Memorials of his Time* (Edinburgh, 1856), pp. 26, 25; and *Life of Lord Jeffrey with a selection from his correspondence*, 2 vols. (Edinburgh, 1852), I, pp. 51-2.

41. Alexander Campbell, 'Ode to Dugald Stewart', 31 December 1806 E[dinburgh] U[niversity] L[ibrary], ms. Dc. 6. 111, ff. 3-4.

42. E.U.L., ms. Dc. 6. 111, f. 11.

43. Robert Heron, *Observations made on a Journey through the Western Counties of Scotand, in the autumn of 1792*, 2 vols. (Perth, 1792), II, p. 493;

Some Account of My Life and Writings: an Autobiography by the late Archibald Alison, ed. Lady Jane Alison, 2 vols. (Edinburgh and London, 1833), I, p. 40; Macvey Napier, 'Stewart's *Philosophical Essays*', *Quarterly Review*, VI (October, 1811), p. 1.

44. John Veitch, 'Memoir of Dugald Stewart', *Collected Works of Dugald Stewart*, ed. Sir William Hamilton, 11 vols. (Edinburgh, 1854-60), X, p. 1vi n.

45. Ibid., X, pp. cxxii, xcccv.

46. Ibid., II, pp. 219-51.

47. Ibid., X, pp. 1xxi, 1xxiii-1xxiv.

48. Cockburn, *Memorials* (1909 edn), pp. 73-4, 78.

49. Helen d'Arcy (Cranstoun) Stewart to William Drennan (M.D. Edinburgh, 1778) of Belfast, 31 December, 1807 (?), E.U.L., ms. Dc. 1. 100², f. 4.

50. *Collected Works*, IX, p. 253.

51. Ibid., VIII, pp. 10, 17; X, p. 60.

52. Ibid., X, p. 87, note G.

53. *Memoirs of the Life of Sir Samuel Romilly, written by himself, with a selection from his correspondence*, ed. by his sons, 3 vols. (London, 1840), II, p. 22. The letter is dated 14 September 1793.

54. K.M. Lyell, *Memoir of Leonard Horner*, 2 vols. (London, 1890), I, p. 17.

55. The consideration of the Bowood circle owes much to J. Derek Jarrett, *The Bowood Circle 1780-1793: its ideas and its influence*, B. Litt. dissertation (Oxford, 1956), and to his section on Shelburne in *Britain, 1688-1815* (London, 1965), e.g. pp. 381, 384.

56. Earl of Ilchester, *The Home of the Hollands 1605-1820* (London, 1937), p. 170.

57. N.L.S., Ms. 2521, ff. 169-70. Letter dated 1 September 1802.

58. See a letter of Lord Minto in *Life and Letters of Sir Gilbert Elliot, First Earl of Minto, from 1751-1806*, ed. Nina, Countess of Minto, 3 vols. (London, 1874), III, p. 361, letter dated 22 August 1805; and Earl of Ilchester, *Chronicles of Holland House, 1820-1900* (London, 1937), pp. 144, 180.

59. Dugald Stewart to Baron de Gerando, 22 May 1816, N.L.S., ms. 5319. f. 57.

60. John Earl Russell, *Recollections and Suggestions 1813-1873*, 2nd edn (London, 1875), p. x.

61. *Letters to 'Ivy' from the first Earl of Dudley*, ed. S.H. Romilly (London, 1905), pp. 106, 168. The letters are dated May 1810 and 6 July 1812. Mrs Apreece (1780-1855), née Jane Kerr, was a distant relative of Walter Scott.

62. *Edinburgh Evidence*, p. 447.

2 THE SCOTTISH ENLIGHTENMENT: THE STUDENTS AND THE LEARNING

I

The Enlightenment in Scotland was especially evident in three university towns — Edinburgh, Glasgow and Aberdeen. Foremost among the
literati were men closely involved with Scottish social institutions,
particularly professors. A consequence of the professorial involvement
was that many students of the era c. 1780-1820 were often imbued
with the philosophical, scientific and medical approaches of the
Scottish Enlightenment at the outset of their careers. Here the concentration, although not exclusive, tends to be on the experience of
Edinburgh students as they provide the best example.

Scotsmen naturally comprised the majority of all at university.[1]
Whereas faculties of divinity and law trained them in the local traditions of Presbyterianism and Scots law, learning in the other faculties
of medicine and arts was more obviously of wider value. A substantial
minority of medical students especially were English, Irish, American,
West Indian, from Europe and beyond. Figures presented to the Royal
Commission appointed to visit the universities of Scotland in 1826 and
1830 are the most reliable available, and while some start from a date
that is a little late for present purposes, the patterns that are illustrated
would have been established by the later eighteenth century, though
they would no doubt have been affected but not dramatically distorted
by particular developments such as the French wars that ended in 1815.

On the basis of the Commission's evidence, the lowest number of
non-medical students matriculated at Edinburgh University between
1790 and 1829 was 757 in 1791, and the highest was 2071 in 1822.[2]
Student numbers by national origin are not available in any but the
medical faculty and there, before 1811, there is only the unofficial
table compiled by James Gregory, Professor of Physic, illustrating the
cosmopolitan character of his class between 1785 and 1790. His average
enrolment was 215, 91 of whom were from Scotland, 55 from England,
35 from Ireland and 12 from each of the West Indies and America.
Others came from English families domiciled in India, and yet others
whose native language was not English came from Portugal, Brazil,
Italy, Germany, Switzerland, Geneva and Flanders.[3] The matriculation
figures presented by the university itself of the national origin of

medical students in the years after 1811, and considering the years only to 1820, are embodied in Table 2.1, which shows Scottish students vastly outnumbering those from other countries.

Table 2.1: Edinburgh Medical Students by Origin, 1811-20

Year	Total no. medical students	Scotland	England	Ireland	Colonies	Foreign
1811	716	458	138	67	37	16
1812	727	478	132	65	28	24
1813	789	557	127	63	23	19
1814	847	579	147	65	39	17
1815	907	559	194	85	54	15
1816	924	523	259	82	44	16
1817	769	439	186	86	34	24
1818	804	391	214	120	59	23
1819	739	345	214	107	50	23
1820	726	361	208	92	44	21

Source: Edinburgh Evidence, p. 129.

Students from countries other than Scotland vastly outnumbered the natives, however, when it came to graduation, the Irish being particularly keen to receive an Edinburgh MD. The indifferent state of the Irish medical schools accounts for the presence of large numbers of Irish students, the lack of cooperation between Dublin physicians and surgeons impeding the establishment of a complete and effective medical education, and the result was the lack of recognition in the public services of Irish qualifications. Consequently, Irishmen came in such numbers that Edinburgh was forced to require of them a year's residence. As the Dean of the medical faculty explained to the Royal Commission:

> latterly it became a practice, which was rather increasing, for men to come here from Dublin who had attended all their time there, and who came here merely to graduate; and, as we had no means of knowing the character of these men, we thought some abuse might be practised in that way, for men might come who had been rejected there, and it seemed desirable to know a little more of their character; that regulation [of a year's residence] was therefore made absolute.[4]

It is, however, important to remember that other graduates in addition to the Irish had not necessarily been exposed to the complete medical curriculum in Edinburgh and, therefore, may not be reflecting as accurately as matriculation figures the different national origins of the medical student body. The numbers in 1777 (the first year given in evidence) and at five-yearly intervals between 1780 and 1820, serve to give an impression that English and Irish graduates at least equalled and frequently outnumbered the Scots (see Table 2.2).

Table 2.2: Edinburgh Medical Graduates

Year	Total	Scots	English	Irish	Others
1777	27	11	7	4	5
1780	24	7	5	9	3
1785	22	4	8	2	8
1790	32	7	7	16	2
1795	44	5	13	15	11
1800	50	14	14	17	5
1805	60	18	10	25	7
1810	55	16	16	15	8
1815	88	39	14	22	13
1820	121	31	34	41	15

Source: Ibid., pp. 149-50.

Table 2.3: Medical graduates whose medical education was partly or wholly carried on at other universities

Year	Total	Edinburgh	Paris and other universities abroad	Partly at Dublin	Partly at Glasgow	Wholly at Dublin
1821	104	67	8	24	5	0
1822	113	75	2	31	5	0
1823	93	63	4	22	3	1
1824	109	65	16	19	5	4
1825	140	92	7	27	7	6
1826	118	77	3	27	4	7

Source: Ibid., p. 150.

The importance to graduates of Edinburgh as a place of medical education can, however, be measured from Table 2.3 which indicates those graduates whose medical education was partly or wholly carried on at other universities. The only figures that the Commission was given were for the years 1821-26 and it may be assumed — perhaps unwarrantably — that they reflect an established pattern. The pattern was that Edinburgh was overwhelmingly the medical school where its graduates had studied.

Table 2.4

Year	Total	Scottish	Irish	English	Others
1796	33	27	3	3	0
1797	24	23	1	0	0
1798	30	25	2	3	0
1799	32	24	3	2	0
1800	35	30	3	2	0
1801	24	22	1	1	0
1802	25	17	5	3	0
1803	25	19	3	3	0
1804	34	28	3	3	0
1805	40	32	4	4	0
1806	44	36	1	4	2
1807	48	32	1	9	1
1808	49	28	16	5	0
1809	82	58	22	2	0
1810	45	30	14	0	1
1811	52	31	17	3	1

Source: *Glasgow Evidence*, pp. 525-6.

The dominance of Edinburgh can be seen if its figures are compared with those of Glasgow and the two Aberdeen colleges (where medicine was a responsibility jointly undertaken). Table 2.4 gives, between 1796 and 1811 only, the annual attendance by national origin of those attending the class of Glasgow's Professor of the Practice of Medicine. Until 1809, very few non-Scots attended, and thereafter, the Scots still vastly outnumbered them. The Commission was also given the national origins of those students of anatomy at Glasgow between 1812 and 1825 which are given in Table 2.5 which shows a similar pattern.

There are equivalent figures for Glasgow medical graduates to those seen earlier from Edinburgh. They are given in Table 2.6 from 1776, the first year given, and then at five-yearly intervals between 1780 and 1820 and once again, Edinburgh's numerical superiority in all columns is evident.

Glasgow was the only university to indicate the national origin of arts graduates, though graduation in arts was uncommon in Scotland during the Enlightenment. However, the national pattern indicated

Table 2.5: Glasgow Anatomy Students, 1812-25

Year	Total	Scottish	Irish	English	Foreign
1812	280	200	61	15	4
1813	351	235	96	14	6
1814	254	163	83	4	4
1815	166	119	39	6	2
1816	140	96	36	6	2
1817	164	118	25	15	16
1818	200	135	43	17	5
1819	215	148	56	7	4
1820	162	119	28	13	2
1821	204	149	41	13	1
1822	186	130	35	14	5
1823	199	136	39	15	9
1824	262	194	39	24	5
1825	277	199	40	28	10

Source: Ibid., p. 525

Table 2.6: Glasgow medical graduates

Year	Total	Scottish	English	Irish	Other
1776	2	1	1	0	0
1780	6	3	0	2	1
1785	13	2	1	6	4
1790	10	2	2	5	1
1795	4	0	1	3	0
1800	7	1	3	1	2
1805	5	5	0	0	0
1810	6	5	0	0	1
1815	8	7	0	1	0
1820	16	8	1	7	0

Source: Ibid., p. 533

again shows Irishmen making as frequent use of a Glasgow MA graduation as Scots. The figures are given in Table 2.7, which gives the figures from 1777, the first year given in evidence, and then at five-yearly intervals between 1780 and 1820.

The figures from the Aberdeen colleges are much less full because they were smaller institutions and medicine, the only subject for which but slight figures on national origins were given, was not provided with several lectureships before 1816-18. Even then, no data on origins were

Table 2.7: Glasgow MA graduates

Year	Total	Scottish	English	Irish	Other
1777	25	10	0	15	0
1780	8	3	0	5	0
1785	7	5	0	2	0
1790	4	2	0	2	0
1795	15	8	1	6	0
1800	8	4	0	4	0
1805	17	6	2	9	0
1810	32	7	2	23	0
1815	31	12	2	17	0
1820	32	20	4	7	1

Source: Ibid., p. 534

provided before 1824 and so no indication of an established pattern for the purposes of this study can be given. For what the figures are worth, of the 53 matriculated medical students in 1824, no less than 51 were Scots. In the 1825 session, 45 out of the 48 were Scots.[5] The absence of medical educational provision in Aberdeen before the end of the French wars did not, however, prevent the colleges awarding medical degrees. Marischal awarded no less than 442 between 1776 and 1830, the highest number of awards in any single year being 26 in 1820.[6] King's College acted in a similar fashion granting 425 medical degrees between 1776 and 1826; of these 164 were to Englishmen, 46 to Scotsmen, 45 to foreigners and 9 to Irishmen.[7] Thirty-three King's alumni subsequently took medical degrees and were examined in the following places: 7 at King's, 14 at Edinburgh, 6 at Edinburgh and London, 1 at London, 1 at Edinburgh and Glasgow, 2 at Aberdeen and Edinburgh; 1 at Aberdeen, Edinburgh and London and 1 at Edinburgh and Paris.[8]

II

Many reasons can be adduced for the presence of non-Scots in the tables of medical students and graduates, especially those who were at Edinburgh: the celebrity of the medical school; the degree or licence that was available for study in the city and which would qualify the Britons among them for service in the medical departments of the army, navy or East India Company; the professional nature of Scottish medical education for which prior qualifications in classics were unnecessary; the comparative ease and shortness of time within which to qualify medically. English Dissenters who aspired to be physicians, but who were legally barred on religious grounds from receiving a university education in their own land and whose own dissenting academies faced doctrinal and other difficulties, found a welcome in Scottish universities which applied no religious test and which were experiencing healthy academic fortunes. The demand was evidently such that, certainly from 1803 and possibly earlier, Edinburgh University specified an oath to be sworn on graduation by members of the Society of Friends 'qui vulgo dicuntur "Quakers" ', although its wording was not noticeably different from that sworn by others.[9]

From the early eighteenth century the Scottish universities and the English dissenting communities demonstrated several common approaches:[10] their traditions were different but allied. At the beginning, both felt harassed — the Scots by the competition they faced from without from the Dutch universities and by the theological disputes within their own bodies; the English by the lack of toleration accorded to Dissenters. William Carstares and Edmund Calamy as well as other representative leaders of the two, did attempt to devise institutional cooperation whereby Edinburgh University would provide an education for English Dissenters but the Edinburgh town council would not support the scheme materially (a hall of residence was required) and the Dissenters felt that Edinburgh, in 1709, was tainted yet by Episcopalianism and Jacobitism.

Carstares' arguments at the beginning of the eighteenth century are interesting as he argued that universities were the pre-eminent sources of learning with advantages which neither private tutors nor academies could offer. Tutors were expensive (especially, one might observe, for the burgeoning middle class of the eighteenth century) and academies did not necessarily provide that pastoral supervision that juveniles required when in a strange place and required to look after themselves. He especially noted that Edinburgh could, potentially, be frequented by those loyal and Protestant subjects of the Queen from all parts of Great Britain who were excluded from the English and Irish universities by tests and oaths. Since proposals had been made in London for Dissenters to come to Edinburgh or Glasgow, and since these proposals had been backed by the offer of funds to support the scheme:

it is hoped that all good men who tend to the education of youth and the advancement of learning and the civil and religious interest of the three nations, and more especially the Right Honourable The

Town Council of Edinburgh as patrons of the University there will think themselves concerned in a suggestion of so great consequence and contribute their endeavours to give parents all possible encouragement in sending their sons hither for a sober and virtuous education.[11]

After 1720, the shared common approach of Scottish Presbyterians and English Dissenters arose from the subscription to common academic ideals. They were then both Calvinistic in character resulting in the practice of catechesis in both the dissenting academies and the Scottish universities. Thereafter, both sets of institutions came to cultivate the liberal arts and certainly the dissenting academies (and arguably the Scottish universities) became less Calvinistic. In the 1730s, both experienced opposition – the Dissenters from Anglican High Church intolerance and the Scottish universities from Calvinist divisions – to both of which their liberal principles made them sensitive. In England, the liberal education offered in the dissenting academies began to be recognised increasingly by the burgeoning middle class as the best available modern education. As in the Scottish philosophy classes, for example those of Dugald Stewart at the end of the century, the emphasis was on the cultivation of moral and intellectual powers. Of the students at Warrington Academy between 1757 and 1782, 393 in all, 22 were entered for law, 24 for medicine, 52 for divinity and 98 for commerce namely, merchants, bankers, brewers, shopkeepers, etc. (197 were not specified). Of the students at Exeter Academy between 1760 and 1793, 6 were attorneys or barristers, 4 ministers, 7 physicians, 24 merchants or in trade, 7 were connected with the navy, 13 esquires, 2 apothecaries and 3 army men.[12] Even before the late eighteenth century, many Dissenters followed a preliminary education in an academy, with a professional education in a degree from a Scottish university, most commonly in medicine.

In the course of the century, many English dissenting teachers and authors were awarded doctors' degrees at Scottish universities – 39 DDs, 10 doctors of civil law and 7 MDs.[13] The awards highlight another shared feature: the Scottish universities and the dissenting academies were both highly dependent on the talents, interests and abilities of individuals. Dissenting academies were privately run by the schoolmasters themselves who established the discipline and who were not responsible to Elders for the execution of their responsibilities. In the earning of intellectual credit for their academies they mirrored the entrepreneurial talents of so many of their pupils' parents. It was these men who, especially after 1750, were rejecting Calvinism and espousing the wider liberal thought. Their counterparts in Scotland were the university professors of the same era on whose reputation their institutions likewise depended. The difference was that the professors, however entrepreneurial in their approach to collecting guineas and promoting the monopoly of their subject, were none the less part of a continuing corporation, financed by town councils, watched over by Presbyteries and were duly provided with successors, albeit of varying calibre.

Among the individuals on whom the dissenting academies of the time depended were John Jennings of Kibworth Academy (1715-23), himself succeeded by Philip Doddridge who broadened the arts curriculum and moved the academy to Northampton and, in other hands, the same academy moved to Daventry. (A characteristic of the academies was their short life and frequent moves, a symptom of social attitudes to Dissenters.) Caleb Rotheram was the key figure of the Kendal Academy; Joseph Priestley of the Warrington (1757-86) and Hackney (1786-96) Academies. Warrington, Hackney and Manchester (from 1783) were Unitarian: the width of their objective had been expressed in the proposals for the Manchester Academy which were for 'a plan of Liberal Education, for young men designed for Civil and Active Life, whether in trade, or in any of the Professions.'[14]

The story of Hackney contains within it the changing circumstances prevailing by the end of the eighteenth century and in which the academies were having to work. Hackney duly had its key teachers, Richard Price and Thomas Belsham: Price, as is well known, argued vociferously against Edmund Burke and in favour of the French Revolution; Belsham believed in the doctrine of philosophical necessity. In the troubled political atmosphere of the early 1790s, their views involved the academy in controversy: a former student was arrested and a member of the college council was tried for treason. So, the death of liberal men of learning in the Doddridge mould who had thrived in the tranquil Hanoverian decades gave way to individuals like Priestley (who emigrated to America) and Price who proved contentious in the very different era of the French Revolution. Contemporaneously in the Scottish universities, there was no immunity from the same suspicion of radicalism and rationalism but the deeper-rooted institutional structures provided some protection for the suspects and also made it possible for established authorities to disburse the patronage of Chairs to safe candidates only, though in the long run this led to the academic decline of the Scottish universities in the 1820s. The Evangelical revival also dealt a blow to the rationalism that had been the hallmark of the academies.

Theological ferment such as that associated with Hoxton Academy led to academies as a whole narrowing their task to that of educating ministers for their own sects. For example, the Manchester Academy moved to York for that purpose in 1803. Being trained as a minister had always interested only a minority of those attending dissenting academies: their higher educational purpose had hitherto been more broadly conceived. Consequently, many would now be looking elsewhere for that education.

The dissenting community had long taken the view that the English universities from which they were barred were licentious pastures that could swallow up fortunes without noticeable benefit to the indulgent, whereas the Scottish universities were thriftily structured through the class fee, non-collegiate system that still permitted a degree of pastoral care in towns where temptation abounded less than elsewhere.[15] The academies, too, were hardly ostentatious and had been built around men of sober habits, sound discipline and similar pastoral care. As the eighteenth century wore on, and certainly in its closing decades, the dissenting academies turned away from the liberal education that had earlier characterised them, for reasons that have been seen, and they became more inward-looking, concerned to train men according to the lights of particular nonconformist sects. They became riven, too, with doctrinal divisions and embroiled in political and theological controversy and effectively collapsed as liberal educational institutions. Consequently, it is not remarkable that the steady trickle of English Dissenters who had, throughout the eighteenth century, sought to crown their educational experience with a Scottish university qualification, turned into a perceptible stream. Medicine in particular proved to be of abiding interest to them, hence perhaps the special graduation oath for Quakers from at least 1803. Traditionally English Dissenters had shared a common outlook with Scottish education, now necessity dictated that they spend some time in Edinburgh or Glasgow. Their growing numbers and aspirations can also be attributed to the increasing self-consciousness of the English provincial (and frequently dissenting) middle-class groups which was a feature of social history certainly from the 1780s and to which this study will subsequently return.

III

Another discernible group in the Scottish student body were the young nobility. They, too, had established a tradition in the eighteenth century of spending some portion of their formal education in enlightened Scotland. Some of the nobility were themselves Scots with homes in Scotland, including town houses in Edinburgh. Others were English and, after a spell at an English public school or at home with a tutor, were sent north as a preliminary to studies at Oxford or Cambridge and the public life they would lead thereafter. The practice was certainly known in English artistocratic circles from the middle of the eighteenth century. When such young men came, they boarded with a professor who undertook full responsibility for them. Professors' houses, at Edinburgh for instance, were commonly in the college buildings or clustered closely around the college.

An early example, from Glasgow, was a member of the Shelburne family of Bowood, Wiltshire. In 1758, the second son of the first Earl of Shelburne, Thomas Petty-Fitzmaurice, was sent to board with Adam Smith while taking classes at Glasgow University. He had been to Eton and was 16 years of age. He had been recommended by a friend of Smith, Gilbert Elliot of Minto, Roxburghshire, who knew his brother, William Petty, Viscount Fitzmaurice (who was incidentally to be prime minister, 1782-83). It was proposed, noted Elliot in a letter to Smith,

that [Thomas] should be in your house and entirely under your direction, and to give you for his board and the inspection of his education a hundred pound a year, or more if it should be thought proper. I understand he is a very good school Scholar, very lively, and tolerably ungovernable, but probably will not give you much trouble, as you will have the total charge and direction without any controul.[16]

Smith obviously took his responsibilities very seriously for he is to be found thereafter in frequent correspondence with his charge's family. Because his tutorship is quite fully documented it may serve as an example of the practice and as an illustration of what was involved in the duties of a professor who admitted boarding pupils to his home. Smith was a bachelor, with no wife to assist in his non-academic responsibilities, but his situation was not unique: John Playfair, with whom Lord John Russell boarded 50 years later, was also a bachelor.

Fairly early in the quite extensive correspondence between Smith and the Shelburne family, Smith is to be found outlining the different ways by which the morals of young students at Glasgow might be guarded. They might, for instance, bring with them their established tutor whose authority already held sway, the measure which Smith regarded as the best; or the family might engage a tutor locally, but it was difficult to find a good one and his fees and living costs would be expensive. A third course was boarding with a professor at a cost of £10 a quarter, which Smith also regarded as expensive.[17] This last method was the course Shelburne had himself adopted, and another letter showed in detail what could be involved when a professor took in a noble boarder. Smith was concerned, first, to account minutely for even the smallest sum of money he spent in carrying out his responsibilities to Thomas Petty-Fitzmaurice: 'I have marked every receipt with a letter of the Alphabet. Your Lordship will find the same letter upon the back of the Account or accounts which correspond to it.' Sometimes, Smith admits, no receipt was possible, as when Fitzmaurice's masters, physician or surgeon were paid, or when he was given pocket-money (around a guinea a month), or bought books for ready money or a set of silver buckles or a case of mathematical instruments. The masters' fees were high, Smith noted, because Fitzmaurice was a nobleman's son; a gentleman's son paid half the amount. Then again Smith has to explain the expense involved in taking Fitzmaurice on two journeys with him, to Edinburgh and to the Duke of Argyll's at Inverary, but his explanation speaks volumes about his approach to the task of guardian and to some incidental benefits to be derived therefrom. In the case of the Edinburgh visit:

> I expected to have brought him back with me for forty shillings; But when I came there I was often obliged either to sup or dine at places where it was improper to carry him. When this happened to be the case, that I might be sure what company he was in in a very dissolute town, I ordered a small entertainment at our lodgings and invited two or three young lawiers to keep him company in my absence. Inverara is two days journey from Glasgow and we happened to be misinformed with regard to Dukes motions and came there two days before him during which time we stayed at a very expensive Inn.[18]

Smith's punctiliousness in accounting was well known to his charge who, nearly three years later, after he had left Glasgow for the prodigiously expensive Oxford, wrote to Smith about a similar letter the professor had sent to the family about a final account in connection with his tutorial and boarding responsibilities:

> had it been for an Affair of £10,000 instead of £200 it could not

have been more accurately drawn up, so anxious were you to clear yourself of what you imagin'd my Lady Shelburne thought was in you unfair dealing, which you were just as clear of before you took that trouble as anything could possibly make you.[19]

Elsewhere in his correspondence, Smith indicated the cost of education in Glasgow: £5-£8 per quarter for board in a common boarding house; 1/10d a dozen for washing; 8-10 guineas for masters' fees; other college dues of about £1 a year; and a 'suit of plain Cloaths of the finest cloth' cost some £5: 'These are all the necessary expenses which any Gentleman's son has occasion to be at while he attends upon this University.' The unnecessary expenses depended upon the habits of the young person concerned.[20] At some point Fitzmaurice must have been so sober in his habits that it occasioned comment from his associates. The consequence was that Smith became more liberal in issuing pocket-money.[21] Numerous letters testify to Smith's meticulous care of his boarder, the young man's health, and, when ill, detailed accounts of his doctors' opinions and of his changing condition, his attitude to his studies, his academic progress, the proposals Smith has to make for his future academic studies.[22] That both Glasgow and Smith were appreciated becomes evident from a lengthy letter to Smith from Shelburne, who compares Glasgow most favourably with Oxford and Cambridge where birth and fortune rather than literary merit are respected. In particular, the Scottish university performs the greatest of services to one on the eve of manhood by inculcating obedience and the conformity of one's own will to that of another, as well as frugal habits, punctuality, sobriety and being methodical. Shelburne went on to say:

The time of my Son's stay at Glasgow, is by no means limited as you seem to think . . . ; I wish him to stay as long as You, Sir, can endure him under your Eye, and so long as he shall continue worthy of your Attention; for my part, having no view to anything but his Improvement, nor any use to make of him until he shall be perfect in those things which I only know how to Admire, but not how to Teach, I shall rejoice at the length of his Absence from me, being much of opinion that great Evils arise by suffering Boys to become Men too soon.[23]

Shelburne further indicated the value his class set by a Scottish university education for their sons by recommending it to others in his social circle.[24]

As for Smith, he found value in his connection with such a political family, not least in its providing him with news of the wider world, both at the time of his stewardship and after Fitzmaurice had left Glasgow. In 1759, for instance, he wrote to Fitzmaurice's older brother, soliciting information on politics in London and commenting on an affair in Portugal then attracting comment in the Scottish press; and in 1767, he is found assisting Lord Shelburne, now Secretary of State, by providing him with some background historical information on the South Seas, then about to be explored by Captain Cook, and on the government of Roman colonies.[25] It is also clear that young Thomas Fitzmaurice, even after he had left Smith's care, continued to value his intellectual mentorship, his time in Glasgow and his contacts there, and that he kept in touch.[26]

The very early example of Smith and the Shelburnes, which can be followed in detail in Smith's correspondence, helps in estimating the value of later instances more pertinent for the current study, because in these instances can also be seen such features as the faith that the English aristocracy had in the Scottish literati, the use that the Scottish literati made of the English aristocracy for furthering their work and the maintenance of contact with his charge by a professor who had had a young aristocrat as a boarder when the young man moved into adulthood and his political inheritance.

The experience of the Shelburne family and their circle shows that the young English aristocracy's practice of spending a formative period in a Scottish university was not at all unknown in the mid-eighteenth century. By the late eighteenth century another factor had entered, which diverted even more of their kind northwards, and that was the turbulent situation provoked by the French Revolution and the ensuing wars. Europe's troubles had for centuries redounded on the Scottish universities: in the later seventeenth and early eighteenth centuries, for instance, the hampering of the traditional traffic of Scottish students of medicine and law to continental universities by the Nine Years' War and the War of the Spanish Succession had contributed to the systematic provision of courses in those subjects, notably in Edinburgh. Now, the Grand Tour of Europe, that traditional feature of the educational programme for young English aristocrats and which usually took place between public school and Oxford or Cambridge, became a hazardous enterprise and was either impossible or much foreshortened. In either event, a sojourn in a Scottish university town — commonly Edinburgh, somewhat less commonly Glasgow, rarely Aberdeen and scarcely ever St Andrews — became an alternative. Incidentally, the cost of a Grand Tour of France, Italy, Germany and Holland was £5000 for three years,[27] considerably more than the cost of a spell in a Scottish university.

A significant group and number of young aristocrats came to board with Scottish professors in the troubled closing decades of the eighteenth and at the turning of the nineteenth century, and they were coming, of course, when Scotland was absorbing the lessons of her own age of Enlightenment as well as the political backwash of the French Revolution and the earliest stirrings of an industrial society. They included no less than three Victorian prime ministers – Lord Melbourne (who boarded with John Millar in Glasgow), Lord Palmerston (who boarded with Dugald Stewart in Edinburgh) and Lord John Russell (who boarded with John Playfair, also in Edinburgh). Their number also included others who were to hold less exalted ministerial office such as John William Ward, 1st Earl of Dudley, Thomas Binning, later 9th Earl of Haddington, Henry Petty-Fitzmaurice, later Earl of Lansdowne and Gilbert Elliot, Earl of Minto, as well as many others who may have been less prominent in political life but who, for example, were not unknown for using their proprietary influence to nominate for parliamentary seats.[28]

The best-documented instance of the relationship that subscribed between one young such nobleman and the professor with whom he was sent to board is that of Dugald Stewart and Henry Temple, later the 3rd Viscount Palmerston and Whig prime minister. Young Harry Temple was one of those who could not, at the very end of the eighteenth century, hope to make a Grand Tour, and his father fastened onto Edinburgh and to Dugald Stewart's pastoral care as a substitute. He was to remain in Stewart's home from 1800 to 1803. In mooting the arrangement, his father wrote:

> He is now coming to that critical and important period when a young man's mind is most open to receive such impressions as may operate powerfully on his character and his happiness during the remainder of his life. At this time, therefore, I think it of the greatest consequence that he should be judiciously directed through such a course of studies as may give full exercise to his talents and enlarge his understanding, and that he should converse as much as possible with persons to whose opinions he must look up with deference, and in whose society his manners would be improved and his morals secured.

The elder Palmerston did not feel that attendance on senior classes of an English public school would attain these objectives because of the common routine of classical instruction and because he would learn nothing beneficial from his classmates. On the other hand, Stewart's character was known to be such as to lead the Palmerston parents to place young Harry under his direction, and Stewart had particularly been recommended by Lords Warwick and Brooke. This was despite the second Lord Palmerston's Pittite Toryism and Stewart's Whiggery. Harry Temple was, therefore, placed in Stewart's house early in November 1800 where he found another noble youngster, Lord Ashburton (heir of John Dunning, the lawyer, who had perceived the increasing power of the Crown in the reign of George III), also in residence as a supervised boarder. After settling his son and seeing his situation for himself, Palmerston noted in his tour journal:

> Mr Stewart takes considerable pains with the young men under his care, if they are disposed to be industrious and, in that case, they may, by his assistance, get much forwarder and draw much more advantage from the lectures of the other professors than they could otherwise do. He sometimes, as an evening amusement, encouraged the young men in his house to debate before him upon some subject previously agreed on.

The cost to Lord Palmerston was £400 for board and Stewart's own fees and in addition there were fees for the other professors and for particular masters. So evidently satisfied was Palmerston that he also sent Harry's brother, William (later Minister Plenipotentiary at the court of Naples) to board with Stewart.

Harry Temple liked the Stewarts 'amazingly' which did not surprise his father: '[Mr Stewart's] character stands so very high in the world, and both he and Mrs Stewart appeared to us so thoroughly amiable and kind, that I had no doubt but that you would all of you be equally well satisfied with each other.' Temple and Ashburton must have approached their studies the same assiduity because Temple is to be found writing of his fellow boarder:

> Lord A improves upon acquaintance, though his oddities and whims are surprising. He has a surprising dread of squinting and he thinks that the study of optics must bring it on, therefore as Mr Stewart in his lecture about the sense of seeing described the anatomy of the eye, he would not go to college that day . . .

Just as Smith had maintained contact with his pupil's family, Stewart wrote to Temple's father, praising his son's conduct, character and abilities. Upon his father's death in April 1802, Lord Malmesbury became effectively his guardian and particularly commended to Palmerston (as he had now become) Stewart's political economy course: 'I have no doubt he will teach it on its right principles and in the way which can the best tend to qualify you to act as becomes in you in the rank you hold in life and in the part you will probably be called upon to act.' Later, on learning of his ward's plan of studies he observed: 'I only fear when you get to Cambridge you will find yourself with nothing to learn, or rather that your tutors will know nothing with which you will not be previously acquainted.'[29] Indeed when, in the 1850s, Sir William Hamilton wished to publish Stewart's political economy lectures for his edition of Stewart's collected works, he sought and received Lord Palmerston's cooperation, by way of comment and the use of his notes from the session 1802-3 (still extant, on microfilm, in the Edinburgh University Library).[30]

Palmerston's life was not, however, all hard study as there are at least two references in different biographies to his high spirits: Lord Buchan recalled being taken as a boy to Stewart's house where he met Henry Brougham, Henry Petty and Harry Temple, 'who beat them all at jumping on the lawn after dinner', and Lady Minto recalled 'the solemn occasion' of a part in the same residence where Temple 'sprained his leg by jumping over Mrs Stewart's Gothic couch in the middle of her drawing room'.[31] Sixty years after his time as a boarder, Palmerston is said to have visited the Canongate in Edinburgh where Stewart's residence had been situated and found a brewery on its site. One surviving relic was, however, the Stewart's old maid whom, when he went to visit her, exclaimed upon seeing him: 'Eh! maister Harry, hae you come back at last!'[32]

William Lamb, later 2nd Viscount Melbourne, was a pupil and boarder for two sessions of John Millar in Glasgow, and had his younger brother, Frederick, as a companion. Frederick's impression was that 'There is nothing heard of in this house but study', and William wrote that he was experiencing 'a course of study and exercise, of debate, doubt, contradiction and examination such as I had never witnessed nor been engaged in before'. He was immersed in lectures and examinations on Justinian, on French and on government, a formal debate every Saturday evening and perpetual discussions and arguments at mealtimes and on walks on religion, metaphysics, law and politics.[33] Millar is also known to have boxed, gloved, with his favourite pupils and

Francis Jeffrey, the editor of the *Edinburgh Review* and Lord Advocate, is quoted as saying in a Glasgow University rectorial address: 'No young man admitted to [Millar's] house ever forgot him, and the ablest used to say that the discussions into which he led them, domestically and convivially, were the most exciting and most instructive exercises in which they ever took part.'[34]

John Playfair superintended Lord John Russell's studies in Edinburgh while he lodged with him, and Russell was impressed by his scientific abilities and his political sympathies. A particular episode in their relationship is of interest: Russell's father suggested in the spring of 1811 that the professor and his charge make a tour of the English manufacturing towns in the summer vacation. This they did and duly visited 'the interesting and busy scenes of Birmingham, Manchester, Nottingham, Sheffield, the great commercial mart at Liverpool. &c'.[35] So, well into the nineteenth century, the same features that were apparent in the mid-eighteenth century between Adam Smith and the Shelburne family can be seen to persist, the perceived value to the aristocracy of studies in a Scottish university guided by a learned professor, an experience encouraged by the practical difficulties for continental travel at the time; close connections were established by the aristocracy with the Scottish literati and intellectual or practical lessons were derived from their professors by the young nobility, which they did not omit to remember later in life.

IV

The students of different social background and national origin came to know each other, and in some instances even became familiar, through the classwork characteristic of the Scottish universities and through such distinctive features of student life as the societies. Even the boarding tradition helped: Professor and Mrs Stewart, for instance, held weekly gatherings in their house for many years 'which happily blended the aristocracies of rank and letters, bringing together the peer and unfriended scholar'.[36] The method of teaching in the Scottish universities, especially teaching conducted by the celebrated professors of the age, actively involved the members of a class rather than simply making them silent note-takers at prelections. The contemporary spokesman for the Scottish system was George Jardine, Professor of Logic at Glasgow University between 1774 and 1827. His explication of Scottish university teaching, *Outlines of Philosophical Education*, was published in two editions in 1818 and 1825. In so far as he treated of teaching methods, and his work went beyond merely them, Jardine wrote of the lecture, catechesis, essays, exercises and prizes as having a place in the good instructor's armoury. Catechesis involved questioning the students about a lecture given earlier to ascertain if they had grasped its purport and provoking arguments with them and among them about its content. In his evidence to the Royal Commission of 1826 Jardine observed that catechesis required much preparation and was most effective in the hands of an experienced teacher who knew what level of question to put to the students of different abilities. He found more talent and, therefore, more competition in bigger classes. As an academic year progressed, so did the catechetical exercises become more difficult, not least because the amount of subject-matter that had been covered was greater. Debates could also be held in class (it has been seen how they were a regular part of life in professorial houses where there were boarders). Essays were set and read out publicly and criticised. The cleverer students might, at the end of a course, be asked to write on topics that a professor had not had time to cover and these essays might also be read out and criticised. Prizes were awarded as an incentive for the students' endeavours.[37]

Jardine also wrote in his book specifically about John Millar's implementation of familiar Scottish teaching methods:

> It was in no small degree owing to his practice of examining, and of prescribing essays on subjects previously discussed in his lectures, that he acquired that high reputation as a professor of law. . . . Every morning, before he began his address from the chair, he endeavoured to ascertain, by putting a number of questions to his pupils, whether they had been able to follow his reasoning on the preceding day, and it was his custom, when the lecture was over, to remain some time in his lecture-room to converse with those students who were desirous of further information on the subject. By engaging with them in an easy dialogue, he contrived to remove obscurities and to correct any errors into which they might have fallen. This meeting was called among the students, familiarly, 'the committee', from which they acknowledged that they reaped more benefit than from the lecture itself.[38]

All these different ways of stimulating the students to learn and of whetting their interest also had the effect of encouraging the students to become aware of and familiar with each other, be they English nobility, gentry or Dissenter, or the more common Scots, from a wide variety of social and economic backgrounds. Arts subjects, such as moral philosophy and logic, or law were not the only ones where teaching methods would have involved whole classes and thus stimulated their familiarity with each other. Natural history, for instance, which was studied by a large number of medical students but also by others with scientific interests, was another subject taught in such a way as to engender a corporate awareness among the students. The Professor of Natural History at Edinburgh from 1804 to 1854, Robert Jameson, taught his subject by conversing with the students one hour before the lecture, and also after it; and by meeting his students in the Natural History Museum which he had refurbished[39] where he enquired as to their progress and set them exercises. These exercises included writing descriptions of objects of natural history which the students would not have seen before and he also undertook field excursions with his students, either in the Edinburgh neighbourhood or to places as distant as the Western Isles. On these expeditions, Jameson taught his students how to examine mineralogical specimens, and he pointed out interesting animals or the significance of particular meteorological occurrences. He also explained the nature of springs, lakes and similar features which occurred on the walks. These practical exercises corrected any erroneous ideas gathered in the classroom and taught the essential habits and methods necessary for the pursuit of natural history.[40]

Most of Jameson's pupils accompanied him on these expeditions during which, in the opinion of the Royal Commissioners who inquired into the state of Edinburgh University in the late 1820s, 'the information is equally shared by all, and an universal feeling of satisfaction and delight is the constant result of these **peripatetic** exercises'.[41] In an obituary of Jameson, an anonymous author gave an evidently informed account of the Saturday expeditions:

> During [them] he made the personal acquaintance of every student and amateur members of his class who displayed a knowledge of, or love for, natural history. Friendships between Professor and pupil then arose, which eventually extended over years, and led to a voluminous correspondence. His advice was eagerly applied for and regularly given, and many of the best scientific writings of his time owe some part of their excellence to his suggestions and revision. The men who became thus attached to him never forgot the college in which they had studied, and from time to time send valuable and

interesting specimens and collections to be applied by their old master to the development of the University Museum.[42]

Men of varied age and experience attended Jameson's natural history classes. Just as mature men in and of the town, in addition to the conventionally matriculated students, attended Dugald Stewart's political economy lectures because of their intrinsic interest, so could Jameson count on the attendance of surveyors, civil engineers, army engineers, silversmiths, jewellers and farmers because of the sheer utility of his training.[43] From among his students up to the year 1826 emerged seven who became university professors of natural history or related disciplines, many renowned geologists and several explorers.[44] One of Jameson's most celebrated students was Charles Darwin (1825 to 1827). In his autobiography appears a passage usually interpreted as critical of the Edinburgh professor and of the teaching he received in the university.

> I gloried in the progress of Geology. Equally striking is the fact that I though now only [seventeen] years old, heard the Professor, in a field lecture at Salisbury Crags, discoursing on a trap-dyke, with amygdaloidal margins, and the strata indurated on each side, with volcanic rocks all around us, say that it was a fissure filled with sediment from above, adding with a sneer that there were men who maintained that it had been injected from beneath in a molten condition.[45]

While the passage is critical of Jameson's particular geological views[46] it also demonstrates that Darwin had been made aware of the great geological debate that consumed Edinburgh from the 1790s until into the 1830s between those who followed the theories of Abraham Werner and those who followed James Hutton. The quotation also provides a picture of a field excursion on which detailed observation and interpretation were offered.

Jameson's teaching of natural history and the encouragement of classroom discussion by arts professors indicate ways in which students of all kinds came to know and be familiar with each other. Facets of the medical education had the same effect: as was indicated in Chapter 1, the emphasis on practice was a special feature of Edinburgh medical education, and the use of botanical gardens, museums, clinical demonstration and experience in a wide variety of institutions associated with public health, would have had the incidental effect of encouraging intimacy and friendship among the students, and an awareness of each other's abilities.

The classroom was, however, only one place where student intimacy was fostered. The students' own societies, where they themselves determined the subjects of interest and the form of their pursuit, were equally significant as assemblies which encouraged talent, association and familiarity. To quote the most recent historian of Edinburgh University, they gave 'coherence to the amorphous Edinburgh undergraduate body', while to a nineteenth-century commentator, they played an important educational element in the Scottish universities, being 'the modern substitute for the ancient and valuable practice of public academical disputation', the chief nourishment of general college life and institutions which liberalised and broadened students' minds more easily than could mere academic studying.[47] The societies also found their origins invariably in the age of Enlightenment during which various societies for the mature community of university towns arose (for instance, the Select Society and the Royal Society of Edinburgh, the Political Economy Club in Glasgow and the Wise Club in Aberdeen) and became fora for the generation and development of new ideas. Students appear to have aped their elders since various student societies were founded, especially in Edinburgh, where in 1720 a student natural philosophy society is known to have existed, the celebrated Royal Medical Society was founded in 1737 and the Royal Physical Society received its charter in 1788, to name but three. There were less avowedly intellectual groups, too, that were deliberately designed to cement relationships such as those designed for particular national groups of medical students in Edinburgh like the American Physical Society which devoted itself to a discussion of medical matters and provided the occasional colonial home-from-home, or the Hibernian Medical Society where the Irish students debated a wider variety of topics such as suicide, education, electricity, the death of Caesar and the peopling of America.[48]

That the activity of student societies were stimulated by classroom teaching is especially to be seen in the number of societies that were founded to pursue chemistry and natural history, subjects that were so much in vogue during the late Enlightenment. Chemical societies in particular were established by students so that they could attempt experiments themselves. One account of activity in chemical society was left by John Thomson, a son-in-law of John Millar and Professor of Military Surgery and of Pathology at Edinburgh between 1806 and 1842. He wrote to John Allen at Holland House:

Lord Lauderdale and I made the galvanic experiment last week, and I exhibited it to the Society on Saturday. We are getting tubes with gold wires and glass stoppers to try its effects on caustic liquids, and we are getting a very broad plate of zinc made, to try whether the increase of power be in proportion to the increase of surface. In that case his Lordship's whole service of plate will be converted into a galvanic battery.[49]

In another chemical society, a participant claimed that a student colleague, who became interested in the solvents of india rubber, discovered that it was soluble in cheap menstruum and coal-tar naphtha, and though he realised cloth could be waterproofed by the solution yet Macintosh gained the credit for the discovery.[50] The natural history society students were allowed by Jameson's predecessor to use his museum, books and specimens. Jameson himself encouraged a student society where the young men could discuss subjects raised in the natural history class or in other classes where natural historical topics had been treated.[51]

The pre-eminent example of a society where students could pursue physical knowledge on the basis of interest stimulated in the classroom, was, however, the Royal Medical Society. Almost all the medical students belonged to this body as well as a few students of other subjects, although its avowed aims were the advancement of medical science and the discussion of purely medical and allied questions. At a business meeting, one or two papers were read, each member in turn being required to submit a paper, the first of which was actually read by the society's secretary. The second paper, however, could be interrupted by objections or by discussion on popular, scientific topics. That there was a mixture of topics can be gathered from John Thomson reading two papers during the session 1790-91, one on catarrh and the other on the natural agents for consolidating terrestrial strata.[52] Henry Brougham, the future radical politician and an arts student at the turn of the century, gave a paper on 'Liberty and Necessity' to the Royal Medical Society, and he admitted that the logic class he was then attending assisted him greatly by providing many of the terms used: 'I not only charged one of my antagonists with *petitio principii*, but had the pedantry to charge another with an *idolum theatri*'.[53]

Dissertations could also be presented to the society and these, too, could be on non-medical topics as when Robert Jameson read a paper, in 1796, on whether or not James Hutton's 'Theory of the Earth' was consistent with fact. Henry Holland, later an influential Victorian physician, made an inquiry in 1810, the year of his presidency of the Royal Medical Society, into the nature and origins of passions in relation to the intellect and bodily economy of man; Richard Bright, who subsequently discovered the disease that bears his name, spoke on gangrene in 1813, and Marshall Hall, afterwards a noted physiologist of the nervous system and Holland's successor as president, also spoke in 1813 on the dispersive and refractive powers of the human eye and on some motions of the iris.[54]

Among those who belonged to the Royal Medical Society in a specimen period from 1790 to 1827, were a number of men who distinguished themselves in their careers, as indicated in the following list, which gives session of membership and their principal professional distinction:[55]

1790-91	Andrew Duncan junior	Edinburgh professor
1793-94	William Woolcombe	noted physician in Plymouth
1794-95	George Birkbeck	adult educationist
	John Yelloly	physician at the London Hospital
1795-96	Alexander Marcet	physician at Guy's Hospital
	George Bell	Edinburgh professor of Scots law
	Peter Mark Roget	physician, medical educator and thesaurus projector
1796-97	John Hume	Inspector-general of Hospitals and Metropolitan Commissioner in Lunacy
	Marc-Auguste Pictet	Professor of Philosophy, Geneva
1800-01	Henry Reeve	Norfolk and Norwich physician
1802-03	Daniel Ellis	horticulturalist
	John Gordon	anatomist in Edinburgh
1803-04	Herbert Henry Southey	Metropolitan Commissioner in Lunacy
1806-07	Henry Holland	Royal physician
1808-09	John Elliotson	London medical professor
1809-10	Richard Bright	medical scientist, educator and Royal physician
	Marshall Hall	medical scientist
1811-12	Robert Grant	comparative anatomist
	Jeremiah Bigsby	botanist
	John Davy	chemist

1817-18	Samuel Hibbert	geologist
	James O'Beirne	Dublin surgeon
1818-19	William Sharpey	physiologist
	James Syme	Edinburgh surgeon
1819-20	John Conolly	mental health specialist
1820-21	Thomas Hodgkin	dermatologist and philanthropist
	Charles Locock	Royal obstetrician
	Robert Carswell	London professor of anatomy, Belgian royal physician
1824-25	William Henry	chemist and student of cholera
	James Kay (-Shuttleworth)	educationist and Assistant Poor Law Commissioner
1825-26	William A.F. Browne	mental health specialist
1826-27	Charles Darwin	author of *Origin of Species*

The most significant of the Edinburgh student societies was the Speculative. Established in 1764 to improve literary composition and public speaking, the society met on Tuesday evenings in a special room in the college buildings. The form of its meeting was to have a paper read and discussed, and then a debate followed on another subject. The range of topics covered included history, politics, legislation and general literature. Specific examples of matters debated in an unknown year during Dugald Stewart's time as a professor included: the mandating of Members of Parliament; the abolition of the slave trade; whether a standing army was the best means of defence; the repeal of the Test Acts; whether preservation of the balance of power was sufficient justification for entering war; the justifiability of impressing sailors; whether it was advantageous to possess territory in the East Indies; whether it was advantageous to educate the lower orders; whether the commercial or landed interest was more favourable to liberty; whether physical causes could account for differences in national character; whether honours ought to be hereditary; whether universal toleration ought to be allowed; whether the union was disadvantageous to Scotland; whether theatrical representations were dangerous to morality; and whether ancient Athens or Great Britain should be considered the better school of eloquence.[56]

A cull of membership lists shows how the Speculative Society enabled students of arts, law and medicine as well as those who were of **aristocratic** and more humble birth to meet and debate with each

clearly club - map that similar to library

other. For example, a very select list of members admitted in a specimen period from 1790 to 1810 (once admitted membership was for life) elicits the following names, with subsequent distinction added:[57]

1790	Walter Scott	novelist
1791	John Thomson	Edinburgh medical professor
1792	Francis Jeffrey	reviewer and politician
1796	Henry Petty	Marquess of Lansdowne
	Francis Horner	reviewer, economic expert, politician
	Charles Kinnaird	8th Baron Kinnaird
	James Loch	estate manager to the Duke of Sutherland
1798	Andrew Duncan Jr	Edinburgh medical professor
1799	Henry Cockburn	memorialist, politician and judge
1800	Charles Grant	Minister in several government departments especially to do with Colonies
	Robert Grant	Governor of Bombay
1802	Henry Reeve	Norfolk physician
1803	Henry Southey	Metropolitan Commissioner in Lunacy
1804	Robert Gooch	physician and Royal librarian
1805	Henry Temple	Lord Palmerston
1806	Henry Home Drummond	Member of Parliament
1809	Cornwallis Hewett	Cambridge medical professor
	Richard Bright	medical scientist, educator and Royal physician
	Lord John Russell	Whig politician

It is clear from Henry Brougham's autobiography that a feature of the society was its capacity for enabling the talented Scot and the aristocratic Englishman to mingle.[58]

In the opinion of Henry Cockburn, the Speculative Society 'trained more young men to public speaking, talent, and liberal thought, than all the other private institutions in Scotland', but it was also a society 'on which age and reputation conferred importance, where the awe of order was aided by hereditary respect for not very flexible rules, and superiority was difficult, and every effort to attain it formidable.'[59] The society became caught up not only in the currents of thought that emanated from Edinburgh classrooms but also in the political controversies of the day. The Whiggery of Stewart and Playfair was shared by the young students leading to 'animated debates and proceedings, which did not occupy the society alone, but the whole College, and indeed all Edinburgh, for nearly an entire session.'[60] The young men antagonised those professors and judges of a Tory persuasion, who, since membership of the Speculative was for life, were entitled to participate in debates. Early in 1799, the Tory Professor of Scots Law, David Hume, nephew of the philosopher, spoke publicly of the young Whigs in the Speculative as 'Those young men, like their masters the French, . . . evidently skilled in political arts.'[61] Hume additionally complained in the University Senate of 'the blasphemous and seditious discourses' delivered at the Speculative.[62] Jeffrey, Horner, Kinnaird and Brougham sought to divide the Speculative Society on whether a message should be sent to Hume complaining of what he had said. In the event, only a minority who attended the division voted to send a message, but that did not prevent the four movers sending one, none the less, and as Brougham later confessed, the message was 'offensive, perhaps hostile'. It asked if Hume had indeed used the expressions, and if he had, the messengers felt bound to declare that the expressions contained a falsehood.[63] The Senate appointed subcommittees to investigate the affairs of the Speculative; these were considered in March and April 1799 and the society was found not to be seditious, though Horner and Jeffrey were to be reprimanded by the Senate, in the person of the University Principal, for their attitude to Hume.[64] In the event, Jeffrey was out of town, Horner and Kinnaird were ill, and so Brougham bore the punishment alone though it was 'most gently administered'.[65] Thereafter, a law was passed prohibiting discussion on political questions of the day and it was not repealed until 1826.[66] The *Edinburgh Annual Register* for 1817, reflecting on the time and on those who were caught up in its preoccupations, commented:

Talent is naturally democratic, spurning at all distinctions not founded on itself. At the private debating societies, into which the students of the Scottish universities form themselves, political discussion became a prominent feature; and it was reported, that the most bold and perilous questions were frequently agitated. The alarm hence felt by the votaries of established order gave rise to a species of proscription, which barred in some degree the first efforts of these young men to bring themselves into notice. The indignation thus inspired failed not, even after their first fervour had been tempered by maturer judgment, to fix them strongly in an opposite interest.[67]

Various early lessons were thus taught in the Speculative Society — those of debating, reasoning, elaborating knowledge introduced in the classroom, the intermingling with students of a different background, the introduction to the passion of politics.

There were many other student societies: the Juridical and the Logical Societies, which merged to form the Philalethic, the Dialectic, Didactic and the Diagnostic Societies were among the better known though not as significant as the Royal Medical or the Speculative. Some societies were very ephemeral — the Azygotic, the Select Literary, the New Logical to name but three. There were societies for the younger students such as the Juvenile Literary Society and the Academical Society, which practised composition and debate in John Playfair's classroom. As has been indicated chemical and natural history societies were also known. One professor voiced the opinion that societies proliferated because of the vanity of being made president, vice-president and secretary.[68] But one other society, the Academy of Physics, a splinter-group of the Literary Society and short-lived, completes a depiction begun by the Royal Medical and the Speculative of the crucial part played by some societies in transmitting the Scottish Enlightenment to a subsequent generation.

The Academy of Physics lasted from 7 January 1797 until 1 May 1800. Its objective was 'the investigation of nature, the laws by which her phemonena are regulated, and the history of the opinions concerning these laws'.[69] The core of its membership included Henry Brougham, Francis Horner, Francis Jeffrey, possibly Sydney Smith, certainly George Birkbeck and Webb Seymour, and also the future Lord Advocate, John Murray. At the time, all were students of Dugald Stewart. Had the Academy not been the precursor of the *Edinburgh Review*, it too would have appeared on a list of ephemeral societies founded to satisfy vanity as much as interest. The significance of the Academy, however, was greater than the brevity of its existence would indicate, not least because it was the first place where George Birkbeck and Henry Brougham, who cooperated so closely in adult education ventures in the early nineteenth century, became associated.

'The Academy of Physics', wrote Brougham, 'was formed here of such men as were attached to philosophical enquiries and saw, with regret, the very little attention which is at present paid to scientific subjects.'[70] So in part, the members, prompted by the emphasis placed by their philosophy classes on induction, wanted to engage in practical science since they were given so few opportunities in the formal classes in which they were enrolled.[71] As Francis Horner wrote:

> the truths of political philosophy, like those of every experimental science, are chiefly to be discovered by analytical generalization according to the rules of inductive logic, and partly also by the synthetic application of general truths, already known, to the explanation of complicated appearances.[72]

And again he wrote of the integrity of all knowledge:

> Without making chemical experiments, it is impossible to study the details of chemical theory: without making experiments of some kind, it is impossible to study the principles of philosophical inquiry; and those of chemistry are, perhaps, the most instructive in this point of view; both because they are most simple, and, at the same time, are susceptible of much variety. . . . I wish to study law as a science; and, for this purpose, it is an essential preliminary, to become familiar with the methods and principles of philosophical investigation, as they have been successfully employed in physics, before I can pretend to apply them to jurisprudence.[73]

The Academy set out to interest itself in pure and mixed mathematics, the physics of matter, the physics of mind (which included metaphysics, jurisprudence and political economy but excluded religious controversies and party politics) and the 'History of Events, Opinions, Systems, &c.[74].' In pursuing these interests, the Academy showed a keen awareness of the contribution of the Scottish Enlightenment in key areas. For example, the Academy was absorbed in the geological controversies current at the turn of the century. Francis Horner wrote in July 1798 to a member who had left Edinburgh:

> You were aware that much of our attention was devoted, last winter, to geology, the various discordant theories which have been proposed, and the evidence from mineralogical surveys and analysis on which we must proceed in order to discriminate their merits.[75]

Brougham had written earlier in the year to a corresponding member, 'At present, the chief objects of our enquiry are the *theory of the earth*, the nature of winds, and the history, natural and civil of the African continent.'[76] At a similar time, Brougham indicated that the Academy was interested in the passing of electric fire through sulphur and iron as well as in the language and manners of ancient Carthage. He also emphasised political economy: 'No part of Philosophy is more interesting, because none is so directly practical and the Academy prizes investigations of excellence on this subject above all the other speculations in Moral Philosophy.'[77] In addition to geology, political economy and past societies, other matters that were elaborated in the Scottish Enlightenment occupied the Academy's attention. The historian of the Academy has noted that one quarter of the subjects discussed pertained to chemistry and the nature of heat, and another quarter to political, legal, economic and social issues such as would have been prompted by Dugald Stewart's teaching.[78]

The Academy met weekly to fulfill two distinct objectives; to carry out original investigations and to appraise investigations carried out and published by others. These objectives were attained by the reading and discussion of two kinds of paper, the first being original dissertations by members, and the second analyses of and remarks on new publications. In addition, the Academy noted the philosophical news of the day and received the reports of committees that had been established to conduct experiments with apparatus or to examine specific phenomena and facts.[79] While it is clear that there is no causal connection between the Academy (which anyway terminated in 1800) and the *Edinburgh Review* which was first published in 1802, there are none the less some features which may demonstrate at least their partial dependence and common origins.

First, there are the personnel involved: Brougham, Horner, Jeffrey, Smith, Murray and Brown between them wrote 77 per cent of the articles that appeared in the first two volumes of the *Review*,[80] and certainly the first three continued to write copiously thereafter. Second, the breadth of the concerns of the *Review* mirror those of the Academy as well as of the Enlightenment: the sciences, especially the mathematical and physical sciences and the geological controversies of the day; travelogues which shed light on the analysis of society that fascinated those who professed and learned eighteenth-century social thought, and political economy. *The Edinburgh Review* introduced the subject of political economy to its reading public. Three renowned political economists of the age wrote for it in its first 30 years, Francis Horner, J. R. McCulloch and James Mill, and all three had learned of the subject from Dugald Stewart. Others with the same experience, such as Henry Brougham and Francis Jeffrey, also contributed articles on political economy as well as on a range of other topics.

A principal characteristic of the *Edinburgh Review* was its Whig politics and this reflects more the activities of its projectors in the Speculative Society than in the Academy of Physics. Confirmed in their Whiggery and in a passion for reform by their experiences in the decade of the French Revolution and wars the *Review* became a potent disseminator of opposition opinion on pressing questions such as the Royal Prerogative, parliamentary reform and education. Yet another characteristic was the innovative character of its essays which could be used by their authors in a number of ways such as popularising a complex topic, expatiating on those contents of a book which interested the reviewer, whether or not they were central to the book itself, and ignoring the book but using the review as an excuse for a reviewer's own views on its subject-matter. The essays were commonly of a length that appealed to the readership. The nineteenth-century essay was, therefore, not a considered piece designed to pass the test of time but often a hurried composition, representing a passing interest and an opinion held only then. Political articles were notably liable to this criticism. The *Review* became merely the first, albeit the model, of numerous reviews which flourished in the Victorian era. There is, therefore, a similarity between the objectives of the Academy, which sought, by the reading of papers, to undertake original work and examine the original work published by others, and the use made by authors of their essays in the *Edinburgh Review*. By means of reviewing books, the *Review* was, in effect, a printed, more mature and more widely disseminated version of an Academy meeting.

An eminent Victorian essayist, Walter Bagehot, attributed what he called 'the eruption of a liberal review' in Scotland to 'the teaching of Scotland' which 'seems to have been designed to teach men to write essays and articles'. Whereas English education could be adequately described as the education of facts, that of Scotland was the education of speculation:

> The particular, compact, exclusive learning of England is inferior in this respect to the general, diversified, omnipotent information of the North; and what is more, the speculative, dubious nature of metaphysical and such like pursuits tends, in a really strong mind, to cultivate habits of independent thought and original discussion. A bold mind so trained will even *wish* to advance its peculiar ideas, on its own account, in a written and special form; that is, as we said, to

write an article.[81]

But, Bagehot continued, the first Edinburgh reviewers were content only with writing a great many articles on a great many topics, and in this respect may have put on the mantle of their mentors, the eighteenth-century Scottish professors, a characteristic feature of whose careers had been intellectual manoeuvrability as they performed the duties of different chairs. The nature of contemporary knowledge did not discourage such practices. Another commentator on the distinctive educational experience that might have led to the equally distinctive character of the *Review* was the future Lord Melbourne. Writing early in 1800 to his mother while still resident in Glasgow, he sought to comment on an observation evidently made to her by the art patron, Lord Egremont:

> I daresay Lord Egremont is right enough about the disputatious disposition of those men who have been so unfortunate as to have been at Millar's. But this I take to be the case throughout the whole university as much as at Millar's, and at Edinburgh still more than here. No place can be perfect; and the truth is, that the Scotch universities are very much calculated to make a man vain, important, and pedantic.[82]

Certainly from their earliest days, the Edinburgh reviewers were known as 'a distinct and marked sect' and renowned for their 'strong mutual coherence'.[83]

There will be cause to return to the *Edinburgh Review* and its authors later in the study: suffice for present purposes to appreciate the background of ideas, experiences, conditions and circumstances from which it sprung, and which made it a bridge between the eighteenth and the nineteenth centuries. When Sydney Smith arrived in London from Edinburgh in the latter part of 1803 he found 'that it is the universal opinion of all the cleverest men I have met with here, that our Review is uncommonly well done, and that it is perhaps the first in Europe'.[84] It may even be argued that the *Review* was a bridgehead, permitting Enlightenment ideas to invade the society that was coming to terms with marked and sustained economic growth. For the moment, it was one of a number of ways that have been indicated here in which various students who found themselves in Scotland, and especially Edinburgh at the end of the eighteenth and the beginning of the nineteenth centuries, took further the lessons of the teachers in the classrooms and deepened their knowledge of each other.

V

The relationships that were struck in their student days by those young men who were active in the classrooms and societies were not merely passing. They were maintained and developed, both with their professors and with each other. The Scottish educational experience could have a lasting impact. A touching instance concerns John William Ward, later 1st Earl of Dudley and Foreign Secretary under Lord Canning. He first lodged with Professor and Mrs Dugald Stewart in the winter of 1797-98, and it is likely that he passed several winters with them. Thereafter, he conducted a regular correspondence with Mrs Stewart, the 'Ivy' of his *Letters to 'Ivy'*. In these letters, apart from giving his observations on a host of different matters, his continued attachment to Stewart and his interest in matters prompted originally by the professor are very evident. For example, when he heard Stewart was retiring in 1809, he wrote,

> I own I am sorry Mr. S has determined to retire from his academical employments. The University is maintained by him and Playfair. It will expire when they cease to labour for it, and they will be succeeded by a brace of Edinburgh parsons ... , and there will then be no place of liberal education in the kingdom.[85]

When at Oxford in 1812, he is anxious to show Stewart's books to leading academics such as Edward Copleston, provost of Oriel, 'who devours eagerly all that proceeds from the pen of Mr Stewart'.[86] He acted as messenger between Stewart and Mme de Staël in 1814, sending back her reply 'that her principal object in going to Scotland would be to see him'.[87] In the same month, Ward reports that he has read the chapter on logic in Stewart's latest book and was struck especially by the remarks on argumentative dexterity. Stewart confirms the view Ward has held for some time:

> The art or knack of disputation I have frequently seen possessed in no inconsiderable degree by very shallow, wrong-headed people, and what is more, I have seen very powerful understandings warped and enfeebled by it. For instance, it always appeared to me that the vast and powerful mind of Mr Fox himself had suffered a little from over-indulgence in the exercise of this faculty. With something less of subtlety (argumentative subtlety, of course, I mean), and something more of philosophy, he would have been a still greater man than he was.[88]

Finally, as an instance, Ward is to be found commenting in July 1814 on Stewart's view that the world is improving: he accepts that Stewart is quite right to make that statement, and adduces in evidence various improvements that have been set in train in France as a result of the Revolution.[89] A friend of Ward's, Henry Home Drummond, later a Peelite MP, observed in his unpublished 'Opinions' that Ward's living with Stewart 'occasioned a certain similarity of ideas, and furnished materials for conversation' which one could have with no other of his contemporaries.[90] Ward represents one kind of continuing relationship between professor and student that was by no means unique.

Francis Jeffrey represents another, much more critical relationship. Not least because he was editor of the *Edinburgh Review*, Jeffrey was the author of a significant body of articles for the journal, spanning an array of subjects. Two, published in 1804 and 1810, sought to attack quite radically what Dugald Stewart had stood for and even to undermine a significant area of eighteenth-century intellectual achievement.[91] In the first article, purporting to review 'Stewart's *Life of Dr Reid*', Jeffrey directed a shaft to the heart of the self-proclaimed achievement of the Scottish Enlightenment, that the literati had become the Bacon and Newton of the social sciences and had put the investigation of moral knowledge on the same footing as the investigation of physical knowledge. In the first of the two sustained attacks asserting the complete inapplicability of Baconian and Newtonian methods to the science of mind, Jeffrey's iconoclasm led him to aver that:

> it does not appear to us that any great advancement in our knowledge of the operations of mind is to be expected from any improvement in the plan of investigation, or that the condition of mankind is likely to derive any great benefit from the cultivation of this interesting but abstracted study.

Jeffrey went on to coin the memorable and pithy phrase, 'We cannot decompose our perceptions in a crucible, nor divide our sensations with a prism.'[92] Metaphysicians could, by analysis, discover nothing new while experimental philosophers could. Whereas experimental philosophy extended knowledge all men were, in practice, familiar with the functions and qualities of their minds even if they were ignorant of the precise words to describe them. The work of the metaphysician was, therefore, no more than that of a grammarian 'who arranges into technical order the words of a language which is spoken familiarly by all his readers', or of a cartographer who draws 'a correct map of a district with every part of which [his readers] were previously acquainted'.[93] Jeffrey's views in the article on metaphysics and on the distinction between observation and experiment were not shared by Sydney Smith, for one.[94]

The second article was a review of 'Stewart's *Philosophical Essays*' in the preliminary dissertation of which Stewart had attempted to reply to the attack of 1804. Jeffrey began by noting how very unfashionable was philosophy of mind and proceeded to devote almost the whole article to countering Stewart's defence. The laws of mental operation had no utility, 'all that is gained by their digestion into a system, is a more precise and methodical enumeration of truths that were always notorious.' After eulogising the achievements of modern physics, Jeffrey noted:

> The knowledge and the power of man over inanimate nature, has been increased tenfold in the course of the last two centuries. The knowledge and the power of man over the mind of man, remains almost exactly where it was at the first development of his faculties.

In sum, Stewart had made a 'lofty estimate' of the utility of his favourite study and this was just 'one of those splendid visions by which men of great genius have been so often misled in the enthusiastic pursuit of science and of virtue.'[95] Not all Stewart's former students were as critical: Sydney Smith wrote to Francis Horner about Stewart's dissertation for the supplement to the *Encyclopaedia Britannica*, remarking how free it was of Stewart's defects:

> No insane dread of misrepresentation; no discussion put off until another time, just at the moment it was expected, and would have been interesting; no unmanly timidity; less formality of style and cathedral pomp of sentence. The good, it would be trite to enumerate:- the love of human happiness and virtue, the ardour for the extension of knowledge, the command of fine language, happiness of allusion, varied and pleasing literature, tact, wisdom, and moderation! Without these high qualities we all know Stewart cannot write.[96]

The two cases of Ward and Jeffrey demonstrate two characteristics of the lasting relationships that subsisted between professors and students, the first a deep personal friendship that was maintained, the second the use of an intellectual training to criticise both outlook and teaching in changed circumstances. Other individuals, even Jeffrey himself, could contain within themselves both a lasting admiration for Stewart and an ability to move with the times. Though formed by a late eighteenth-century perspective they were yet able to adapt to the numerous challenges of the nineteenth century.

If Ward and Jeffrey show different instances of the continued intercourse between professor and former student, there were others between the students themselves as may be glimpsed from the relationship between Francis Horner and John Archibald Murray. Horner (1778-1817) has figured thus far as a member of student societies and of the group that founded the *Edinburgh Review*, one of those able Scots who benefited from the academic prelections of enlightened professors and from the institutions of extra-curricular life which led him into close contact with others of that talented and influential student body that congregated in Edinburgh especially from the 1790s. His father was an Edinburgh merchant, he studied with Dugald Stewart, was closely attached to the professor personally and intellectually, and determined on a career in law. Political historians of Scotland have noted how certainly by the 1790s, for a number of reasons, the perceptions of Scotsmen were much more British and Horner sought to make his career in England possible in this atmosphere. He was also following a long and honourable tradition of his countrymen in forsaking Scotland to find work and in England met up with many with whom he had studied. Certainly the increase of Scots business in the House of Lords that was evident by 1802 afforded good prospects for a Scots lawyer, who had made a reputation in the Edinburgh Court of Session, who was familiar with its forms and who was now prepared to reside in London.

Horner left permanently for London in March 1803, though he had first gone to a tutor there for two years between 1795 and 1797. Then he had left behind close friends of his own age who were not prepared to follow careers in England. One contemporary so left was John Murray (1779-1859), who had been with Horner at the Edinburgh High School as well as the university, a member with him, too, of the Juvenile Literary and the Speculative Societies. In 1799, Murray went to the Scottish Bar, contributed frequently to the *Edinburgh Review* in its early years, became MP for Leith in the 1830s and Lord Advocate. Almost immediately Horner had gone to England in 1795 he was writing to Murray:

I see nothing to prevent us carrying on our *Disputationes Academicae*, though we are four hundred miles asunder — Metaphysics can wax loud enough, and I can get franks every week. Come, I order you in the name of Hume, and Smith, and Dugald Stewart, to select a question immediately, and to begin upon it in your very first letter.[97]

Subsequent correspondence with Murray and others contained the debates: Horner and Murray were not merely full of good intentions and it is significant that they conjured up the spirit of the great figures of the Scottish Enlightenment.

The lasting impact of his educational experience on Francis Horner is particularly well documented. When he returned from his first foray south, he wrote to his old tutor in England saying how he wished to treat law in that philosophical way prescribed by the literati of the Scottish Enlightenment:

I am labouring to study [law] as a science, and by writing it with philosophical history so render it an exercise of the reasoning and arranging faculties, not of mere memory. I can find very few authors indeed who teach me anything in this way; I should wish not only general results, but to be taught the *habit* of generalising and the logic (as it were) of legislative science.[98]

The value of 'reasoning and arranging' noted here was obviously not shared by Jeffrey but Horner was nearer to Ward, perhaps, in his veneration for Stewart. He commented from London to his brother in 1803 that no political economy was taught there, though there was plenty of chemistry: 'We are very fortunate if we have one Stewart in the course of a century.' To Horner, it was if he was enchanted by Stewart and Stewart's mentor, Francis Bacon: 'Lord Bacon and Dugald Stewart have made me a little of a visionary. . . . But I have not yet reasoned myself out of those shades; the 'fantastic spell' is unbroken.'[99]

A year later, from Hampstead, Horner wrote a lengthy account of his hopes for Stewart's influence in a letter to Thomas Thomson, an Edinburgh advocate who had sent an account to Horner of Stewart's plans for a book:

I should like to have *all* his metaphysics, and I should like to have all his literature, and I should like to see him pay both these debts that he might proceed forthwith to discharge his farther engagements in political economy. On all of these subjects, his views are original and profound; and their originality consists so much in the comprehensive form which they have assumed in his mode of conceiving them, that it can be preserved only in his expressions. His writing on literary and moral topics is the most popular in this part of the world, but Stewart ought not to write for this part of the world or for this age of the world' he is bound to feel more courage, professing the art of writing as he does which always makes such a conquest over time, to say nothing of that loftiness and sensibility which pervade his philosophy, and must insure its success for ever, if England has any pretensions to immortality. If I could have my own wishes gratified, I confess I should desire that he would make his view of mind, intellectually considered, as enlarged as he has ever considered it, including all his valuable suggestions for the improvement of logic in the various sciences, even tho' he sh*d* not have perserverance to mould these into a systematic shape and that he would proceed immediately to political philosophy, in which I am confident he would produce a work that would excite great attention, and impress a lasting influence. After all the mischief that has been done of late years, I am thoroughly convinced that the public mind in England at least is still sound and susceptible.[100]

Stewart's lectures produced the great effect of sending out every year a certain number of earnest pupils who had imbibed his spirit: for this reason alone Horner regretted hearing in November 1804 that the enrolment in the political economy class had dropped so that there was a possibility of Stewart giving it up.[101] When Stewart finally decided to retire in 1809, Horner wrote to Mrs Stewart sympathising with the reasons for the decision but bemoaning the decline of the university that must necessarily result and the solitude in which John Playfair would be left 'among the ignorant and illiberal priests'. He hoped that Stewart would fulfill his public duty and his duty to posterity by writing.[102] This the philosopher did and not without help from former students, including Horner. Horner supplied him with facts for a paper on a boy born blind and deaf which Stewart read to the Royal Society of Edinburgh in 1812 and ensured that he was in possession of a copy of the Bullion Committee Report for the House of Commons (1810) of which Horner was an author. He considered that the greatest favour Stewart could perform was to comment on those points on which he disagreed with the committee. Horner implied clearly he had had to restrain himself in several parts of the Bullion Report because the general public in England were not yet ready for thoroughgoing principles of political economy that Stewart had inculcated in Horner and that he would find had been muted.[103] A number of letters record Horner's pleasure with each new publication that Stewart produced, including in 1814, his comments on the second volume of *Elements of the Philosophy of the Human Mind*. He thought that the disputation on Aristotle 'can hardly fail to have some salutary influence upon education in England, provided it provokes anger at Oxford'[104] (a reference to Edinburgh university opinion that Oxford scholarship was moribund).

There are other instances of Horner's and others' continued interest not merely in individuals and ideas but also in the institution of Edinburgh University. In 1804, Horner, Lord Lauderdale, John Thomson, Sir James Mackintosh, Webb Seymour and Henry Brougham all sought, unsuccessfully, to counter the system of hereditary professorships that they felt had of late caused the university's standards to deteriorate. In 1809, Horner is bemoaning the university's failure to distinguish itself by chemical discoveries as in the past. In 1805, Horner and Mackintosh were very interested that Stewart and Playfair's campaign to defeat the moderates and to see John Leslie installed in the Chair of Mathematics should triumph, and Horner again watched anxiously in 1810 for the success of two other liberal professorial appointments. He further demonstrated his continuing interest in Edinburgh intellectual life by writing to his brother in 1811 about Playfair's book on James Hutton's Theory of the Earth.[105] So there is no doubt that the educational experience had a lasting impact on significant students and once they were making their careers in England, mutual interests and talents nurtured in their student days were brought to bear on their new involvements. The personal ties initiated by their Scottish university education were carried forward into a wider world. The common experience of their youth was to prove durable even in the new settings and their challenges. 'I have a very sincere attachment to Scotland', noted Sydney Smith, 'and am very much interested by Scotch news. 5 of the most agreeable years of my life were spent there, and there I have found many friendships which I am sure will last as long as I live.'[106]

Notes

1. R.D. Anderson, *Education and Opportunity in Victorian Scotland: Schools*

and Universities (Clarendon Press, 1983), pp. 27-38 is a recent coverage of the Scottish universities in the age of Enlightenment. On 'catchment areas' in earlier times, see Robert Noyes Smart, 'Some Observations on the Provinces of the Scottish Universities 1560-1850', *The Scottish Tradition: Essays in Honour of Ronald Gordon Cant*, ed. G.W.S. Barrow (Scottish Academic Press, 1974), pp. 91-106.

2. *Edinburgh Evidence*, p. 128.

3. Ibid.

4. Ibid., p. 206.

5. *Aberdeen Evidence*, p. 217.

6. Ibid., p. 295.

7. Ibid., p. 222.

8. Ibid.

9. *Nomina Eorum qui Gradum Medicinae Doctoris in Academia Jacobi Sexti Scotorum Regis quae Edinburgi est adepti sunt 1705-1845* (Edinburgh, 1846), p. vi.

10. See Peter Jones' helpful study 'The Politics Academy and the Presbyterians, 1720-1770', *New Perspectives on the Politics and Culture of Early Modern Scotland*, ed. John Dwyer, Roger A. Mason and Alexander Murdoch (John Donald, n.d. [1982]), pp. 156-77. Aspects of connections between educational thinking in Scotland and dissenting academies in England are also discussed idem., 'The Scottish Professoriate and the Polite Academy, 1720-1746', *Wealth and Virtue: the Shaping of Political Economy in the Scottish Enlightenment*, ed. Istvan Hont and Michael Ignatieff (Cambridge University Press, 1983), pp. 89-117.

11. William Carstares, 'Considerations and Proposals for Encouraging of Parents in sending their Sons to the University of Edinburgh', E.U.L. ms. La. II 407/1-13, in Jane Rendall, *The Origins of the Scottish Enlightenment* (Macmillan, Press, 1978), pp. 51-2.

12. Irene Parker, *Dissenting Academies in England: their rise and progress and their place among the educational systems of the country* (Cambridge University Press, 1914), pp. 159-60.

13. Nicholas Hans, *New Trends in Education in the Eighteenth Century* (Routledge & Kegan Paul, 1966), p. 247.

14. Quoted in Brian Simon, *Studies in the History of Education 1780-1870* (Lawrence & Wishart, 1960), p. 60.

15. A good account of the sober Edinburgh student life, even for the more mature gentlemen, is to be found in D.B. Horn, *A Short History of the University of Edinburgh*, pp. 91-2, and Professor Horn gave a reference (on p. 91 n) to *Anecdotes and Egotisms of Henry MacKenzie*, ed. H.W. Thompson, (Humphrey Milford, London, 1927), pp. 74-90 for a full and contemporary account of the games played in eighteenth-century Edinburgh. Round tours to pick Penicuik strawberries and billiards appear to have been the worst vices that were indulged. As a contrast, the observations on Cambridge of the Duke of Bedford to his son, Lord John Russell, might be noted: 'I can see no possible benefit likely to result from it, except you call the various excellences attending the sciences of horse-racing, fox-hunting, and giving extravagant entertainments, an advantage, as these, I believe, are the chief studies of our youth at Cambridge', quoted in Spencer Walpole, *The Life of Lord John Russell*, 2 vols. (Longmans, 1891), I, pp. 59-60.

16. *The Correspondence of Adam Smith*, ed. E.C. Mossner and I.S. Ross (Clarendon Press, 1977), Letter 27, 14 November 1758, p. 27.

17. Ibid., Letter 37, to Lord Shelburne, 31 August 1759, p. 45.

18. Ibid., Letter 42, to Lord Shelburne, 29 October 1759, p. 59.

19. Ibid., Letter 64, Thomas Fitzmaurice to Adam Smith, 26 February 1762, pp. 81-82.

20. Ibid., Letter 35, to Lord Shelburne, 23 July 1759, p. 41.

21. Ibid., Letter 51, to Lord Shelburne, 15 July 1760, pp. 70-1. The same letter speaks of a spell in Glasgow proving to be the death of 'a sort of flippant smartness' 'learned at Eton'.

22. On health, for example, ibid., Letters 45-9 and 51-3, 10, 12, 15, 17, 19 March 1760 and 15 July 1760 and 11 November 1760 (2), pp. 62-7, 69-73; on the other aspects of Smith's care see, for example, Letters 28-30, 42, 43, 51, 21 February 1759, 10 March 1759, 4 April 1759, 29 October 1759, 3 December 1759, 15 July 1760, pp. 28-32, 58-62, 69-71. Smith's pastoral concern is also discussed in R.H. Campbell and A.S. Skinner, *Adam Smith* (Croom Helm, 1982), pp. 41-5.

23. *Correspondence*, Letter 32, Lord Shelburne to Adam Smith, 26 April 1759, pp. 36-8, with the quotation from p. 38.

24. See, for example, ibid., Letter 35, Adam Smith to Lord Shelburne, 23 July 1759, p. 41.

25. Ibid., Letters 28 and 101, 28 February 1759 and 12 February 1767, pp. 28-9, 122-4.

26. See, for instance, ibid., Letter 64, Thomas Fitzmaurice to Adam Smith, 26 February 1762, pp. 81-4.

27. Roy Porter, *English Society in the Eighteenth Century* (Penguin, 1982), p. 179.

28. Some impression of who these aristocrats were can be gained from the list below, drawn from a variety of works, of young nobility who attended classes in Edinburgh and Glasgow in the years of the French wars, giving the title inherited where possible:

Edinburgh
Lord Ancram, 6th Marquis of Lothian
Richard, 2nd Baron Ashburton
Lord Brooke, 3rd Earl of Warwick
Charles, 2nd Baron Calthorpe
Lord John Cuninghame
Basil, Lord Daer, son of 4th Earl of Selkirk
Michael Hicks-Beach
Lord Kileen, 9th Earl of Fingall
James Ochoncer, 17th Baron Forbes
Charles Grant, Baron Glenelg
Thomas Hamilton Binning, 9th Earl of Hamilton
Charles, 8th Baron Kinnaird
Henry Petty-Fitzmaurice, Marquis of Lansdowne
Sir Alexander Muir MacKenzie of Delvin
Gilbert Elliot-Murray-Kynymond, 2nd Earl of Minto
Richard Wingfield, 5th Viscount Powerscourt
William Pleydell-Bouverie, 3rd Earl Radnor
Lord John Russell, Earl Russell
Thomas Douglas, 5th Earl of Selkirk, 13th Baron Sempill
Lord Webb Seymour, brother of 11th Duke of Somerset
Hon. Charles Stourton, 3rd son of 16th Baron Stourton
(Lawrence Sulivan, son-in-law of 2nd Viscount Palmerston)
Henry Temple, 3rd Viscount Palmerston
William Temple, son of 2nd Viscount Palmerston
John William Ward, 1st Earl of Dudley

Glasgow
Henry George, 4th Earl Bathurst

William Lennox, 5th Earl Bathurst
John Campbell, 2nd Marquis of Breadalbane
David Erskine, Earl of Buchan
Frederick Lamb, 3rd Viscount Melbourne
William Lamb, 2nd Viscount Melbourne

29. See Brian Connell, *Portrait of a Whig Peer: compiled from the papers of the second Viscount Palmerston 1739-1802* (André Deutsch, 1957),pp. 425, 426, 431, 432, 433, 441, 444, 445, 461. The quotations are from Mr Connell's rendering of letters and journals in Broadlands mss. For the debt of Lord Ashburton to Dugald Stewart, see *The Letters of Sydney Smith*, ed. Nowell C. Smith, 2 vols. (Oxford University Press, 1953), I, pp. 80-1, Letter 76 to the Hon. Caroline Fox.

30. Microfilm no. M136.

31. Alex Ferguson, *The Honourable Henry Erskine Lord Advocate for Scotland with notices of certain of his kinsfolk and of his time compiled from family papers and other sources of information* (Blackwood, 1882), p. 190, and *Life and Letters of Sir Gilbert Elliot*, III, pp. 231-2.

32. James Lorimer, 'Letters and Discoveries of Sir Charles Bell', *Edinburgh Review*, CXXXV, p. 407.

33. Philip Ziegler, *Melbourne: A Biography of William, Lamb, 2nd Viscount Melbourne* (Collins, 1976), p. 30.

34. Quoted in W.C. Lehman, *John Millar of Glasgow*, p. 33. The reference to boxing is in Lord Cockburn, *Life of Lord Jeffrey*, I, pp. 10-11.

35. Walpole, I, pp. 57-9, with the quotation from p. 57.

36. Sir William Hamilton, 'Memoir of Dugald Stewart', *Collected Works of Dugald Stewart*, 11 vols. (Edinburgh, 1854-60), X (1858), p. lix.

37. An account of Jardine's own teaching is given by a former student in *Edinburgh Evidence*, p. 174; Jardine's own account is to be found in his book, and also in *Glasgow Evidence*, p. 514.

38. Quoted in Lehmann, pp. 32-3.

39. See Anand C. Chitnis, 'The University of Edinburgh's Natural History Museum and the Huttonian-Wernerian Debate', *Annals of Science*, XXVI (1970), pp. 85-94.

40. *Edinburgh Evidence*, pp. 141-2.

41. *Report*, p. 138.

42. 'Biography of the late Professor Jameson', *The Monthly Journal of Medical Science*, XVIII (January-June 1854), p. 574.

43. *Edinburgh Evidence*, p. 142.

44. See Chitnis, *Edinburgh Professoriate*, pp. 209-11.

45. *The Life and Letters of Charles Darwin, including an autobiographical chapter*, ed. Francis Darwin, 3 vols. (London, 1887), I, pp. 41-2.

46. See Chitnis, *The Scottish Enlightenment*, pp. 229-32.

47. Horn, p. 93, and *Collected Works of Dugald Stewart*, X, pp. xxvii-xxviii.

48. See C.P. Finlayson, 'Records of Scientific and Medical Societies preserved in the University Library, Edinburgh', *The Bibliotheck: A Journal of Bibliographical Notes and Queries mainly of Scottish Interest*, I (1958), pp. 15-16.

49. John Thomson to John Allen, 12 June 1801, in 'Biographical Notice of John Thomson', John Thomson, *An Account of the Life, Lectures and Writings of William Cullen, M.D.*, 2 vols. (Edinburgh, 1832-59), annexed to II (1859), p. 17.

50. *The Life of Sir Robert Christison, Bart.*, ed. by his sons, 2 vols. (Edinburgh and London, 1885), I, pp. 61-2.

51. The Society was the Plinian; see *Edinburgh Evidence*, pp. 145-6.

52. Thomson, *Cullen*, annex to II, p. 12.

53. *The Life and Times of Henry, Lord Brougham written by himself*, 3 vols.

(Blackwood, 1871), I, p. 81.

54. *Dissertations by Eminent Members of the Royal Medical Society*, (Edinburgh, 1892), pp. 32-9, 40-63, 64-83, 84-94.

55. The list is culled from *General List of the Members of the Medical Society of Edinburgh*, (Edinburgh, 1887), pp. 23-44.

56. A selection made from Edinburgh University Library ms. Dc. 6. 111, ff. 163-4.

57. Compiled from *History of the Speculative Society of Edinburgh from its institution in 1764* (Edinburgh, 1845), and *A General List of the Members of the Speculative Society* (Edinburgh, 1814).

58. *The Life of Lord Brougham*, I, pp. 86-7.

59. Cockburn, *Memorials* (1856 edn), p. 74, and *Life of Lord Jeffrey*, I, p. 53.

60. Cockburn, *Memorials*, p. 74.

61. *Brougham*, I. p. 52.

62. Horn, p. 40.

63. *Brougham*, I, p. 52.

64. *[Edinburgh] College Minutes*, Edinburgh University Library, II (1790-1811), pp. 160-71, 12 and 28 March, 8 April 1799.

65. *Brougham*, I, pp. 52-3.

66. W.K. Dickson, *The History of the Speculative Society 1764-1904*, (Edinburgh, 1905), p. 23.

67. *Edinburgh Annual Register for 1817*, X (Edinburgh, 1821), p. 148.

68. John Leslie, Professor of Natural Philosophy to the Royal Commissions of 1826 and 1830, *Edinburgh Evidence*, p. 132.

69. David Welsh, *Account of the Life and Writings of Thomas Brown*, (London, 1825), p. 77.

70. *Correspondence Book of the Academy of Physics*, Edinburgh, National Library of Scotland, MS. 755, p. 29, 21 February 1798.

71. G.N. Cantor, 'The Academy of Physics at Edinburgh 1797-1800', *Social Studies of Science*, V (1975), pp. 117-18.

72. Quoted ibid., p. 119 from his commonplace book in the Kinnordy mss.

72. *Memoirs and Correspondence of Francis Horner, M.P.*, ed. Leonard Horner, 2 vols. (London, 1843), I, pp. 114-15, entry dated 20 July 1800.

74. Welsh, p. 499.

75. Francis Horner to Thomas Logan of Dunglass, 21 July 1798, National Library of Scotland, ms. 948, no. 76.

76. Henry Brougham to William Manchester, 12 February 1798, *Correspondence Book*, ms. 755, p. 10.

77. Ibid., 6 and 20 February 1798, pp. 1-3, 25-6.

78. Cantor, pp. 123, 128.

79. *Correspondence Book*, ms. 755, 20 February 1798, pp. 24-5.

80. Cantor, p. 132 n. For a recent account of the origins of the *Review* see Allan Bell, *Sydney Smith* (Clarendon Press, 1908), pp. 34-7. Smith edited the first issue.

81. Walter Bagehot, 'The First Edinburgh Reviewers', *Literary Studies*, ed. R.H. Hutton, 2 vols., 2nd edn (Longmans, 1879), I, pp. 24-5.

82. William Lamb to Lady Melbourne, 8 February 1800, *Lord Melbourne's Papers*, ed. Lloyd C. Sanders, (Longmans, 1889), pp. 19-20.

83. Cockburn, *Jeffrey*, I, p. 142.

84. Smith to Francis Jeffrey, 30 November 1803, *The Letters of Sydney Smith*, no. 87, I, p. 91.

85. *Letters to 'Ivy'*, p. 64, letter dated 1 February 1809.

86. Ibid., p. 177, letter dated December 1812.

87. Ibid., p. 231, letter dated 8 February 1814.

88. Ibid., pp. 233-4, letter dated February 1814.

89. Ibid., pp. 245-6.

90. Henry Home Drummond, *Opinions*, II, pp. 25-6, Abercairny Papers, no. 1032, Scottish Record Office, and written towards the end of 1808.

91. I have surveyed the Jeffrey-Stewart debate in another context, in *The Scottish Enlightenment*, pp. 214-17.

92. *Edinburgh Review*, III, (1804), pp. 273, 275.

93. Ibid., III, pp. 275-76.

94. Smith to Jeffrey, February 1804, *The Letters of Sydney Smith*, no. 89, I, p. 93.

95. *Edinburgh Review*, XVII (1810), pp. 183-6.

96. Smith to Horner, December 1816, *The Letters of Sydney Smith*, no. 272, I, p. 272.

97. *Memoirs of Francis Horner*, I, p. 9.

98. *Horner Collection of Manuscript Correspondence and Papers,* British Library of Political and Economic Science, 8 vols. (subsequently *Horner Collection L.S.E.*) I, Letter 49, n.d. [late 1798?].

99. Ibid., II, Letters 27 and 70, 5 November 1803 and 13 September 1804.

100. Ibid., II, Letter 107, 8 August 1805. The impression of Stewart derived from Horner is tempered somewhat by Sydney Smith's noting that when he visited the philosopher in 1808, he found him 'fat and agricultural – fond of indecent stories as ever' (quoted in Bell, p. 81).

101. Ibid., II, Letter 80, 21 November 1804.

102. Ibid., IV, Letters 6 and 8, 25 and 27 January 1809.

103. Ibid., Letter 126, 16 November 1810.

104. Ibid., VI, Letter 14, 25 February 1814.

105. Ibid., II, Letters 36-9, 5, 7 and 10 January 1804; IV, Letter 8, 27 January 1809; II, Letter 95, 8 April 1805; IV, Letters 98 and 99, both 8 May 1810; and V, Letter 36, 3 September 1811.

106. *Letters of Sydney Smith*, I, p. 217, Letter 212 to J.A. Murray, 6 December 1811.

3 INTO ENGLAND AND THE NINETEENTH CENTURY: 'ONLY CONNECT...'

Edinburgh had never contained such a concentration of young men as now inspired it, of whose presence the Review was only one of the results. They formed a band of friends all attached to each other, all full of hope and ambition and gaiety, and all strengthened in their mutual connection by the politics of most of them separating the whole class from the ordinary society of the city. It was a most delightful brotherhood. But about the end of 1802 it began to to be thinned by emigration, and this process went on until 1806.

Henry Cockburn, *Memorials of his Time*
(Edinburgh, 1856), p. 176)

I left Edinburgh with great heaviness of heart: I knew what I was leaving, and was ignorant to what I was going. My good fortune will be very great, if I should ever again fall into the society of so many liberal, correct and instructed men, and live with them on such terms of friendship as I have done with you, and you know whom, at Edinburgh.

(Sydney Smith to Francis Jeffrey, [August] 1803, Letter 78 in
The Letters of Sydney Smith, ed. Nowell C. Smith, 2 vols.
(Oxford University Press, 1953), I, p. 82)

I

The students that are of concern here, be they Scottish, English, aristocratic or dissenting, were those who took 'Scotch knowledge' to England at the end of the eighteenth and at the beginning of the nineteenth centuries. It may be useful to define here more precisely, on the basis of what has gone before, what 'Scotch knowledge' can be said to mean, rather than rely on the mere impression of it conveyed by Lord John Russell before he went to Edinburgh. It can most obviously consist of a body of knowledge, such as that social philosophy and political economy associated with leading thinkers of eighteenth-century Scotland and incorporated into lecture courses at the Scottish universities from that time. It can also subsist in another area of endeavour,

79

then just as unique, namely the systematic medical curriculum pursued at Edinburgh and to a lesser extent at Glasgow. It subsists, too, in the educational experience generally available in the Scottish universities, not merely the content of teaching to which a student might be exposed, but the methods of teaching in and out of the classroom, and the extra-curricular opportunities that could abound, with the chances they gave to develop talents and to become known in a wide circle. Whether the exposure was to philosophy, medicine, or both, as well as the overall educational experience, general and specific principles were conveyed and, in some instances, so too were specific methods of tackling specific problems.

It will become an important component in the developing analysis to show that the furtherance of the lessons and influence of 'Scotch knowledge' depended on the connections that were forged between an array of individuals during their time in a Scottish university. So much was this so that it is possible to detect a coherence and a network among Scottish alumni. In some literature, both of the time and since, the network has been described in a variety of ways that amount to 'the school or disciples of Dugald Stewart'. Such a description can detract from the influence of other teachers in other universities and narrow the influence to those in politics and public life, obscuring the strong 'Scottish' element among medical practitioners and their significance for provincial life and culture.

There is, therefore, a ubiquity about 'Scotch knowledge' and an influence can be ascribed to it as significant as the Clapham sect, the Unitarians, the utilitarians and the Statistical Movement, of which groups (in particular the last three) 'Scots'[1] were members and with whom they regularly cooperated in a number of causes. 'British individualism', wrote Elie Halévy, 'is a moderate individualism, a mixture whose constituents are often mingled beyond the possibility of analysis, a compound of Evangelicalism and utilitarianism.'[2] One of Halévy's great capacities, as has often been recognised, was that of comprehending and unravelling the texture of English life, the detection of and interaction between the different religious sects and intellectual côteries. It is true that some of the subtleties escaped him, particularly his identification of the single, unvaried term Methodism with all Evangelicalism, but he never left the allegedly significant power of utilitarianism in isolation. One of the influences Halévy detected and expounded in this crucial section of his book was that of the Scottish universities, and he highlighted the influence of Dugald Stewart on those English aristocrats and Dissenters who went to Scotland to study.[3] Only the narrow religious vocabulary requires to be tempered in Halévy's assessment of the Scottish contribution to England:

> the Scottish Presbyterians, hard on others, hard on themselves, unwearied thinkers, contributed to nineteenth-century England an element of intellectual virility which would have been wanting had the country been abandoned entirely to the emotionalism of the Wesleys and the Wilberforces.[4]

Once the secular character of the 'Scots' is appreciated, they can be seen as a vital element in Coleridge's clerisy, the intellectual élite.

There is evidence that the 'Scots' were aware of the differences between their approach and that of others. When, for instance, Francis Horner saw that Henry Brougham was cooperating with Evangelicals in such matters as the abolition of slavery he wrote:

> But the Saints are not properly a political set of men; and their character is so entirely cast from their religious zeal, that there can be little community of sentiment between them and Brougham, when the object that at present brings them together is once gained.[5]

Horner was also critical of Bentham: '[his] name is repulsive . . . for tho' I am satisfied the system is quite devoid of enlarged views and comprehensive principles, there are possibly minute details both ingeniously contrived and admitting of practical applications'.[6] Sir James Mackintosh found Bentham and his disciples intensely arrogant:

> He and they deserve the credit of braving vulgar prejudices, so they must be content to incur the imputation of falling into the neighbouring vices of seeking distinction by singularity — of clinging to opinions, because they are obnoxious — of wantonly wounding the most respectable feeling of mankind — of regarding an immense display of method and nomenclature as a sure token of a corresponding increase of knowledge — and of considering themselves as a chosen few, whom an initiation into the most secret mysteries of Philosophy entitles to look down with pity; if not contempt, on the profane multitude. Viewed with aversion or dread by the public, they become more bound to each other and to their master; while they are provoked into the use of language which more and more exasperates opposition to them.

Bentham himself, hermetically sealed off from all but his own circle, was aware only that his proposed systems were being totally disregarded and he himself treated with disdain the ideas of others: 'He is too little acquainted with doubts to believe the honest doubts of others, and he is too angry to make allowance for their prejudices and habits.'[7] John William Ward, Earl of Dudley, recounted a story which revealed Dugald Stewart's predilections:

> I was going to call on Mme. de Staël so I had an opportunity of immediately delivering Mr Stewart's message to her. She seemed very much pleased and desired me to say that her principal object in going to Scotland would be to see him . . . I wish, however, you had heard the scream of joy she gave when Mackintosh told her that Mr Stewart is hostile to the 'Principe d'Utilité'. By the bye, What with Paley, and what with Bentham, we are converts to it here, so if he means to set us right he had better lose no time.[8]

In their self-awareness, the 'Scots' were bemused at the integrity ascribed by the English to particular aspects of 'Scotch knowledge', notably metaphysics, and at the lack of appreciation of the differences and debates between Hume and Reid and Smith. One of Horner's letters conveys the impression gained:

> Metaphysical thinkers here . . . may be described as belonging, more than they will always confess, to the Scotch school, by which I take the liberty of understanding the school founded by David Hume, and not the Aberdeen foundation.. I suspect they are not always aware of the merit which I must ascribe to Reid, and they certainly are not sufficiently apprised of what was done by Smith's book to the natural history . . . of the mind.[9]

None the less, that the Scots specialised in metaphysics (whatever it meant and to whatever school they belonged) was a common impression in England. It was an impression fostered by such wits as Sydney Smith who were familiar with the cultures of both countries. He sent some game to Holland House on his return from a visit to Scotland with the following note:

> I take the liberty to send you two brace of grouse, curious, because killed by a scotch metaphysician; in other and better language they are mere ideas, shot by other ideas, out of a pure intellectual notion

called a gun . . . The modification of matter called grouse which accompanies this note is not in the common apprehension of Edinburgh considered to be dependent upon a first cause, but to have existed from all eternity.

He frequently delivered such affectionate jibes as 'those compositions of itch, oatmeal and metaphysics, the Scotch philosophers'.[10]

The Scots themselves, though, may have helped give the impression of a social if not an intellectual clannishness by the creation of particular focal points. One was the King of Clubs. It was founded by Sir James Mackintosh and Sydney Smith's brother, Robert, in February 1798 as a dining club for 'Scots' of liberal views. Such dining clubs were commonplace for distinct groups: Sir Francis Burdett, the Radical, had a dining club for his closest friends called the Rota, another was the Eumelian, and there were many more. The King of Clubs met monthly, beginning in Mackintosh's home, moving to the Crown and Anchor in the Strand and then migrating from hotel to hotel. It continued even during Mackintosh's time in India as Recorder of Bombay between 1804 and 1811, and did not die out until 1823.[11] By 1802, the King of Clubs was being described by Horner as having been formed by those Whig Scots who had been to Edinburgh and had now removed to London, and that the names of the members would be obvious to one of his friends who was still in the Scottish capital.[12] The members included Henry Petty, Sydney Smith, John William Ward, Henry Brougham, William Lamb, Francis Jeffrey and John Playfair (made a member just two years before he died, doubtless while on a visit to London and out of the regard in which he was held).[13]

If the King of Clubs was fairly exclusive another focal point, Holland House, was not, though the 'Scottish' contribution was prominent in its deliberations and activities. Like the King of Clubs, however, Holland House was politically liberal; a not invariable characteristic, of the 'Scots' was their tendency to Whiggery. At Holland House, the fulcrum of the Whig Party, their coherence among the *habitués* prompted the close definition used by others to describe them, namely 'the Edinburgh reviewers'.

II

Situated two miles from Marble Arch on the road west out of London, Holland House, as a social and political institution, lasted from 1797, when Lord and Lady Holland contracted their scandalous but highly successful marriage, until 1840 when Lord Holland died. Described as 'something of a shrine' to the archetypal eighteenth-century Whig, Charles James Fox, the house was maintained by Lord Holland, Fox's nephew and political heir, as 'the forum in which memories of Fox could be kept alive and where his views could be retailed to new generations.'[14] Holland House was a salon in the European mould, that is a means of wielding political power, of being the hub of political wheels, of attracting young men of talent who would then be found patrons and thereafter remain in debt to the promoters of their political career. For an older historian of the house, it was 'a political council-chamber and meeting-place where the few matured plans and the many made acquaintances', and Holland's wide social relations made him an unrivalled political intelligence officer for Whig leaders.[15] For its most recent analyst the very holding of a salon 'implied the wish to meddle' though the House was simultaneously 'one of the great social centres of early nineteenth-century London'. There was no paradox here for since the parliamentary session and the London season were coterminous, the political and the social could be brought together. At the same time, the integrity of the Whig Party during its lengthy period in the political wilderness was ensured by Holland House since its social functions kept the party together: its 'political function' in this respect was 'of the greatest importance'. But the description 'salon' has cultural rather than social or political connotations: it has been further shown that the Hollands saw an intimate connection between literature and politics, and literature was certainly their favourite leisure pursuit. Consequently, Holland House 'acquired a quite extraordinary pre-eminence and popularity', 'represented a self-conscious attempt to bring the powerful and the best together', and Lord and Lady Holland have been assessed as 'intellectual impressarios' of a 'self-conscious élite'.[16]

Holland's political views remained static; to some extent this was because the French Revolution and its aftermath caused the main political issues to remain the same for some 40 years but also he took very seriously his position as the representative of his uncle's tradition. The perpetuation of the memory of Charles James Fox took numerous forms including the foundation of Fox clubs and the holding of annual Fox dinners throughout the country on his birthday. Whigs in Edinburgh particularly revered Fox's memory. Holland's view of his inheritance did mean, however, that he continued to fight the battles of the 1780s and 1790s against the Royal Prerogative and executive power into the 1820s and 1830s. He viewed all insurrections against authorit-

arianism as worthy of support and as heralding the dawn of constitu-
tionalism, whichever country might be in a state of revolt. In the era of
the French Wars, Holland was always far more suspicious of those
instances when executive power was demonstrated than of instances of
radical activity or civil disturbance. He also viewed the war as a means
of asserting the Royal Prerogative, thus rendering himself rather
isolated from most politically-recognised opinion in those years. His
failure to move with the times clearly reflected poorly on his judgement
and affected his and his party's standing. Holland explained the rise of
radicalism by the assertion of executive power and, therefore, he saw
some virtue in leaning towards support for radicalism in the face of the
executive. The task was for the property-owning aristocracy to act as
a balance between the two extremes and in practice, since the executive
was the more powerful, the aristocracy should tend to radical opinion.
A reformed House of Commons, for instance, was seen as one important
way of countering royal power over ministers, especially since the
massive increase in the members of the Lords between 1784 and 1801
meant that that chamber could no longer be viewed as unequivocally
suspicious of the King. In his espousal of the rights of the people, however, Holland's interpretation of 'the people' was only that of the
political nation, that is property-owners. Parliamentary reform was to
make possible the proper representation of the political nation.[17] To
this static Foxite approach the Edinburgh reviewers brought the
dynamic ideas of the social thought of the Scottish Enlightenment.

Whoever was welcomed into Holland House came on the Hollands'
terms. If the hosts' creed, political tactics or exclusiveness proved
unacceptable, or if ingratitude were shown (often in the form of an
ambition that did not require or depend on the Hollands) then once-
honoured guests could quickly be viewed as nuisances or at least cause
bewilderment. For these reasons, relations proved not to be smooth
between the Hollands and their kinsmen the Lansdownes, or with
George Canning and Henry Brougham. Incompatibility ruled out any
mutual interaction between Holland House and Bentham and the
Clapham sect, though they did ally with the latter over the slave trade.
Hence it appears that the only intellectual current of the day which
impinged at all on Holland House between 1797 and 1840 was that of
the Scottish Enlightenment, and the Edinburgh reviewers were the
link between the two. Most were part of that young talent and ability
that the Hollands were always anxious to search out and to patronise.
Jeffrey wrote of the 'ever loved and honoured Holland House', and
Lord Byron's celebrated lampoon on the *Edinburgh Review* assumed

the relationship between Holland House and the *Review* to be so close that the attack made on him had been determined editorially at Holland House.[18] Two areas of concern to the *Review* made no impact on the Hollands, political economy and education and, indeed, they were topics that positively repelled them as did the detail of 'Scottish' philosophy.

Ideas on property in Scottish social thought, however, proved invaluable to Holland House's contribution to the interminable debate over parliamentary reform. For instance, eighteenth-century Scottish thought had shown scientifically that the number of property-holders would naturally increase as society advanced. If this was coupled to Holland's view that the franchise was a trust inherent in property-holding, then there was bound to be an incorporation of more people into the political nation over time. Holland came to see through the reviewers that rather than being static, society was in motion; additionally he could see that the *Review*, by espousing his brand of Whiggery, was a powerful means of disseminating it. Jeffrey was a most faithful correspondent and ally. In sum, to quote Leslie Mitchell,

> Holland House remained one of the principal meeting places for London Whigs and Scots reviewers. The interchange between them was supervised and encouraged by the Hollands. The Foxite core of the party was thereby immeasurably enriched'.[19]

The ideas, however, penetrated Holland House because of the close ties forged by individuals. Pre-eminent was John Allen (1771-1843). His father had been a Writer to the Signet in Edinburgh and he commenced medical studies at Edinburgh University in 1786, studying anatomy and surgery, medical theory and practice, chemistry, materia medica, clinical practice, and botany until 1791. He matriculated for three courses each session except that of 1791 when he took five.[20] While some sources suggest that he took an Edinburgh MD in 1791, this cannot be substantiated from the records. He is, however, recorded as a Fellow of the Royal College of Surgeons of Edinburgh, and between 1798 and 1801 he set himself up as a private lecturer on physiology and animal economy at the time when the numbers flocking to Edinburgh for a medical education soared. Henry Cockburn heard from a noted Edinburgh medical authority that 'Allen's single lecture on the circulation of blood contained as much truth and view as could be extracted by an intelligent reader from all the books in Europe on that subject'.[21] Politically a Whig, he realised then that he stood no chance of a Chair at the university since such posts were in the gift of a Tory town council. He had associated with the Edinburgh reviewers (he had been a member of the Speculative Soicety since 1791) and one of them, Sydney Smith, together with the political economist Lord Lauderdale, wrote him letters of reference to Lord Holland then seeking a medical attendant on a projected tour of Spain. So in 1802 he made his first appearance at Holland House, went on a three-year tour with the Hollands during which he made himself indispensable, and on the return, he was invited to remain as librarian, a post he held till his death. For Cockburn, the association was 'at far too high a price when it lost him the glory of being the first medical teacher in Europe'[22] though, ironically, the partisanship of the Edinburgh town council was instrumental in spreading the Scottish Enlightenment far wider than it might otherwise have been and certainly to where it was needed.

Allen's duties included the preparation of the lists of those who were to dine at the house, which rooms visitors should be allocated, and he acted as companion to the Hollands on numerous European tours, including that on which the young Lord John Russell was taken in 1809. Outside the house, he was warden of Dulwich College (1811-20) and then Master until his death. The Hollands regarded him as a valued literary and political adviser. For a few months in 1806 he served as Under-Secretary to the Commissioners treating with America of whom Lord Holland was one. But for present purposes his most significant function was as the link between Edinburgh and Holland House, introducing there the first reviewers and thereafter those he considered to be the latest talent produced by the Scottish capital where he went trawling for talent in 1814, 1818 and 1822.[23] Sydney Smith wrote how Lady Holland 'has taken hugely to the Edinburgh reviewers, particularly to little John Horner — whose reputation as well as Brougham's are so high for political oeconomy that they are fêted everywhere.'[24]

Holland enjoyed the political tutoring of the young men from Scotland, especially Francis Horner and Lord John Russell, perhaps because his own son jibbed at the thought of a political career. Brougham, however, proved an awkward pupil, partly because his ambitions went beyond those limits thought proper for one of Holland House's creatures, partly because he disliked being ordered about by Lady Holland, partly because he was unstable, inconsistent, meddlesome. None the less, he was sufficiently countenanced at Holland House on and off through the years to reinforce the 'Scotch' presence there, though he was not really understood. On one occasion Sydney Smith wrote to J.A. Murray of Brougham's dissociation:

Brougham I am truely sorry to say has abandoned Holland House entirely, the house into which he stept on his getting out of the Scotch mail upon his first quitting the north; an house which is always open as you know to men of character and genius, and where he has been uniformly treated with the greatest indulgence . . . I really like Brougham and regret most heartily that he will not walk thro' life in a straight path.[25]

Brougham was, in fact, omitted deliberately by Walter Bagehot in his celebrated essay on 'The First Edinburgh Reviewers' because his inclusion would have marred the unity of his article: 'He was connected with the Whigs, but he never was one. His impulsive ardour is the opposite of their coolness; his irregular, discursive intellect contrasts with their quiet and perfecting mind.'[26] To a more recent scholar, however, 'perhaps no one can appreciate his career, or fathom his motives, who has not had the experience of having his abilities confined within the constricting mediocrity of men more timid and time-serving than himself.'[27] Jeffrey was always welcome at the house when infrequently in London but his principal contact was by his frequent correspondence with Allen. As for the aristocratic element in the 'Scotch' connection, Lords Minto, Lansdowne, Palmerston, Melbourne and Dudley were all familiars of the Hollands: Minto, successively President of the Board of Control and Governor-General of India, had rented a house in Edinburgh in 1801-02, while his son Gilbert Elliot (Lord Privy Seal 1846-52) was studying at the university. Minto senior not only made friends with Stewart, but in January 1802 spent a week with Gilbert and with Henry Temple going to chemistry, philosophy and particularly Stewart's political economy classes.[28]

Henry Petty, 3rd Marquis of Lansdowne, was a cousin of Lord Holland, and various close family arrangements existed between them, including Petty's accompanying of Lord Holland on one of his continental tours. But political differences subsisted too, stemming from Petty's father's time when questions began to be raised about whether the Landsownes could always be relied on to distance themselves from Fox's political enemies and the questions remained unanswered virtually through the lifetimes of Henry Petty and Lord Lansdowne. Foxite exclusiveness was breached, for instance, when Lansdowne agreed to serve under first Canning and then Goderich in 1827. Away from the susceptibilities of the Hollands, Lansdowne was perceived to have become more grave and cautious when he inherited the marquisate in 1809. His espousal of moderate policies thereafter contrasted with the more dashing figure he cut as Chancellor of the Exchequer in 1806-07. Later, as Lord President of the Council and Minister without Portfolio he served to temper reform legislation, political and social. After 1830, he could have had any of the major offices of state but he was content with the Lord Presidency and acting as a maker of mid-century ministries. 'Whilst honest as the purest virgin', Lord John Russell is said to have written, 'Lansdowne was too yielding, too mild, and most unfit to deal with men in important political transactions.' 'You may be sure', Lansdowne himself is said to have assured an admirer in 1851, 'that if any strong measure was to be contemplated by the Cabinet, I should walk out of it.' His residences, Lansdowne House and Bowood, were rallying points for that part of the Whig opposition who found Lansdowne's approach congenial, and Bowood maintained its reputation acquired in the late eighteenth century for being, like Holland House, a great cultural centre.[29]

Lord Palmerston was another of the Whigs who inclined to Canning but yet frequented Holland House, even at times of ministerial dissension. The most difficult phase of Palmerston's relationship with Holland was in the 1830s when Palmerston was Foreign Secretary and Holland a Cabinet minister conducting foreign relations as if oblivious to the policy of the actual minister. Holland meddled and consequently battled with Palmerston. As Leslie Mitchell has written:

> In government or out of it, the Hollands too easily turned their dinner guests into couriers, agents and sources of intelligence. At times, it was hard to know whether their first loyalty lay with the British government or with some larger commitment to European liberalism.[30]

Palmerston married Melbourne's widowed sister, Melbourne being another who served Canning, as Irish Secretary, and who was an intimate of John William Ward, Lord Dudley. Both were evidently frequent and familiar faces at the Holland House dinner-table. In the 1830s, if not before, Holland House was the Whig ministerial headquarters,[31] it was, therefore, also 'an avenue of promotion'[32] and like the Edinburgh student societies before it, promotion was eased by the facility it provided for social and political intermingling. That political promotion for 'Scots' individuals indeed followed will be demonstrated shortly. Suffice it for now to see Holland House as a ready, potent and receptive force for the promotion of Scottish ideas. The most recent student of the Hollands writes:

The Foxite creed, which had been static in terms of a restatement of the politics of the 1970s, now also began to be defended as a reflection of a society in motion . . . . [R] elief for Roman Catholics or the claims of the Parliamentary Reformers could now be based on the idea of a movement in society which could be scientifically demonstrated, as well as on traditional Foxite views.

And he concludes:

The weight of family tradition contributed to the very odd intermingling of old myths and new ideas that constituted Holland House conversation. Their involvement with the *Edinburgh Review* and the enduring presence of John Allen guaranteed a lively interest in the concept of progress and movement in society.[33]

III

As has been implied, for all their appeal to the greatest Whig name of the recent past, the Holland House Whigs were but a part of a multi-faceted party. There was a clear divide politically between the pure Foxite Holland and those who did not carry on vendettas over generations and who were, therefore, prepared to cooperate with those tainted by Pittite connections. The Party also contained all shades of opinion from that of the most high aristocratic Whiggery to that bordering on popular radicalism. Socially two distinct groups populated the Party; the aristocrats and professional men, especially lawyers. Despite the power wielded by the aristocracy on the basis of their land-ownership, they still needed the talent of the professional men, not least because of the knowledge they possessed. The professionals tended to be on the liberal wing of the Party, were often lawyers, and they also tended to be 'Scots'. Yet for all the very real tensions and frustrations within the Party, and all were compounded by the interminable period in opposition, it is possible to discern a common body of opinion; detestation of the Royal Prerogative and of war, not least its expense and its enrichment of profiteers. Liberalism was to be found in the Party's attitudes to religious intolerance, their opposition to high taxes, and their espousal of a free press and reform of the legal code.

The central feature of Whig ideology was the Revolution of 1688-89, though there were divergent attitudes to it at the time that persisted certainly until the Reform Act 1832. In brief, the Revolution was seen by some Whigs as an act to preserve rights and by others as an opportunity to extend rights. In the working-out of the inheritance of 1688, the landed Whigs stressed the importance of family, the professional Whigs the importance of principle. Given the opinions they held, the professional 'Scots' could only hope to make a political career in the Whig Party, though the lawyers among them could not, as a result, expect much preferment. The Party itself, as Holland recognised, could well do with their knowledge and abilities, notably as debaters, so the landed interest were prepared to find them parliamentary seats leading to the paradoxical situation that those who most vigorously attacked the unreformed parliamentary system themselves sat for rotten boroughs. Despite astute distribution of patronage, some magnates rarely forsook the arrogant interpretation which they put on 1688: in the era of the French revolutionary and Napoleonic Wars they saw the radicals as serving the pretensions of the Crown by both questioning the Whig leadership and protesting, since the consequence in each instance was to strengthen the power of the Crown. Professional Whigs, on the other hand, which included the Edinburgh reviewers, were not bound by family history to such an outlook but rather were informed by the historical approach of the Scottish Enlightenment with its awareness of social and economic change. They used their expertise and access to the journalism of the day to assert a more dynamic Whiggery: 'The strength of intellectual Whiggism lay in its writers, men educated mostly in the universities of Scotland, who brought the party a sense of purpose and an eager articulateness which the traditional leadership could not bring.'[34]

An examination of one of the mechanisms of patronage in the early nineteenth century, namely clientage, illustrates how the 'Scots' were able to bring their knowledge to bear. Of the different mechanisms of control that flowed from the oligarchic rule of Britain,[35] clientage was the one that was most commonly used to forward the careers of the Scots-educated. Clientage has been defined as 'the informal process whereby men with national or local power fostered the careers of less powerful individuals who, in return, could be expected to uphold their patron's influence'.[36] The most common form that the patronage took was the provision of a parliamentary seat, but in the 1830s and 1840s senior positions in the expanding government service also came the way of 'Scots'. Whereas in 1793 71 peers nominated 88 MPs and influenced the election of 72, in 1816 87 peers nominated 88 MPs and influenced the election of 103.[37]

Francis Horner is a case in point. He had left Edinburgh in March

1803 to settle in London. Allen duly introduced him to Holland House, and he practised law at Chancery and in the House of Lords. Then in February 1806, the Earl of Minto procured for Horner a seat on the Board of Commissioners of the East India Company (the Carnatic Commission). (Minto, it will be recalled, was a friend of Dugald Stewart, had attended briefly the political economy classes in 1802, and had placed his son under Stewart's tutelage. Minto was later Governor-General of India, his son Lord Privy Seal.) The Commission involved much work adjusting the disputed claims of the creditors of the Nabob of Arcot. The appointment was quickly followed by a seat in Parliament from October 1806: his first was at St Ives which he held for a year, till the election of May 1807. His patron was Charles, Baron Kinnaird (1780-1826). Kinnaird had studied with Horner at Edinburgh, where they had been friends, though Horner felt that 'he had prematurely attained all that he was destined to acquire, and accordingly has been at stand for some time.'[38] After his studies Kinnaird had been found a safe Whig seat in the Commons by his father, and he was an active Party member. In 1806, a year after his father died and the year Horner entered the Commons, he was elected a Scottish representative peer. Horner was to write from Truro of canvassing in his first election:

> I shook every individual voter by the hand, stinking with brine and pilchard juice, repeated the same smile and cajoleries to every one of them, and kissed some women that were very pretty.

In accepting Kinnaird's offer, Horner wrote that 'I shall have the satisfaction of acting along with men of my own age, whom I have long known as thinking alike upon all the great questions in our politics.'[39]

In July 1807 Lord Carrington found Horner a seat at Wendover which he held till October 1812, when his new patron's nephew came of age and when his patron's son-in-law lost his seat at Hull. He then found a third patron in the Marquis of Buckingham whose seat at St Mawes he accepted in March 1813. In Parliament, he promoted and supported a wide range of liberal measures, but his outstanding contribution was to the debates on currency. He was one of the three authors of the Bullion Committee Report of 1810, and his familiarity with political economy and his advocacy of setting economic matters in a broad social context won his much respect amongst his parliamentary colleagues from the traditional élite. Between 1813 and 1815 he was a staunch opponent of the Corn Laws and he led the parliamentary battle in May 1816 for the Bank of England to resume cash payments, quite possibly because he believed that the Bank should keep the public informed of its activities.

Horner was a commoner patronised for his abilities certainly at the beginning of his career by his Edinburgh connections. Henry Petty affords an instance of an Edinburgh alumnus whose parliamentary career was more predictable and secure but whose early days in the Commons were closely watched by his fellow, less privileged, 'Scots'. In June 1798, Horner wrote that as Murray frequently saw Petty, he should remember Horner to him. 'He is one of those I respect and admire much, for his great and original good sense, and for an affability of manners far superior to what one usually finds in those of his rank at his age.'[40] Three years later, he wrote again to Murray in Petty's praise:

> there cannot be a more agreeable companion. If Lord Henry has con-
> tinued to improve that very strong understanding, and to augment
> that store of valuable information which he appeared to me to
> possess when I had the pleasure of knowing him, his society must be
> equally instructive and pleasing. Partiality aside, would you still
> distinguish him by a cool, clear-thinking head, a plain, firm, manly
> judgement?[41]

When Petty first entered the House of Commons, Horner remarked to Murray what a good figure he had cut there. One of the reasons Horner felt this was clearly expressed in a letter to his brother, Leonard, which neatly combined the intellectual and personal Scottish links:

> It is a curious proof of the degree in which Adam Smith's specu-
> lations and others of the kind are studied by the young men in
> Parliament, beyond the attention that was paid to such topics by the
> politicians who were educated at an earlier period of the last
> century.

Politicians were now realising the importance of economic knowledge, as exemplified by a number of parliamentary committees, and he noted how Petty was one of those drawing the attention of leading parliamentarians to the matter.[42]

On 8 April 1805, Petty attacked Lord Melville in a speech in Parliament. Horner wrote to Mackintosh to share with him an interest in their fellow alumnus's progress:

> I have heard several persons say, that Fox's compliment was

seriously deserved, when he called it the best speech that was made that night. Lord H. is moving very steadily on to a high station, both in the public opinion, and in office. His discretion, his good sense, his pains in acquiring knowledge, and the improvement of his power as well as taste in speaking, make such a prophecy with respect to his future destiny very safe.[43]

Horner relayed a similar view at great length to Murray early in May 1805:

All that I can learn about the nursery of our great families gives no promise of such an appearance [of a rival to Petty]. If he remains steady to the principles and general views of his present party, he will soon possess that sort of character which is more efficient in England than the fame of original uncertain genius.[44]

Early in 1806, Petty was trying for the Cambridge University parliamentary seat vacated 'on the death of Pitt, and opposing Lord Althorp. Horner wrote a number of letters canvassing for him, including one to Dugald Stewart. He assured Stewart that Petty had 'a firm attachment to Fox and his maxims of government', even though Petty in fact thought he was over-rated. Still he had numerous qualities that would enable him to be an eminent statesman if only he preserved his consistency and probity. Stewart was being involved in the election for reasons that became clear in a letter from the same batch to John Murray: 'There are probably a good many medical men who have been both at Edinburgh and Cambridge; take what mode seems to you most effective for getting at their names, and then inclose a list of them to John Allen.' The Edinburgh names were to be sent to Dugald Stewart who, with a medical professor, John Thomson, had offered to help.[45] Petty duly won handsomely by 331 to 144 votes and Stewart was informed: he was also told how Petty had been accused during the election of being not only a deist but an atheist.[46] Petty then became Chancellor of the Exchequer in the 'Ministry of All the Talents' (1806-07), and showed some interest in the subject of medical reform. A few years later Horner was writing to Murray about Lansdowne's (as Petty had now become in November 1809) views on parliamentary reform: 'there is no difference whatever between him and Lord Grey on any of the subjects that were discussed; at least none that I am aware of and I have lived a good deal with both lately, particularly with Lansdowne.'[47]

Once the Edinburgh alumni were into the higher realms of society and government is is clear that they did not forget their *alma mater* nor the associations that had arisen during their time there. What might almost be considered nepotism or, in twentieth-century terminology, an old-boy network, was evident as can be seen from the letters in Francis Horner's collection.

In December 1803 or 1804, Horner was soliciting the vote of his former tutor, Mr Hewlett, for a Dr de Rockes, a Genevan educated at Edinburgh, who was seeking the post of physician to a dispensary of which Hewlett was a governor.[48] Early in 1804, Horner was campaigning for John Allen to be appointed to the Edinburgh Chair of Natural History. He had gained the support of Sir Thomas Maitland, the Earl of Lauderdale's brother, in whose hands Scottish patronage was, Charles James Fox and the Duchess of Devonshire. Dugald Stewart was to interest Lords Ancram (a former student) and Castlereagh. The campaign was being led by Lauderdale and the idea was to outwit Lord Melville. (They failed.) Other correspondence on the same matter involved John Thomson, Sir James Mackintosh, Webb Seymour and Brougham. Mackintosh saw Addington, the Prime Minister, to point out 'that that university had suffered much of late years by an absurd system of hereditary professorships, and several unfit nominations of the Town Council', and Addington had asked about Allen's politics.[49] Attempts were also made to secure a pension for Thomas Campbell, the Edinburgh-educated poet and later prime mover of a university in London, through the good offices of Lady Holland.[50]

A patronage network was openly believed to facilitate the solution of problems by means of 'Scotch knowledge'. For example, in April 1805, Mackintosh had been sending Horner details of a famine in the Mharatta country, near Bombay, where he was recorder. Drought and civil war had been partly responsible, but also the refusal of corn dealers at Poona to sell corn at a maximum price laid down by the local British resident: 'They ran away, and there was no grain in the market next day'. Horner had sent the details on to Stewart. He believed it was important to give 'the element of liberal opinion, or if you will the dogmas of the right school, to men who have . . . trusts'. Hence, he was trying to secure for 'Campbell' (probably Thomas, the poet) the professorship of moral philosophy and political economy in the India College at Hertford, so that the subjects could be taught with particular application to an Asiatic government. Mackintosh was also carrying out a statistical survey of the island of Bombay. For his part, Horner was interested in Mackintosh's applying theories of political economy to Bombay, to see if Bombay bore out Britain's general experiences. Did, for example, price rises in India, like Britain, bear a relationship to a change in the supply of precious metals?[51]

The Edinburgh Whig set were also concerned and interested in news of their *alma mater*. Horner was to tell Mackintosh, for example, of Leslie's case, noting that Leslie had been a tutor to the Wedgwoods:

> I must not let you remain ignorant of certain ecclesiastical intrigues, and metaphysical treacheries, that have been lately practised at Edinburgh — that eye of Greece — mother of arts — native to famous wits or hospitable in her sweet recess.

He went on to comment that in William Robertson's time the moderates in the Scottish Kirk had justly been called moderate and liberal, as their wish had been to relax the stiffness of Presbyterian discipline; but now the Evangelicals had exactly changed places with them in championing Leslie's appointment.[52] In 1809, Horner was writing to Webb Seymour bemoaning Edinburgh's failure to make the chemical discoveries of former days,[53] and to Allen and Dugald Stewart in 1810 triumphing over two particular professorial appointments at Edinburgh that marked victories over the clergy and for liberality. He had feared 'the disappearance of all moderate notions on liberty'.[54] Horner's continuing interest in work originating from the Scottish Enlightenment is further demonstrated by a letter to his brother in 1811 containing thoughts on Playfair's book on James Hutton's Theory of the Earth.[55]

The perpetuation of what Dugald Stewart had taught and news of the philosopher himself also illumine Horner's papers. For example, about a year after Horner first returned to Edinburgh from London, he was writing to Hewlett, his tutor, about his wish to treat law in that philosophical way prescribed by the literati of the Scottish Enlightenment:

> I am labouring to study [law] as a science, and by uniting it with philosophical history so render it an exercise of the reasoning and arranging faculties, not of mere memory. I can find very few authors indeed who teach me anything in this way; I should wish not only *general results*, but to be taught the *habit* of generalising and the logic (as it were) of legislative science.[56]

He also showed his immersion in philosophic history in a later letter to John Murray on Napoleon's invasion of Russia:

Surely there is nothing in history so delightful to read or witness, nothing so useful in its example, as the successful resistance of foreign invaders; whether it be by the patriotism of a civilised and free state, or by the instinct of barbarians and slaves.[57]

Not only did Stewart convey desirable cast of mind as evidenced by the quotations, he positively whetted Horner's appetite for commercial and political tracts. Horner wrote to Murray in 1801 of the degree of assiduity with which he was attending Stewart's lectures on the corn trade and the Poor Law. He asked Murray to send him any associated pamphlets to add to his collection and continued in a vein that shows the interconnections between French and Scottish Enlightenment thought, and the concern for that thought by the practical politicians at Lansdowne House:

If you are ever at any of the French booksellers, I wish you would make enquiries about a translation of *Smith's* Wealth of Nations, which was published at Paris in 1790, in three volumes 8vo; the translator's name is B(?r)oucher, but there is a volume of notes professedly by *Condorcet*. . . . It is probable that Condorcet's name may have been given to notes which he did not compose; he is said to have been guilty of this trick upon other occasions: I have not yet asked Dugald Stewart about it — perhaps you may have the opportunity of putting the question at Lansdowne House, where these things are well known.[58]

If the *alma mater* and its associations were not forgotten, it is also clear from the instance of Francis Horner that the Edinburgh experience and contacts of certain young men permitted them to take particular turns of direction. First, Horner's studying under Stewart and the philosophy and political economy he learned from him greatly influenced Horner's later thoughts and opinion. Secondly, his involvement with Jack Allen meant he was introduced, as were others, to the foremost Whig house in London. Thirdly, his part in founding the *Edinburgh Review* permitted his contribution with others to the shaping of Whig political opinion and his writing on political economy. Fourthly, in 1806 he first entered Parliament, as did others, through the bounty of an Edinburgh connection: once he had shown his paces in the Commons, the aristocracy, the astute amongst whom had a ready eye for professional talent, saw to it that he was rarely without a seat until his death. As Horner noted to his friend J.A. Murray when explaining that he had thrown in his lot with the Foxites, his education did not fit him to be 'at the tail of a party'.[59]

Horner is a well-documented example of the conscious transmission, through connection, of 'Scotch knowledge' to England. Once there, it set to work through the media of individuals' writing, especially in the *Review*, and activities. It is to non-medical 'Scotch knowledge at work' that this study now turns.

Notes

1. I am so describing former students of Scottish universities because while a number were indeed Scotsmen, the aristocrats and Dissenters who figure too were commonly English.

2. Elie Halévy, *England in 1815*, trans. E.I. Watkin and D.A. Barker (Ernest Benn, 1961), p. 587.

3. Ibid., pp. 466-7, 538-43.

4. Ibid., p. 467.

5. *Horner Collection, L.S.E.*, II, Letter 57 to John Murray, 8 June 1804.

6. Ibid., II, Letter 20 to Thomas Thomson, 15 August 1803.

7. 'Dissertation on the Progress of Ethical Philosophy, chiefly during the Seventeenth and Eighteenth Centuries' [originally preface to the 7th edn of the *Encyclopaedia Britannica*], *The Miscellaneous Works of the Rt Hon. Sir James Mackintosh*, ed. R.J. Mackintosh (London, 1851), pp. 89-90.

8. Ward to Mrs Stewart, 8 February 1814, *Letters to 'Ivy'*, pp. 230-31.

9. *Horner Collection, L.S.E.*, II, Letter 73, Horner to John McFarlane, Advocate, 27 September 1804.

10. Quoted in Alan Bell, *Sydney Smith* (Clarendon Press, 1980), pp. 82, 100.

11. See *The 'Pope' of Holland House: Selections from the Correspondence of John Whishaw and his Friends 1813-1840*, ed. E. Seymour (London, 1906), pp. 333-40; Lloyd C. Sanders, *The Holland House Circle*, 2nd edn (Methuen, 1908), p. 258; William Thomas, *The Philosophic Radicals: Nine Studies in Theory and Practice 1817-1841* (Clarendon Press, 1979), pp. 62, 62 n.; and Bell, pp. 46-7.

12. *Horner Collection, L.S.E.*, I, Letter 70, Horner to James Loch, 27 May 1802.

13. *The 'Pope' of Holland House*, p. 335.

14. Leslie Mitchell, *Holland House* (Duckworth, 1980), pp. 54-5. The book contains much of direct relevance to my topic and I am particularly indebted to it, as will become apparent.

15. Sanders, p. 56.

16. Mitchell, pp. 22, 34, 59, 36, 172-173, 175, 37, 302, 303.

17. See ibid., Chs. 2 and 3.

18. Quoted ibid., p. 187.

19. Ibid., p. 190.

20. *List of Medical Students*, I, 1783-90, and II, 1791-95, unnumbered pages, E.U.L. mss. room.

21. Cockburn, *Memorials*, p. 177.

22. Ibid., p. 178.

23. Mitchell, p. 186.

24. Quoted in Bell, p. 48.

25. *The Letters of Sydney Smith*, I, p. 199, Letter 196 to J.A. Murray, 17 January 1811.

26. W. Bagehot, 'The First Edinburgh Reviewers', *Literary Studies*, I, p. 40.

27. William Thomas, *The Philosophic Radicals*, p. 51, to which I am indebted, particularly in section III of this chapter. There was clear personal rivalry between Brougham and Horner which was fanned by at least one of their mutual friends, Sydney Smith. Smith noted that whereas both might be original, liberal and independent, Horner was not arrogant and therefore less likely to offend or to fail in his public career. Subsequently, Smith chronicles Brougham's frustration at entering Parliament after Horner, sometimes unwarrantably suspecting that Horner had been brought in by the administration. *The Letters of Sydney Smith*, I, pp. 102, 120, 278, letters 102 and 120 to Francis Jeffrey dated 16 February 1805 and 21 December 1806, and letter 278 to Lady Holland dated 31 July 1817. See also Henry Richard Vassall Fox, *Further Memoirs of the Whig Party 1807-1821 with Some Miscellaneous Reminiscences*, ed. Lord Stavordale (London, 1905), p. 45 and note.

28. *Life and Letters of Sir Gilbert Elliot*, 3 vols. (London, 1874), III, pp. 231-4.

29. See Mitchell, pp. 124-6, 144; Sanders, pp. 144-7.

30. Mitchell, p. 279.

31. Sanders, p. 348.

32. Mitchell, p. 176.

33. Ibid., pp. 184-5, 306.

34. Thomas, p. 56.

35. See A.D. Harvey, *Britain In The Early Nineteenth Century* (Batsford, 1978), Part I, Ch. I, pp. 6-37.

36. Ibid., p. 12.

37. Ibid., p. 18.

38. *Horner Collection, L.S.E.*, I, Letter 57, Horner to J.A. Murray, 10 April 1801.

39. Ibid., III, Letter 45 to J.A. Murray, 4 November 1806, and III, Letter 41 to Charles Kinnaird, 23 October 1806.

40. Ibid., I, Letter 45, 16 June 1798.

41. Ibid., I, Letter 57, 10 April 1801.

42. Ibid., II, Letter 44, 17 February 1804 to J.A. Murray and the quote is from Letter 51, n.d. [April 1804] to Leonard Horner.

43. Ibid., II, Letter 97, 19 April 1805.

44. Ibid., II, Letter 99, 4 May 1805.

45. Ibid., III, Letter 3, 23 January 1806 to Dugald Stewart and Letter 4, 21 January 1806 to John Murray.

46. Ibid., III, Letter 10, 12 February 1806.

47. Ibid., IV, Letter 109, 26 June 1810.

48. Ibid., II, Letter 25, 23 December 1803 or 1804.

49. Ibid., III, Letter 3, 23 January 1806 to Dugald Stewart and Letter 4, 21 January 1806 to John Murray.

50. Ibid., II, Letter 124, December 1805 to Lady Holland.

51. Ibid., II, Letter 95, 8 April 1805. The quotation is from a letter from Mackintosh to Sydney Smith, in *Memoirs and Correspondence of Francis Horner*, I, p. 293 n.

52. Ibid., II, Letter 95, 8 April 1805.

53. Ibid., IV, Letter 8, 27 January 1809.

54. Ibid., IV, Letters 98 and 99, both dated 8 May 1810.

55. Ibid., V, Letter 112, 8 December 1812.

56. Ibid., I, Letter 49, n.d. [late 1798?].

57. Ibid., V, Letter 112, 8 December 1812.

58. Ibid., I, Letter 57, 10 April 1801 and the lectures are published in Stewart's *Collected Works*, Vols. VIII and IX.

59. Horner Collection, II, Letter 70 to J.A. Murray, 13 September 1804.

4 'SCOTCH KNOWLEDGE' AT WORK I

'Scotch knowledge' was politically at work within a confined area. Being but leaven within the Whig Party, itself in opposition for a considerable time, 'Scotch knowledge' was one of a number of reforming approaches within the minority party and could be limited still further to a particular aristocratic set and their entourage. The question of parliamentary reform, to take an instance, gave the opportunity for the 'Scotch' approach to be aired vigorously within these confines for a long time. It illuminates how intellectual background and personal networks were brought to bear on a pressing issue of the day.

The *Edinburgh Review* was the distinctive forum which propounded 'Scotch' ideas on the subject and, in so doing, revitalised the demoralised party with which it sided. Articles on parliamentary reform blended 'Scotch' philosophic history with contemporary concrete circumstances. In his article, 'The Dangers of the Country', published in 1807, for instance, Francis Jeffrey wrote passages that echoed the writing of John Millar in his *Origin of the Distinction of Ranks*, exemplified by his account of the beginnings of governmental administration:

> The most famous warrior would be king; the next in prowess and reputation would be earls and generals; he who could write best would be chancellor; and he who had the greatest gift of prayer, would be court chaplain or archbishop. The same principle would regulate all the inferior conditions: the first captains . . . were taller and more expert than the serjeants; and they than the soldiers in the ranks. The acquisition of wealth, and the establishment of hereditary right, made a great change in these particulars. A cast, called nobility, was formed, from which alone all the great functionaries of government could be appointed in most countries of Europe; and in process of time, the more important charges could only be given among a small number of families.[1]

From the analysis, Jeffrey moved to concrete results and the event which overshadowed the whole history of his age. He pointed to two evil effects of the system whose evolution he had just traced: the number of people from whom a suitable appointment could be made was diminished, and incentive and the effort necessary to satisfy ambition was removed. This last development led to a repression of talents. Consequently those with talent and intelligence mocked their rulers and felt keenly the disparity between themselves and those with talent and privileges. In France, that had led to revolution. While the situation was not as bad in England, similar problems were having to be faced:

> Those who are in possession of power, and entitled to nominate to the great and influencing employments in the government, cannot be expected to bestow them on their political enemies; and thus one third part of the whole population of the country, comprehending perhaps a still larger proportion of its talent, is lost to the public service, and as completely proscribed and excluded as the plebeian classes are in the old aristocratical governments of the Continent.[2]

The remedy to the disparity between talent and power in Britain was to employ men of political talents rather than partisans to form a strong ministry.[3]

Some of what Jeffrey and others wrote in the *Review* can be put down to ambition, to the high opinion in which they held their own abilities, and to a natural tendency on the part of opposition to criticise those in power. On the other hand, the need to combat the popular radicalism of William Cobbett, his thoroughgoing criticism of the Establishment, and his impatience with theory was well perceived. The *Review* put forward an alternative people's champion, Henry Brougham, and yet recognised the place of the aristocracy in the constitution. This was a political balancing act of some delicacy. Jeffrey wrote another article in 1807 on 'Cobbett's *Political Register*'. In it, he attacked Cobbett for his pernicious and reprehensible doctrines and for begetting distrust and contempt of every individual in public life (except for Sir Francis Burdett). By way of summarising Cobbett's view, Jeffrey said that the evils under which the country groaned were due to the improper composition of the House of Commons especially. Members were not chosen fairly by the people but by the influence of families or by purchase from venal electors; placemen also were allowed to sit. Thus far, it is hard to discern a massive gulf between the views of Cobbett as represented by Jeffrey and those of Jeffrey himself earlier in the year. Jeffrey proceeded to say, however, that the situation could be worse and that a struggle ought to be maintained to keep the balance of such good as there was. Revolution was abhorrent and would lead to the loss of liberties. While there was a scrambling for places and emoluments and a selling of votes, placemen were better in Parliament than elsewhere, the influence of great families was beneficial rather than pernicious and the sale of boroughs did not hazard the constitution.[4] He continued:

> The most perfect representative legislature must be that which reunited in itself the greatest proportion of the effective aristocracy of the country, or contained the greatest proportion of the individuals who actually swayed the opinions of the people, by means of their birth, wealth, talents, or popular qualities.[5]

His defence of an aristocracy with a variety of interests and, therefore, enriching the political process was in marked opposition to Cobbett's views and may have owed much to the association with Holland House:

> that country is happiest, in which the aristocracy is most numerous and most diversified as to the sources of its influence; that government the most suitable, secure and beneficial, which is exercised most directly by the mediation of this aristocracy. In a country where rank, wealth and office, constitute the chief sources of influence over individuals, it is proper that rank, wealth and office, should make the greatest number of its legislators.[6]

Parliament existed to preserve the freedom of the people, it was the spirit and intelligence of the people that caused their liberties. Parliament, therefore, was to have a sufficient number of a sufficient variety of persons so that every class and party in the country could have an expounder and advocate of its views and sentiments. Despite placemen, there were, in Jeffrey's view, a sufficient number and variety of persons to propound different viewpoints.[7]

This line of argument led Jeffrey to favour a balance of the three great national classes in the community — the sovereign, those with hereditary property and its accompanying rank and influence, and the people, especially those who aimed for office on the basis of talent, industry and popular qualities. The three groups are rivals, and in the constitution they compromised or were balanced in the Commons.[8] In making this point, Jeffrey was echoing the political economy lectures of his mentor, Dugald Stewart. When encompassing the subject of government, Stewart had noted that all governments in history had been more or less mixed, being varieties of one or more of the simple forms monarchy, aristocracy and democracy. He defined mixed governments as 'constitutions which professedly share, by their fundamental principles, the *supreme or legislative power* among different orders of the community', and pointed to 'the constitution of our own country, so strikingly distinguished from all others, by the systematic rigour by which it requires, in every legal enactment, the cooperation of all its three branches'.[9] Balance was explained by Stewart as very necessary:

> As the possession of power, however, is to the best of men a source of corruption, the general utility requires that some checks should be imposed on the pretensions of the aristocracy; and the only effectual checks may be easily perceived to be, a *popular assembly*, on the one hand, to secure the enactment of equal laws, and a *single magistrate*, on the other, possessing the sole executive power, to prevent the competitions and rivalships [sic] among the order of nobility.[10]

He elaborated later on the justification for balance 'so that if either [sic] of the three branches should attempt to extend its power too far, the other two might be expected to unite in opposing it'. He continued:

> If the King should attempt to render himself independent of the House of Commons, the Lords (however little interested they might feel themselves in the cause of general liberty) would see the danger with which their own order was threatened. It is from the weight which the people have in the Constitution that the Peers derive their legislative authority; and if the House of Commons were annihilated, they would feel themselves degraded from the important station they now hold, to the insignificant distinction of adding to the parade of a despotic court. If, on the other hand, the Commons should attempt to reduce too far the King's prerogative, he might reckon with certainty on the support of his nobility. The attachment which they may all be supposed to feel to the monarchy from which they derived their titles and rank, and with which their titles and rank must inevitably fall, will, independently of better motives, secure their exertions in defence of the Constitution. Lastly, if we could conceive it to be possible, in the present state of society, for the House of Lords to revive their old aristocratical pretensions, the Crown and the People would unite in resisting a power, by which the one has in former times been so often insulted, and the other

oppressed.[11]

That, however, was the theory: nowadays, neither the monarch nor
the Lords possessed the kind of independence and importance implicit
in the theory. As a consequence, 'the whole practical efficiency of our
Government is either centred within the walls of the House of
Commons, or operates by the intermediation of that assembly.'[12] The
Commons was now a blend,

> an assembly which is no longer composed of men whose habits and
> connexions can be supposed to attach them exclusively to *the
> people*, but of men, some of whom, from their situation, may be
> presumed to lean to the regal part of a government, others to the
> aristocratical; while, on important questions, the majority may be
> expected to maintain the interests of the community at large.[13]

Just as the Lords now contained peers who were neither great, landed
proprietors nor men of noble descent but mere pensioners of the
Crown, public servants and ministerial favourites, so too the Commons
has contributed to standing the constitution on its head by having as
members great landed proprietors from ancient families and men whose
dignity gives them right of precedent over a great many peers. This
gives the monarch and aristocracy 'a very great *indirect* influence' on
Commons' proceedings and contributes to making the Commons the
location of 'the whole efficiency of government'. He then brings his
argument about balance to a conclusion:

> if each has a certain influence, the three powers may balance each
> other, and may produce the happy result aimed at in the theory of
> our constitution, in a way still more advantageous than if it were
> exactly realized, by saving the machine of government from those
> violent shocks it must occasionally suffer if king, lords, and
> commons were openly and avowedly to draw, in any instance, in
> different directions.
>
> The perfection of our government, while its present forms
> continue, consists in properly balancing these influences, by giving
> to the Sovereign a sufficient degree of parliamentary weight to pro-
> duce a *general* support to public measures, without an implicit con-
> fidence in ministers; — to the Aristocracy such a weight as may be
> necessary to secure a due respect to landed property, and to ancient
> establishments; — and to the People such a preponderance as may

enable them to secure equal liberty and impartial justice to every subject, without permitting them to run into the extravagances of popular tumult and violence.[14]

This teaching of Dugald Stewart was purveyed to the early nineteenth century by Jeffrey's articles in the *Review*.

In an article specifically entitled 'Parliamentary Reform' and published in 1809, Jeffrey again blended Scottish philosophic history with analysis of the contemporary political situation. The contemporary evils were the burden of taxes, the dominant influence of the Crown as manifested in establishment and patronage and the monopoly of political power concentrated in a small part of the nation and the jealousy it prompted.[15] He then constructs an argument designed to show a central feature of Scottish Enlightenment thought, that the institutions of society require to keep in harmony with changing circumstances of the people. He shows how much of eighteenth-century learning he has absorbed by the phraseology he uses:

> In all new governments, superior fitness and ability are the sole recommendations to office and employments. In old governments, hereditary wealth and rank are apt to have too great an influence. The former, therefore, are commonly administered with more vigour and ability; but the latter are, for the most part, more stable and secure. This advantage they derive from the natural tendency of the influence derived from wealth, to settle and consolidate into a sort of patriarchal chieftainship, which gains strength by descent and duration; while the influence derived from more personal talents or accomplishments necessarily perishes with the individual by whom they were possessed.[16]

There were only two sources of influence in society, personal talents and property. The first cannot be transmitted to heirs, the second can. Not only is property transmitted but it acquires greater strength through the generations — 'thus the aristocracy of personal merit is gradually supplanted, or at least overtopped, by the aristocracy of hereditary wealth. This is the first step in the history of civilized society.'[17] What is now happening in the Europe of Jeffrey's time is that the aristocracy that grew up in feudal and early modern Europe, who maintained 'a tranquil and unquestioned supremacy over their natural inferiors', were being reduced by luxury from the accomplishments which gave them rank while improvements in education and their circumstances gave the peasantry intelligence, skill and ambition. An aristocracy of merit was arising and for government to be secure and peaceful, the two aristocracies of merit and of wealth must be united. This unity can be accomplished if the hereditary chieftains yield up a large share of political power to those now their equals in personal endowments.[18]

In Britain, continued Jeffrey, posts of importance are monopolised by the majority in the House of Commons who use patronage. Heredity secures election and office. The monopolists are not aware, nor do they seek to make themselves aware, of public opinion which is seen as interference with their peculiar privileges, and anyway, they are too immersed in public business:

> it is . . . very much owing to the multiplication of those pert, practised, and narrow-minded politicians, that the repulsive tone of contempt has been adopted towards the people, which has been repaid, upon their side, with retorted scorn and resentment.[19]

Four developments have assisted in bringing about this contempt and scorn — the French Revolution, which causes a dread of popular insurrection and an arrogance in the aristocracy; the length of Pitt's administration which has alienated it from popular sentiments; the replacement of distinguished and popular leaders by lesser-known but pretentious men utterly subservient to the Crown, and the lack of success of public measures in foreign affairs and in Ireland, for instance, which have excited distrust and disrespect for rulers.[20]

All this served as background to Jeffrey's prescription for parliamentary reform: he favoured it because it would restore the confidence of the people in their rulers. On the other hand, reconciliation between government and people would not be achieved by the measures then being proposed, the abolition of rotten boroughs, the enlarging of the elective franchise and shorter parliaments. Jeffrey wanted a diminution in the inequality of constituencies (whereby five voters, for instance might merit two MPs), and the pecuniary qualification to be raised and estimated on all kinds of property, not merely land. The landed interest would, however, have a lower qualification because of their 'superior weight and respectability'. The tumult and disorder at elections was also to be ended by the ballot. He admits that such reforms would not touch either taxation or influence and he would not wish to exclude from the Commons those there by the interest of the ministry or noble families as such an exclusion would deprive the constitution of all its practical benefits.[21]

These benefits were, of course, embodied in balance: 'distractions and dreadful conclusions' would ensue if the three branches of the legislature were kept practically apart. They checked and controlled each other, they could concert and cooperate. If the yeomanry alone were represented in the Commons and given the power of supply, government would degenerate into mere democracy. If there was no monarchical or aristocratic interest in the Commons the only response to Commons' Bills could be rejection, and civil war would ensue. If there was no influence for the sovereign or his servants, control of the Executive would be abandoned. Consequently, the Crown had to have influence in the Commons. Jeffrey saw no intelligible ground for excluding nobles or opulent commoners since their interests were indistinguishable. Unless nobles have a say in the Commons they would have no say in government since the whole force of a government actually resides in the Commons.[22] Here was Dugald Stewart's efficient and perfect government.

The Holland House influence came at the end. It was argued that Cobbett's and Burdett's proposals would lead to the revival or active development of the Royal Prerogative. Cobbett was portrayed as saying that the Commons should no more choose the king's ministers than his footmen, and Burdett as wanting to restore the sovereign the prerogative of determining what boroughs should return MPs. and which should be deprived of the privilege. Tampering with the notion of the Commons as representing interests, freeing it of all but popular influence, would lead to the revival of the Royal Prerogative and the people should remain ever vigilant to encroachments of power.[23] The article encapsulates 'Scotch knowledge', early nineteenth-century England and the mediation of one to the other by the Holland Whig interest.

By 1810, Jeffrey was perceiving the crucial part played by the mediating group at a time when 'the great body of the nation appears to us to be divided into two violent and most pernicious factions; — the courtiers, who are almost for arbitrary power, — and the democrats, who are almost for revolution and republicanism'. The 'old constitutional Whigs of England', 'the friends of liberty and order', stood between the two, talented, well-intentioned but denied power and popularity and loathed by the extremes. Both the constitution and liberty were under threat: indifference among the great body of the people, evident at the time when Wilkes challenged Bute, has been transformed by a combination of the rise of intelligence, the success of plebian insurrection, repression, the multiplication of offices and patronage, bad government and taxation. This has led to antipathy on the part of the 'courtiers' who have responded by repressing popular agitation, thus creating a real threat of popular insurrection.[24] The justification of the crucial part Jeffrey saw for the Whigs owed much to the philosophy of his educational background:

> The stability of the English constitution depends upon its monarchy and aristocracy; and their stability, again, depends very much on the circumstance of their having grown naturally out of the frame of society — upon their having struck their roots deep through every stratum of the political soil, and having been moulded and impressed, during a long course of ages, by the usages, institutions, habits and affections of the community. A popular revolution would overthrow the monarchy and the aristocracy; and even if it were not true that revolution propagates revolution, as waves give rise to waves, till the agitation is stopped by the iron boundary of despotism, it would still require ages of anxious discomfort, before we could build up again that magnificent fabric, which now requires purification rather than repair; or secure that permanency to our new establishments, without which they could have no other good quality.[25]

The small group of talented and reputable, if hardly popular, Whig royalists are the group who could provide the remedy because while they could never forget that government derives from the people and is for the people, yet they realise that the rights and liberties of the people are best safeguarded by a regulated hereditary monarchy and a large, open aristocracy. They 'are as much averse, therefore, from every attempt to undermine the throne, or to discredit the nobles, as they are indignant at every project to insult or enslave the people.'[26] These Whigs should associate themselves with the popular party because that is from where the immediate danger comes, because the people would willingly be led by 'a legitimate Whig Chieftain' and because anyway the Whig Party should only exist with popular affection and approbation and Whig leaders have tended to alienate the people by their haughtiness and disdain. They should also associate with the popular party because most of the demands of that party are legitimate, the need to reduce expenditure, to punish delinquent statesmen (Jeffrey had the Walcheren expedition in mind) and to reform the representation of the people. Jeffrey concluded with specific proposals: to secure retrenchment by abolishing sinecures, economising on magnificence, making an example of one statesman who retires with honours and riches after the grossest mismanagement (he noted that a delinquent physician was punished as a murderer and wondered why a delinquent politician was not), investigating and punishing blunder, disenfranchising rotten boroughs and enfranchising a great number of respectable citizens.[27]

In 1811, Jeffrey was writing jointly with Brougham on parliamentary reform and asserting that their prime objective was to curb the power of the Crown. The article represents the 'middle way' that was being advocated by the *Review*.[28] The article also makes clear the authors' ideas on property and how property related to the franchise, though its burden is an attack on the corrupt use of property: 'the natural and inevitable influence of property in elections, is not only safe, but salutary; while its artificial and corrupt influence is among the most pernicious and reprehensible of all political abuse'. The distinction drawn between 'natural' and 'artificial' may have originated from Jeffrey and Brougham's shared philosophical and educational background. Natural influence, for instance, was explained on the basis of a man spending a large income in his place of residence and so contributing to local facilities, local charities and having accounts with local tradesmen. A person exercising this sort of influence is bound to have the goodwill of the local electors and it would be absurd to forbid it, say Jeffrey and Brougham, because it arises from the nature of men and affairs. This influence originates from property and not from venality or corruption. Artificial influence, on the other hand, is the wilful and direct employment of property to purchase or obtain political power.[29]

Their distinctions become fine when applied to specific arrangements. For example, they assert that privately-owned boroughs cannot be seen as criminal corruption but are cases of the fair influence of property:

> though we admit them to be both contradictory to the general scheme of the constitution, and subversive of some of its most important principles, we think they are to be regarded as flaws and irregularities brought on by time and the course of events, rather than as abuses introduced by the vices and corruptions of men.

The remedy was to take away the right of election from such boroughs, not to rail against individual owners or impose penalties on them.[30] Treasury boroughs — those especially in Devon and Cornwall and containing between 150 and 500 electors — were different. Defined as 'boroughs that are sold by usurping and intriguing agents, partly for money paid over by the candidate, and partly for offices and patronage corruptly promised and distributed by ministers', they were also too large to be the property of an individual and too small to have a popular spirit or opulent independence.[31] The real evil for Jeffrey and Brougham was the influence of the Crown, — 'the most distressing symptom of our present malady'. Therefore, placemen and minor officials had to be excluded and sinecures abolished. Seats were to be redistributed from decayed boroughs to great towns to increase the feeling of political right among the people.[32]

The philosophic history emerged when the authors perceived that all political societies were divided into governors, those opposed to the governors and those who counted for nothing:

> In rude and early ages, this last division includes by far the greater part of the people: but as society advances, and intellect begins to develop itself, a greater and a greater proportion is withdrawn from it, and joined to the other two divisions.

Advances, such as the diffusion of knowledge and improvements of education 'necessarily raise up more and more of the mass of the population from that state of brutish acquiescence and incurious ignorance in which they origianlly slumbered'. If government were mild and equitable those now awakened would come to support it, but if government were capricious or oppressive, a greater number of those awakened might try to correct or subvert it. The history of Europe since c. 1770 is to be explained by the unwillingness of people grown strong to submit to the folly and corruption of long-established governments. As the increased strength which was proving a danger was to be found in intellect not wealth, it was preposterous to increase Crown patronage: 'If a greater proportion of our population be now capable and desirous of exercising the functions of free citizens, let a greater number be admitted to the exercise of these functions.'[33] As Jeffrey alone was to write the following year, when a nation has ultimately attained a full measure of civility and intelligence, then substantial power is invested in the nation at large. Parliament ought to reflect on how the power of the state resides in the great body of the people, especially the wealthy and intelligent.[34]

Similar themes were taken up by Sir James Mackintosh in 1818 when he wrote an article attacking Bentham's plan for universal suffrage.[35] Once again, property was central to the analysis: if the labouring classes were all given the vote, then there would grow up a permanent animosity between opinion and property, and in any contest, property will, as ever, prevail, leading to violence, to the removal ultimately of all restraint on authority so that it can deal with the violence, and thence to the curtailment of that liberty which has taken six centuries to establish. Rather, the objects of government and representation need to be borne in mind: government was to provide security against wrong and 'Most civilized governments, tolerably secure their subjects against wrong from each other'. Therefore, the representative assembly must contain all the different interests and qualifications needed to serve the general interest. The objects of representatives were to make good laws and resist oppression. While the right of suffrage enables the lowest classes to have their voices heard, the men of popular talents who are elected as a consequence require to be kept in check and restrained by others of a different charcter: 'an assembly exclusively composed of them, would be ill-fitted for the duties of legislation'. There are certain 'natural' principles of authority, talent, skill, popularity, fame, property, liberal education:

> As far as an assembly is deprived of any of these natural principles of authority, so far it is weakened, both for the purpose of resisting the usurpations of government, and of maintaining the order of society.[36]

Mackintosh was of the view that the English nobility had preserved their distinctive character, their preference for country life rather than being sycophantic at Court, because their power had depended on elections. He argued for a variety of electoral processes so that in some elections great weight would be given to property whereas in others, there would be universal suffrage with variations in between: 'if representation be proportioned to numbers alone, every other interest in society is placed at the disposal of the multitude.' Town would dictate to country. Mackintosh also opposed the ballot: he did not believe that it would remain a secret process and it would remove from the voter incentives for voting such as to gain the favour of his superiors, the kindness of his fellows and the gratitude of the candidate. Thus, only public duty would be left as an incentive: 'If such a principle could be trusted, laws would be unnecessary.'[37]

Mackintosh favoured the middling classes because they had 'the largest share of sense and virtue' and 'the most numerous connexions of interest with the other parts of society'. After all, 'Perhaps there never was a time or country in which the middling classes were of a character so respectable and improving as they are at this day in Great Britain.'[38] Francis Horner also laid an emphasis on what he called 'the middling order'. He was convinced that they constituted a broad foundation for a popular party and genuine democracy, and he defined them as those with 'the opinions, interests and habits of those numerous families who are characterized by moderate but increasing incomes, a careful education of their youth, and a strict observance of the great common virtues.' Jeffrey concurred:

> I agree with you entirely in thinking that there is in the opulence, intelligence, and morality of our middling people a sufficient quarry of materials to make or repair a free constitution; but the difficulty is in raising them to the surface. The best of them meddle least with politics; and, except as jury men or justices of peace, they exercise scarcely any influence upon the public proceedings of the society.

He also recognised the inherent difficulties that had grown up with the 'constitution' and that were implicit in attempts at reform:

> The antiquity of our government, to which we are indebted for so many advantages, brings this great compensating evil along with it; there is an oligarchy of great families — borough-mongers and intriguing adventurers — that monopolises all public activity, and excludes the mass of ordinary men nearly as much as the formal institutions of other countries. How can you hope to bring the virtues of the people to bear on the vices of the government, when the only way in which a patriot can approach to the scene of action is by purchasing a seat in Parliament?[39]

The present concern is to point out how Scottish eighteenth-century philosophy informed *Review* articles on the subject of parliamentary reform. At the time, however, the articles were invariably viewed by radicals as specious arguments produced by Whigs for their own self-interested purposes of undermining both the monarchy and the populace while masking their intentions by talking about popular rights or the need of the Whig Party to associate itself with the popular party.[40] Equally, it was also unlikely that the aristocratic leadership of the party would happily associate with the radicals, as advised by the *Review*. Even a reviewer, Sydney Smith, chastised Jeffrey for overestimating the sentiments of the commercial and manufacturing areas of the country, and underestimating the tendency of the mass of landed proprietors to rally round the constitution and moderate principles.[41] While these considerations are important in assessing the political history of the time, they must still be seen alongside the intellectual origins of much that was written in the *Review*. Dugald Stewart had observed that 'the perfection of political wisdom does not consist in an indiscriminate zeal against reformers, but in a gradual and prudent accommodation of established institutions to the varying opinions, manners and circumstances of mankind.'[42]

This outlook was shared by others of Stewart's former students. In 1809, for instance, Francis Horner was writing to John Ward about the urgent need to reform sinecures and Parliament, of the need to make considerable concessions to popular sentiments and of 'the living principle of [the constitution] which has always consisted in prudent and timely reforms'.[43] He advised Jeffrey prior to the writing of the article of 1809 on parliamentary reform urging the same degree of prudence. He believed, no doubt, that caution in agitated times was necessary not least after the uproar following the controversial 'Don Pedro Cevallos' review written by Jeffrey and Brougham in October 1808. He doubted whether the Commons had, at any previous period, 'approached nearer . . . to the theory of our constitution as drawn by general writers. With all this, I have a strong bias in favour of the proposition for rendering the representation more adequate and agreeable to that theory.' His was almost the epitome of the safe Whig line:

> in England I would give members to some important classes of the population who can scarcely be said to be represented. It is at the same time a perilous thing either to change the qualification, or to take away franchises, or by compensations to recognize such a principle as the acquisition of that kind of property. I see a great deal of practical benefit result, even to the interests of liberty and popular rights, from the most rotten parts of the constitutional body.[44]

He again revealed his intellectual pedigree when he wrote to John Murray in May 1810:

> The peculiar character of the English constitution is, that that portion of discretionary power is shared among the several constituted authorities, instead of residing in one; and the chances

of an improper exercise of it are lessened, by the checks which are thus established.[45]

Two months later he was again writing to Jeffrey that the partisan line the *Review* was taking was impairing the journal's previous authority and was even worrying Holland and Allen; then he reiterated his caution about making overtures to the popular will.[46]

The issue of Roman Catholic emancipation, which ultimately proved to be the dyke that, once breached, permitted parliamentary reform to proceed, was the cause that all Whig factions agreed upon. A letter of Horner's from 1812 illustrates again his view that there should be harmony between law and changing social circumstances, using the Church of England's opposition to Catholic emancipation as the butt of his criticism and his example:

> They come from their monastery in St Paul's Church Yard with opinions which all the rest of the world have rejected or begin to be ashamed of and while our laws are in a constant flux, adapting themselves slowly indeed but surely to the changing circumstances of mankind, we have the Doctors always telling us that the acts of parliament which exist form the whole constitution; and in the last triumph of every innovation, some dignitary of the consistory court is still found clinging to the wisdom of former times.[47]

Arguments and events had moved by 1819-20 when the Whigs began to elaborate a defence of virtual representation. In his article, 'Parliamentary Reform', published in the *Review* in 1820, Mackintosh praised Lord John Russell's plan of December 1819 to disfranchise rotten boroughs and enfranchise great towns as combining 'the prudence of a Statesman with the enlarged views of a Philosopher'. The historical dimension was crucial to Mackintosh's approach: revolution does not bestow liberty; it is difficult to construct governments because they are the product of time and, he noted in this context, how easy it was to burn a bad house, how difficult to build a new one. He went on to argue on the basis of history, particularly the Chester Act passed in the reign of Henry VIII, that representation belonged to districts, communities, to all classes and interests but not to all men who were represented virtually:

> it was not, however, till the great impulse given to English industry, in the middle of the eighteenth century, that the disparity between

the old system of representation, and the new state of society, became very remarkable. This was very soon followed by the sudden and enormous growth of the manufacturing towns. Then, for the first time, were seen several of the most important places in the kingdom, without any direct share in the national assembly. The new manufacturing interest itself was left without any additional provision for its adequate representation. The original defect of our representative system, which, while it provided for the influence of great property, and secured a regard to the voice of the multitude, did not allot a sufficient share of power to the middle class, became in this state of things, more apparent and more humiliating.[48]

So Stewart's point about the institutions of society requiring to be in harmony with the social circumstances of the people underlies the specific instance Mackintosh gives.

Since the Revolution [of 1688] a far greater diffusion of property and intelligence has produced a new struggle. Class after class, as they rise to consequence, become ambitious of a larger share of that collective power which the body of the Commons gained from the Crown.

Just as the curbing of the Royal Prerogative proved safe, so too would a return to the principle of the Chester Act whereby virtual representation implied some share of actual representation. Mackintosh also asserted that elections would no more provoke riots than the absence of elections had hitherto, and that Russell's moves would help counter the growing power of the Crown in the Commons exercised through placemen: 'the House of Commons can have no safety but from a new infusion of that popular spirit which once enabled them to resist and depose kings, and call new royal families to the Throne.' Even if it is considered by some insufficient to add only 20 seats to popular representation, that 20 would none the less strengthen the 'democratical' principles of the House of Commons. Mackintosh's condemnation of non-resident freemen roving in the towns also highlights the importance he gives to property: their rights did not arise from the permanent influence of property, from the respect in which they were held as social superiors or out of gratitude for kindnesses they had done, but rather because of 'an indisguised triumph of money alone over every sort of natural influence'.[49]

It is not a cause of wonder, therefore, that even some 18 years before the publication of the article, Sydney Smith was writing that he 'never saw so theoretical a head which contained so much practical understanding'. For him, Mackintosh

> has lived much among various men with great observation, and has always tried his profound moral speculations by the experience of life. He has not contracted in the world a lazy contempt for theorists, nor in the closet a peevish impatience of that grossness and corruptibility of mankind, which are ever marring the schemes of secluded benevolence. He does not wish for the best in politics or morals, but for the best which can be attained.[50]

Mackintosh's line concerts with the 'middling way' of thinking on parliamentary reform that had been established earlier by Jeffrey and that bore the hallmarks of its debt to the Scottish Enlightenment.

II

The strand of reforming opinion that was informed by the Scottish Enlightenment was one of several, though it did contribute distinctively to the aspirations of Whig grandees. There was another area where 'Scotch knowledge' operated but was, in its origins, unique, namely classical political economy. The lineage from Adam Smith to Dugald Stewart and thence to the Edinburgh reviewers was clear and uninterrupted. Classicism in economics lay in the influential writing of Smith's immediate successors who pursued inquiries that both concerted with and diverged from his principles.[51] Noted political economists of the early nineteenth century from the Edinburgh stable included Francis Horner and John Ramsay McCulloch, others were the 8th Earl of Lauderdale and James Mill, and Jeffrey, Allen and Brougham wrote on the subject, too, in the *Review*. While others wrote on the topic in the journal from other backgrounds, such as Thomas Malthus, it is scarcely surprising that political economy was viewed as a 'Scotch' science. The *Edinburgh Review* gave greater attention to economic matters than any other journal in the early nineteenth century so that one commentator has described its reviews as an essential source of authority and influence for the development of economic theory in early nineteenth-century England and for appraising changes in public opinion that brought about a revolution in economic policy in the first half of the century.[52] The function of the *Review* in economics, as in other complex matters such as science, was to provide a comprehensible summary of the principal arguments and issues revealed in economic literature, as they pertained to the relevant issues of the day. In the first half of the nineteenth century, these issues included the monetary standard, banking policy, taxation, the Corn Laws, population, the Poor Laws, the economic condition of Ireland, the monopoly of the East India Company and the Combination Acts. There were to be crucial developments in each of the areas in the period.

Some flavour of the critical tradition which subsisted between the Scottish political economists can be gathered from a letter Horner wrote in 1803 to an advocate friend of his, Thomas Thomson, about his refusal to furnish notes for a new edition of the *Wealth of Nations* and is, perhaps, accounted for by youthful self-regard:

> I should be most reluctant to expose Smith's errors before his work has operated its full effect. We owe much at present to the superstitious worship of Smith's name; and we must not impair that feeling, till the victory is more complete. There are few practical errors in the Wealth of Nations, at least of any great consequence; and until we can give a correct and precise theory of the Nature and Origin of Wealth, his popular & plausible & loose hypothesis is as good for the vulgar as any other.

Later references to Smith are much less critical, however; one reference might even be described as hypocritical, bearing in mind what has just been noted, and was Horner's comment, less than a year later, to Jeffrey on Lauderdale's book on political economy:

> The manner in which Smith is spoken of is the most reprehensible feature of the book . . . . Our gratitude can never exceed the benefits which we owe to Smith; and if the peer does not in time acquire more reverence for his memory, and a juster sense of his merits, he will remain, what he is at present with all his acuteness and readiness, a political speculator of the third or fourth class.

A month later, he was noting to his brother how a particular discussion in Parliament was 'a curious proof of the degree in which Adam Smith's speculations and others of the kind are studied by the young men in Parliament, beyond the attention that was paid to such topics by the politicians who were educated at an earlier period of the last century.' In August 1805 he was wondering to the historian, Henry

Hallam, if there were more than a very few people who realised all that Smith had done for them and signed off with, 'Forgive me, . . . for being so very Scotch through my whole letter; but with you, I forget these distinctions now and look upon you as one of *us*.' Finally might be noted his recommendation to Richard Sharp, the hatter, MP and frequenter of Holland House, who had asked for a list of political economy books: '*Smith's* name must be at the head of the list, though I should not have thought of mentioning him to you, were it not that one must come back to that book after every other, or rather carry it always on in examining any other.'[53]

That Sharp was asking Horner for a list of such books at all testifies to his reputation in the economic field. Even Ricardo is reported early to have admired his *Edinburgh* articles.[54] It was they which stimulated so much interest in monetary and banking policy and he carried on his campaigns in Parliament, though his editor notes that his approach and vision were broader in philosophic outlook than that of Ricardo.[55] The specific issue, however, on which Horner made his reputation was that of the suspension of cash payments by the Bank of England. The measure, in addition to the cost of the war, led to a decline in the foreign exchanges and a rise in the price of bullion. Other contributory factors were an increase in note issue as a result of a misconceived discount policy, inflationary government borrowing, poor harvest, subsidies made to allies by the government, military expenditure abroad and the impact on exports of the Continental system and the American boycott. To maintain exchanges, it would have been necessary to reduce domestic prices and incomes to below pre-war levels and this could only have been done by a contraction of credit with its resulting tensions.[56] The suspension of the Bank of England's specie payments for all but the armed forces overseas, and which effectively applied to the country banks too, lasted from February 1797 until 1821.

About half-way through the period of suspension voices of protest at the high price of bullion became particularly noticeable. This was because whereas the years 1793-1801 had seen economic difficulty, there had been a cyclical fluctuation which persisted up to 1812, during which taxes exceeded war expenditure and harvests were ample. That economic difficulties were again on the horizon was perceived by 1809-10 and expressed by David Ricardo in letters to the *Morning Chronicle* and by Francis Horner in the Commons. Pressure led to the appointment of the Select Committee on Bullion, chaired by Horner, which produced a Report in June 1810, it was published in August of the same year but not discussed until May 1811.[57] In the event the Committee's recommendation to return to specie payment within two years whether or not the war continued to be waged was rejected, but the Report itself, when considered alongside the work of another member of the Bullion Committee, Henry Thornton's *An Inquiry into the Nature and Effects of the Paper Credit of Great Britain* (1802), promoted an awareness of technical economic knowledge at a time when the economy was becoming increasingly complex. Horner's lengthy review of Thornton in the first volume of the *Edinburgh Review* was part of the process that increased awareness. Horner himself excused his review on the grounds of Thornton's prolixity and obscurity which marred the value of the book and masked the new information it contained. He believed anyway that the large number of publications on political economy liberalised the practitioners — 'It is in this manner, that every period of dearth has contributed in some degree to alleviate subsequent years of scarcity, by the instruction which it yielded against popular prejudice.'[58]

Horner did admire Thornton's explanation of the relationship between the quantity of money in circulation and the velocity with which it circulated: 'A high and prosperous state of mercantile confidence quickens it; and it is apt to be retarded, during the intervals of distrust and alarm.'[59] On the question of the effect of the quantity of paper-money in circulation on prices, Horner is concerned to distinguish two cases which Thornton confounds — bullion or the general price of goods and their local price in paper currency.[60] He praises Thornton's analysis of the prevailing system of credit and circulation, the banking system, commercial transactions and disorders that can occur: 'such dissected exhibitions of our commercial economy prepare, with necessary knowledge, those more active citizens who undertake the discussion of the national counsels.'[61] When Horner comes to Thornton's account of the circumstances in 1797 that caused the suspension of cash payments, he criticised the view that the war and the economic events leading up to it were directly responsible, and is concerned to lay some considerable responsibility on the directors of the Bank. He believed that the diminution of the quanity of notes was due to the directors, indeed they told Parliament that they felt embarrassed by their unprecedented advances on Treasury bills which was not permitted by their charter. The Bank's difficulties were caused by a progressive drain of specie because the Bank failed to put sufficient specie into circulation. Further, the Bank had limited discount of commercial paper-money for some time because it had given so much more leeway to the government; hence followed mercantile distress and difficulties in financial arrangements. Pressure on the situation was increased by the restriction of credit. Government loans 'did tend to distress the circulation by rendering that sum of notes less adequate to the wants of commerce, than if they had flowed into the market through the usual channel of discounts.' Horner regarded Thornton's view as fallacious that 'it is the total quantity of circulating notes, and not the manner in which they come into circulation, that is the material point.'[62] He agreed with Thornton, however, that an extravagant issue of paper would raise the price of commodities and depreciate currency in its bullion value. He stressed that last point rather than the other causes suggested by Thornton and gave figures to prove that there had indeed been an extravagant issue of paper.[63]

Less than a year later Horner was most favourably reviewing Lord King's *Thoughts on the Restriction of Payments in Specie at the Banks of England and Ireland* because its arguments showed that 'nothing but a derangement and depreciation of our currency can explain the appearance, continued since 1799, of an exchange against us'. By the end of the article, Horner was praising Lord King for an achievement beyond that of merely elucidating a particular economic case with which he agreed and the praise may equally be applied to Horner's own *Edinburgh* articles:

> we have always thought, that such writers as undertake to inform the public mind upon measures of temporary interest, render themselves doubly and eminently useful, when they seize every opportunity of expounding those more extensive truths, which, though in possession of the learned, are not yet insinuated into popular conviction. It is by innumerable repetitions of this sort, that an impression may at length be made, even on vulgar and understandings, in favour of an enlightened policy; and the assent of the multitude habituated to the results of that genuine philosophy, whose high aim is to emancipate mankind from practical error, and to ameliorate their political condition.[64]

Horner's mentor, Dugald Stewart, while retired and not active in the debate about specie and paper, none the less sent extensive notes in exchanges on the subject in the spring of 1811 with the Earl of Lauderdale, another author on political economy from the Edinburgh stable. They amount to more than 20 pages of very small print in his *Collected Works*, and Stewart had serious reservations about the Bullion Committee's Report. First there was the matter of circulation;

he felt that there was a lack of relationship between the comment that gold would rise above its mint price if excessive local currency was issued and price rises were caused, and the observation made on the effects of quick and slow circulation:

> It is, at least, a *possible* case then, in theory, that, on the one hand, an increase in the quantity of money may be so counterbalanced by a decrease in the rate of circulation, as to leave the relation between money and commodities the same as before; and that, on the other hand, the quantity of money may remain unaltered, (nay, may suffer a great diminution,) while in consequence of an accelerated circulation, its influence upon prices, and upon everything else, may be increased in any given ratio.[65]

Stewart questioned if a high state of confidence quickened the circulation of bank notes. In a period of confidence money was no longer passing rapidly through the same number of hands but through the many more hands which were now sharing in prosperity.[66] The circle through which money passed was enlarged in such a period. However, Stewart believed it was far more likely that money would circulate more quickly in a time of alarm. In such times, everything must be paid for in cash because there is a lack of trust and the consequence of speeding up circulation multiplies the currency and exacerbates the existing evil. Stewart could not accept the view of the Committee that circulation was slowed down by distrust.[67] He agreed with the Committee that increased issues of notes had caused the currency to depreciate and prices to rise but he differed from the Committee over the manner in which the situation arose.[68]

For Stewart, the radical evil was not the mere over-issue of notes, but the anomalous and unchecked extension of credit which produced a sudden increase in prices by a sudden increase in demand.[69] So he disagreed strongly with Thornton, the Bullion Committee, and implicitly with Hume in his essay on Money:

> the increased issues of paper currency since the year 1797, have operated on the prices of commodities chiefly by means of that sudden extension of *credit* which they necessarily suppose; and of the communication of this credit to those classes of individuals whose capitals have the greatest influence on the state of the market.[70]

He therefore pinpointed the difference between the view expressed by Thornton and the Bullion Committee and his own view by saying that they wanted credit limited by a well-restricted currency while he wanted currency limited by 'a well-regulated and discriminating credit'.[71] In his final note of comments on the Bullion Committee's Report, Stewart renewed his case for credit being the cause of price rises rather than the amount of notes issued: 'it is the rise of prices produced by the extension of credit and the creation of fictitious capital implied in the enlarged issues, that gives full employment to the same issues considered in their capacity of circulating medium.' Indeed, price rises 'occasion a *scarcity* rather than a superfluity of circulating medium'.[72]

From credit, Stewart moved on to a criticism of Ricardo and Malthus who argued that the same principles of circulation apply to money (whether in paper or specie form) as to any other commodity, namely that it is depreciated by excess and raised in value by deficiency, in other words its value is subject to the principles of supply and demand.[73] Stewart objected to a circulating medium being regarded as a commodity and excused Thornton and others for their intellectual laxity in so regarding it by referring to the language which had for so long been applied by political economists to the corn trade. The principles of supply and demand were indeed applicable to corn because the demand was constant and because it is necessary for the supplies to bring corn quickly to market, given its perishable nature and the expense involved in storage. Wine, on the other hand, is different: it can be kept at no expense, its value increased with age and, given a moderate demand and an abundant supply, wine keeps its price for years.[74] (Stewart was, of course, writing of wine in his own time!) There is also the case of water, the supply of which in Britain is inexhaustible and the consequential exchange value of which is negligible. Water illustrates the care which must be used when referring to the principles of supply and demand, the nature of which are dependent on what experience teaches us is reasonable. Money, therefore, may still be called a commodity but a special sort of commodity none the less: a man will only borrow the amount of money he needs or can invest profitably and he will give a higher interest for it if his needs are pressing or the likelihood of profit great. The rate of interest charged is determined by the demand and by the availability of supply. In Britain in 1811, the maximum rate of interest was fixed by law; if the Bank regulated its issue of money solely by demand:

The inevitable consequence of this is, a general rise of prices, (or what amounts to the same thing,) a depreciation in the value of our circulating medium; — a *depreciation*, however, I must again repeat, which is not (like the fall in the price of wheat after a plentiful crop) the immediate or necessary consequence of mere superabundance, otherwise the same effect might have been produced (which it manifestly could not) by slipping a twenty shilling note into the pocket of every inhabitant of the kingdom.

Stewart recognised that, by asserting such a view, he was contradicting Adam Smith who said that precious metal abounded in a country because of increased production from mines, leading to the diminution in the value of the metal. Stewart asserted that the low cost of living in Ancient Rome that accompanied ample supplies of money was due to the cultivation of land by slaves — 'the plenty of the precious metals does not *necessarily* raise prices, and that *these* are influenced by many other circumstances of a perfectly different nature.' Smith also noted that the discovery of rich mines in America seemed to have been the sole cause of the decline in the value of silver in relation to corn. But Stewart asserted that a variety of other highly potent causes were operating and, without them, 'the discovery of the American mines would no more have raised the price of corn in modern Europe, than the sudden influx of wealth from the conquered provinces did in ancient Rome.' The discovery probably retarded the development of banks and paper currency which facilitated real wealth and prosperity.[75]

The concluding paragraph of Stewart's comments is of interest for the light it shed on the relationship between himself and Horner — 'I have sometimes wished that I had seen the *Report* before it was printed, as nothing would have given me greater pleasure than to have contributed anything, however trifling, towards its improvement.' But even now, he told Lauderdale,

If I have stumbled upon anything that you think worth shewing to Horner, I can have no objection to your communicating my papers, either in whole or in part, to one in whom I have so entire a confidence, provided only you mention to him my anxiety that nobody whatever shall hear of such a communication.[76]

It may be reassuring to the contemporary reader to reflect, after considering the points rehearsed in the debate by Thornton, Horner

and Stewart, that *plus ça change*. One historian of the Bullion Committee, however, in appraising their report criticised their view that
the fall in exchanges was due to an excess of currency. The Committee
was thus implicitly calling for a reduction of currency and passing over
lightly the impact of deflation on all sectors of the economy. They did
not examine the mechanism whereby a reduction in money supply
affected prices and so greatly underestimated the difficulties that
would ensue.[77] Yet the general principles of the Bullion Committee
were sound, for instance that the discount policy of the directors was
incompatible with the maintenance of cash payments. Their biggest
achievement has been regarded as the application of their theory of
money prices to the working of a central bank. Future experiments
were in part made possible by their theoretical demonstration of 'the
need for an active policy of credit regulation by reference to the
exchanges'.[78]

In the furtherance of crucial economic inquiries, it is significant to
note the shared interests and convergence of views of the Clapham
Sect (Thornton was an Evangelical MP), whose influence on the burgeoning Victorian age has long been recognised, and of the 'Scots'.
Both played an inestimable role in informing the public on political
economy. As Dugald Stewart observed in his lectures, in the decade
before the Bullion Committee even existed:

> The progress made in Political Economy during the course of the
> last century, affords the most luminous illustration of the truth of
> some of the foregoing remarks. Every step which has hitherto been
> gained in that science, has discovered to the world some delusive
> project or erroneous opinion, counteracting human happiness, and
> even counteracting the partial interests of those by whom the pro-
> ject or opinion was fostered and encouraged. And in proportion as
> its general principles assume somewhat of a systematical form, the
> connexion between the interests of individuals and the national
> prosperity, and the still more unexpected connexion between the
> prosperity of nations and that of neighbouring communities,
> becomes more and more apparent.[79]

Lord Holland was duly impressed by the work of his political protegé.
He wrote, after the work of the Bullion Committee had been com-
pleted, that Horner's

was a determined enquiry into matters which, little attractive in their nature, led him, as he well knew, to conclusions unpalatable to powerful individuals as well as to the Bank and the Government. . . . The dread of the consequences of fair dealing and honesty, or rather the persuasion of the convenience of paying for everything in fluctuating and depreciating paper, was not confined to the vulgar. All the supporters of the war, and some who, without approving its origin, profited by the spirit of speculation to which its continuance gave occasion, were for preserving a hazardous and dishonest system.[80]

Moreover in June 1819, with the conversion of the anti-bullionists, Lord Dudley wrote to the Bishop of Llandaff, Edward Coplestone:

To me who am apt to laugh, it appears laughable, and to those of a more serious turn, it must be provoking, to see persons who after being a long time in office, come down to Parliament gravely to declare, that they have just condescended to learn about as much political economy as was usually known to the junior students in the University of Edinburgh twenty years ago, and to lend the sanction of their authority to the opinion of wiser and better men.[81]

Horner was not the only publicist of political economy to emerge from a Scottish university lecture room. After Horner died in 1817 John Ramsay McCulloch, first editor of *The Scotsman*, dominated the writing of articles on political economy from 1818 until 1838. While McCulloch has been criticised for unoriginality of mind and for a poor literary style, his reputation was as a staunch follower of Ricardo in the cause of whose doctrines he was a dogged propagandist. He disseminated the ideas not only in *The Scotsman* and the *Edinburgh Review* but also in his article on 'Political Economy' in the supplement to the *Encyclopaedia Britannica*. He joined the Political Economy Club, founded by James Mill in 1821, and he and Mill were known for bringing a Scottish religious zeal to their proselytising.[82] McCulloch campaigned ceaselessly for the recognition of political economy as a distinct subject in both Edinburgh and London. In 1824, he was lecturing on political economy in London: 335 people attended his classes, five of whom were peers and 15 MPs and the auditors included the Earl of Clarendon, Mr (Thomas?) Baring and Sir James Mackintosh. In 1825, it was being mooted that a separate Chair of Political Economy be

established at the University of Edinburgh, and while McCulloch felt
that the plan might be obstructed by the Scottish authorities, especially
Lord Melville, he none the less had hopes of preferment to the prospec-
tive Chair. Dugald Stewart was much in favour, and his wife wrote to
Macvey Napier that her husband 'says he must be cautious in any direct
interference in favour of Mr McCulloch, lest it should be said, as it most
undoubtedly would, that he was influenced by personal hostility to Mr
Wilson.'[83] Mr John Wilson ('Christopher North' of *Blackwood's Magazine*) was, by 1825, Professor of Moral Philosophy and a Tory in his
politics, quite the reverse of the Whig Stewart, his predecessor-but-one.
He opposed the plan because, he said, it was the prerogative of the
holder of the Moral Philosophy Chair to give lectures on political economy, and his political stance would indeed ensure the support of Lord
Melville for his opinion. Consequently, the plan failed, but McCulloch's
efforts to be recognised were eventually crowned in 1828 with his
appointment as first Professor of Political Economy at the new university in London.

III

It has been written that James Mill's *History of British India* (1806-17)
is a key document for assessing what each of Mill and Bentham contributed to Benthamic doctrine, and that it is a work in the Scottish
philosophic tradition in that it used the comparative method and was
concerned with general truths of use to contemporaries. Mill, as a
devoted admirer of Adam Smith, wanted to illustrate his economic
principles by studying a monopolist commercial company like the
East India Company.[84] Mill had been enabled to study at Edinburgh
from 1790 through the patronage of Sir John Stuart of Fettercairn, to
whose daughter he had been tutor, and his education was made possible by a fund, established by Lady Jane Stuart, for the training of
ministers. Moral philosophy was a compulsory subject for Divinity
students, but the subject and its praelector proved irresistible anyway:

> All the years I remained about Edinburgh, I used, as often as I
> possibly could, to steal into Mr Stewart's class to hear a lecture,
> which was always a high treat . . . The taste for the studies which
> have formed my favourite pursuits, and which will be so till the end
> of my life, I owe to him.[85]

Mill studied arts subjects from 1790 to 1793 and Divinity for four winters thereafter. A later editor has pointed to Mill's relatively neglected writings in the period 1803-08 as manifesting 'the first fruits of his Scottish education and the beginnings of many of his later interests' (the *History of British India* was one such work). The editor continued: 'His main sources at this time are those Scottish authors who made up his intellectual diet as a student; the questions which occupy his attention are those concerned with the science of Man.'[86] The eighteenth-century Scottish philosophers' idea of progress was never abandoned by Mill; it has been said to explain his taste for sweeping generalisations and dogmatism because he felt history supported his notions of tolerance, freedom, reform and especially reason. The comprehensive and attractive treatment of history in Millar's works and his liberal outlook were an enduring influence on Mill. Millar's sociological history of the development of law and government formed Mill's earliest political views,[87] for instance, Mill classified nations according to a position in a scale of civilisation.[88]

Mill was, however, writing after the outbreak of the French Revolution, in a very different atmosphere from that in which the philosophers of the Scottish Enlightenment had written and when he himself was undervaluing and suspicious of philosophers.[89] He illuminates, however, another facet of the connections between the eighteenth and nineteenth centuries. Not only was the *Edinburgh Review* a bridge between the two eras, but a melting-pot in which the ideas of the Scottish Enlightenment continued to simmer and from which emerged, among other developments, James Mill and others who were Bentham's disciples. As will be seen, the *Review* and the Benthamites collaborated in various educational schemes, and also in law reform.

IV

Sydney Smith's lectures were another, quite different way in which the 'Scotch knowledge' which had been imparted to him in Edinburgh was in turn passed on to others in London. Like Francis Horner, he sought to inform. His lectures on moral philosophy were given on Saturdays at the Royal Institution, in three courses, between November 1804 and spring 1806. Smith himself was modest about his abilities and aspirations but they were well judged in level and presentation for their audience, and were popular and well received. In April 1805, between

600 and 800 attended, though a year later the numbers had fallen substantially.

As for the content, the lectures were privately published in 1850 and, while unoriginal, gave rein to Smith's wit and to his powers of arrangement and argument. These powers show what he had learned from Dugald Stewart and others, and his most recent biographer has observed that 'Perhaps the most important historical contribution of the lectures is their communication of contemporary Scottish thought to a general London audience'. He quoted Reid, Stewart and others frequently in the lectures and his definition of moral philosophy was that broad area of knowledge that was not concerned with natural philosophy.[90] Smith's enterprise illustrates the nooks and crannies of England into which 'Scotch knowledge' could be taken by means of the enterprise, talents and personal qualities of former students.

Notes

1. Francis Jeffrey, 'The Dangers of the Country', *Edinburgh Review*, X (1807), pp. 11-12.

2. Ibid., X, p. 14.

3. Ibid., X, p. 17.

4. Francis Jeffrey, 'Cobbett's *Political Register*', ibid., X, pp. 399, 405-7.

5. Ibid., X, pp. 407-8.

6. Ibid., X, p. 408.

7. Ibid., X, pp. 408-9.

8. Ibid., X, pp. 409, 411.

9. *Collected Works of Dugald Stewart*, IX (1856), pp. 403, 406.

10. Ibid., IX, p. 417.

11. Ibid., IX, pp. 430-1.

12. Ibid., IX, p. 444.

13. Ibid., IX, pp. 445-6.

14. Ibid., IX, pp. 448-50.

15. Francis Jeffrey, 'Parliamentary Reform', *Edinburgh Review*, XIV (1809), p. 278.

16. Ibid., XIV, p. 290.

17. Ibid., XIV, p. 291.

18. Ibid., XIV, pp. 291-2.

19. Ibid., XIV, pp. 292-4.

20. Ibid., XIV, pp. 294-7.

21. Ibid., XIV, pp. 298, 299, 300.

22. Ibid., XIV, pp. 300, 301.

23. Ibid., XIV, pp. 303, 305.

24. Francis Jeffrey, 'The State of Parties', *Edinburgh Review*, XV (1810), pp. 504-8.

25. Ibid., XV, p. 512.

26. Ibid., XV, pp. 512-13.

27. Ibid., XV, pp. 513-17, 519, 520.

28. Francis Jeffrey and Henry Brougham, 'Parliamentary Reform', *Edinburgh Review*, XVII (1811), pp. 253-90.

29. Ibid., XVII, pp. 266-7.

30. Ibid., XVII, p. 269.

31. Ibid., XVII, pp. 270-1.

32. Ibid., XVII, pp. 277-8.

33. Ibid., XVII, pp. 282, 283, 288.

34. Francis Jeffrey 'Leckie on the British Government', *Edinburgh Review*, XX (1812), pp. 327, 329-34.

35. James Mackintosh, 'Universal Suffrage', *Edinburgh Review*, XXXI (1818), pp. 165-203.

36. Ibid., XXXI, pp. 172-3, 174, 175, 176, 177.

37. *Edinburgh Review*, XXXI, p. 195.

38. Ibid., XXXI, pp. 178-9, 182, 186, 187, 191, 192.

39. *Horner Collection, L.S.E.*, III, Letter 36 to Francis Jeffrey, 15 September 1806, Jeffrey's reply is in Cockburn, *Life of Lord Jeffrey*, II, pp. 110, 112.

40. See Harvey, pp. 226-7.

41. *Letters of Sydney Smith*, I, p. 186, Letter 181 to Francis Jeffrey, soon after 17 April 1810.

42. *Collected Works*, II (1854), pp. 229-30.

43. *Horner Collection, L.S.E.* IV, Letter 28 to John Ward, 25 May 1809.

44. Ibid., IV, Letter 36 to Francis Jeffrey, 12 June 1809.

45. Ibid., IV, Letter 102 to John Murray, 18 May 1810.

46. Ibid., IV, Letter 110 to Francis Jeffrey, 16 July 1810.

47. Ibid., V, Letter 66 to John Murray, 5 February 1812.

48. James Mackintosh, 'Parliamentary Reform', *Edinburgh Review*, XXXIV (1820), pp. 461, 468, 475, 477, the quotation is from p. 479.

49. Ibid., XXXIV, p. 479, 480, 483-6, 492.

50. *Letters of Sydney Smith*, I, p. 63, Letter 58 to Francis Jeffrey, postmarked June 1801.

51. Jacob H. Hollander, 'Adam Smith 1776-1826', *Journal of Political Economy*, XXXV (1927), pp. 176-7.

52. F.W. Fetter, 'The Authorship of Economic Articles in the *Edinburgh Review*, 1801-1847', ibid., LXI (1953), p. 232.

53. *Horner Collection L.S.E.*, II, Letter 20 to Thomas Thomson, 15 August 1803; II, Letter 47 to Francis Jeffrey, 29 March 1804; II, Letter 51, to Leonard Horner, April 1804; II, Letter 106 to Henry Hallam, 2 August 1805, III, Letter 18 to Richard Sharp, 20 March 1806.

54. *The Economic Writings of Francis Horner in the Edinburgh Review 1802-1806*, ed. Frank Whitson Fetter (London, 1957), p. 2.

55. Ibid., pp. 14-15. 18-19.

56. E. Victor Morgan, *The Theory and Practice of Central Banking 1797-1913* (Cambridge University Press, 1943), p. 73.

57. Ibid., pp. 34 and 40.

58. Francis Horner, 'Thornton on the Paper Credit of Great Britain', *Edinburgh Review*, I (1802), pp. 172-201. References here are to the more accessible Fetter edn of Horner's economic writings (see note 54 above), which in this instance is on p. 28.

59. *Economic Writings*, p. 33.

60. Ibid., p. 39.

61. Ibid., p. 42.

62. Ibid., pp. 52-4.

63. Ibid., p. 55.

64. Francis Horner, 'Lord King on Bank Restrictions', *Edinburgh Review*, II (1803), pp. 401-21. Reprinted in *Economic Writings*, in which these two quotations are on p. 95.

65. *Collected Works*, VIII (1855), p. 432.

66. Ibid., VIII, p. 433.

67. Ibid., VIII, p. 434.

68. Ibid., VIII, p. 436.

69. Ibid., VIII, pp. 440-1.

70. Ibid., VIII, p. 442.

71. Ibid., VIII, p. 443.

72. Ibid., VIII, p. 450.

73. Ibid., VIII, p. 444.

74. Ibid., VIII, pp. 446-7.

75. Ibid., VIII, p. 448.

76. Ibid., VIII, p. 452.

77. Morgan, p. 73.

78. Ibid.

79. *Collected Works*, IX, p. 348.

80. Vassall Fox [Lord Holland], *Further Memoirs of the Whig Party 1807-1821*, pp. 103-4.

81. John William Ward [Earl of Dudley], *Letters of the Earl of Dudley to the Bishop of Llandaff* (London, 1840), pp. 222-3.

82. Fetter, 'Economic Articles in the *Edinburgh*', p. 239; and Elie Halévy, *The Growth of Philosophic Radicalism*, trans. M. Morris (London, 1952), pp. 342-3.

83. McCulloch to Macvey Napier, 23 April 1825, *Selections from the Correspondence*, pp. 45, 48. Of the members of the Baring family of financiers mentioned in the *Dictionary of National Biography*, it seems most likely that it was Thomas who attended McCulloch's lectures. Helen d'Arcy Stewart's letter to Napier was written on 21 May 1825 and is to be found in *Selections from the Correspondence*, p. 47.

84. Thomas, p. 98.

85. James Mill to Macvey Napier, 10 July 1821, *Selections from the Correspondence*, p. 30.

86. *James Mill: Selected Economic Writings*, introd. and ed. Donald N. Winch (Edinburgh and London, 1966), p. 4.

87. Ibid., pp. 6-8.

88. Thomas, p. 105.

89. Ibid., pp. 99-100.

90. Bell, pp. 53-7, with the quotation from p. 57.

5 'SCOTCH KNOWLEDGE' AT WORK II

The previous chapter was concerned with knowledge related to the teaching of moral philosophy in the Scottish Enlightenment and how it informed political, economic and intellectual matters in the early nineteenth century. The emphasis now is rather on a number of different ways in which 'Scotch knowledge' interacted with society by means of Scottish-trained doctors and others who furthered educational developments and social administration.

I

In enlightened Scotland, science was so integral a part of intellectual life that historians have seen no specific need to explain its pursuit in social terms. However, some historians have suggested that in later eighteenth-century England especially there was an increased concern for science. Three explanations commonly adduced for the increased concern are the utility of science in the early stages of industrialisation, the part played in the promotion of scientific knowledge by the rationalism of Dissent, and the alternative progressive culture which science provided for the emergent middle classes of burgeoning provincial towns. Such explanations have, however, been questioned and it has been proposed instead that English greater scientific concern was an evolving part of the country's distinct expression of the Enlightenment. Since it was believed that England already possessed constitutionality and freedoms, her philosophers did not need to be preoccupied with political questions. The emphasis of the English Enlightenment was different:

> Educated and propertied élites were most concerned to establish the validity of egoistic individualism, the liberty to improve one's lot and pursue happiness through knowledge, industry, enterprise, the free use of capital, science, skill. But desiring to secure the peaceful enjoyment of these, they were also committed to public harmony and order, a stability which would partly flow from individual progress, and which partly was to be imposed by the exercise of rationality, moderation, politeness and humanitarianism.

133

For many provincials, science could play a large part in both of these quests.[1]

The desired location of the endeavour was the town: rusticity was barbaric, urbanity civilised — 'Only in towns could man achieve taste, elegance, society, knowledge, science.'[2] The standard of culture that was adopted in the towns was that of the metropolis, London: towns were defined in terms of their distance from London, they named their pleasure gardens and theatres after those of London, and some built new towns in the style of metropolitan neoclassicism. Science was but part of the culture that was adopted in provincial towns and it was cultivated by local fashionable men and women long before the need for utility in industry or the assertion of the dissenting ethic were felt.[3] Indeed, the definition of science itself was broad: it did not have to be useful for economic life but could include such interests as botany or astronomy, and early in the nineteenth century included phrenology, animal electricity and mesmerism. A tradition of urban scientific interest was established from quite early on in the eighteenth century: it developed over time and took different forms well into the nineteenth century — 'The founding of formal scientific societies was the climax of a very long, cumulative, tradition of scientific lecturing, instruction, teaching, showmanship, gentleman's clubs, medical societies, etc.'[4] By the late eighteenth century, then, science had played a longstanding part in the fashionable culture of both the capital and provincial towns. The social significance of scientific interest over time depended on the character of the individual town.

Former students of Scottish universities are the focus of the present study: it is predominantly those among them who were medical practitioners who have been recognised as key figures in actively fostering urban science from the later eighteenth century. Science here becomes intimately involved with the cultural and social context in which these men found themselves. Reasons were seen earlier why, from the later eighteenth century especially, Dissenters sought a Scottish medical education and how they came in perceptible numbers. Indications were also given earlier of the number of Scots who sought a medical education and how, in 1826, one-third of those in the army, navy and East India Company medical service were said to have spent some time studying in a Scottish medical school.[5] By the time of the Royal Commission on Scottish Universities (1826 and 1830) the Director-General of the Medical Department of the Army, Sir James McGrigor, could remark on the advantages of the Chair of Military Surgery, which had been established in 1806:

> Besides wounds, and what is termed Military Surgery, the economy
> of Hospitals, and of Hospital arrangements, is in this school taught
> by a gentleman who has served much in the field and in various
> climates. At the end of the last war, upwards of 300 medical officers
> of the Army were placed on half-pay and it is within my knowledge,
> that many of them profited greatly by attendance on this class, and
> before they returned to employment on full-pay.[6]

Those with medical training from a Scottish university were not
immune from the tendency, noted among Dugald Stewart's students, to
seek careers furth of Scotland. The medical alumni conformed to the
long-established pattern of Scottish university students of taking their
knowledge and skills elsewhere. In the case of the medicals, their social
background and training was very different from that of the fashionable
doctor in Bath: James Hamilton, professor of midwifery, told the
Royal Commission how those who had graduated from Edinburgh since
he had been appointed 26 years before, had included 600 Scots, 627
Irish and 500 Englishmen:

> Now, a very large proportion of Scotch and Irish are poor men, who
> cannot afford to pay what is absolutely necessary: it is with diffi-
> culty scraped together; they sink their degree; they go into the Army
> or Navy as Hospital Mates and Surgeons' Mates; they take up labora-
> tories in different quarters of the kingdom, or keep druggists' shops,
> with the degree of M.D. in their pocket. That is destroying the
> proper distinction there ought to be.[7]

Before any examination of their relationship to scientific culture in the
provinces can be resumed, however, it will be assisted by an analysis of
the tensions the Scots-trained experienced in their profession before
and after 1815.

As the contrast between Bath, Scottish and Irish doctors suggests,
the eighteenth-century medical profession was stratified, and the strati-
fication was bound up with social attitudes. The profession consisted
of physicians, surgeons and apothecaries. Physicians were controlled by
their Royal College, itself governed by its fellows. Fellows were
essentially gentlemen, defined as graduates of Oxford or Cambridge
who had received the classical education of those universities (there was
no medical education offered in either institution until well into the

nineteenth century), who were Anglicans and who did not engage in any manual work involved in medical treatment. Exceptions to these rules were extremely rare. Surgery and the compounding of medicines, the work of the other two branches of the profession, were regarded as manual occupations, whereas physicians prescribed the drugs to be compounded and superintended surgical operations. Even midwifery was regarded as degrading because it necessitated manual dexterity. The precondition of an Oxford or Cambridge degree invariably served to bar from fellowship of the college Dissenters and also those, whether Anglican or not, who had received a professional medical education, rather than the classical education of the English universities. Between 1771 and 1833, 130 out of 149 fellows admitted were graduates of Oxford or Cambridge.[8] The fellows of the Royal College of Physicians technically controlled practice throughout England and Wales through their granting of a required licence, but enforcement of the requirement was really only possible within seven miles of London. As a consequence some decades before the start of the nineteenth century, tension grew between the fellows and licentiates, and on occasion hostilities broke out. Between 1800 and 1825 258 out of 371 MDs who became fellows, licentiates or extra-licentiates (those with a licence to practise outside the London area) were Scots-educated,[9] indicating that a crucial element in the tension was the nature of medical education they had received and the social and cultural/professional difficulties they faced in thir careers. Physicians traditionally practised among the social élite and their dependants.

The history of the surgeons in the eighteenth to early nineteenth centuries, despite its intrinsic interest, does not bear as directly on the situation of the Scots-educated medical practitioners as the history of the apothecaries. In England the training for both surgeons and apothecaries depended heavily on a system of apprenticeship until 1813-15. The Company or Society of Apothecaries had, by the eighteenth century, accreted to itself the right not merely to compound or dispense medicines but also to offer treatment. Apothecaries could not until 1829, however, charge for their medical advice, only for the remedies they supplied. After 1800, it was also commonplace for apothecaries to take the licence of the College of Surgeons, giving rise to a breed of practitioner called the surgeon-apothecary. Certainly by 1815 surgeon-apothecaries were, in the words of one pamphleteer, 'the most numerous part of the profession in town and country'. Another pamphleteer observed that the conjunction or separation of different branches of medicine depended on the degree of wealth and on the

population size of the area of practice. Separation tended to be the rule
in cities, conjunction in rural areas. There were exceptions, however:
'in Edinburgh we find, that in consequence of the want of sufficient
wealth, an intimate coalition exists between surgery and pharmacy.'[10]
Apothecaries came from a very different part of the social spectrum
than the physicians, being mainly sons of small shopkeepers, yeomen
and respectable craftsmen. As to the social composition of their
patients, two works written in 1773 and 1795 respectively noted that:

> Apothecaries have got physic principally into their own hands: this
> is evidently the case, especially in the country, where the Physician
> seldom visits any but such as are in opulent circumstances; the poor,
> alas, scarce ever! It is much the same in London (allowance being
> made for those that are in hospitals); so that Apothecaries have by
> far the greatest number of patients under their own care.

And that:

> In this city [London?], where a physician attends one patient, an
> apothecary attends twenty; and in the country this proportion is
> more than doubled . . . . Huts, hovels, and cottages, which, through-
> out the whole country, but more especially in large manufacturing
> towns, inclose such infinite numbers of human beings, and feed . . .
> diseases of the most infectious and fatal tendency, compose almost
> exclusively the walk of the apothecary. To him is likewise allotted
> the care of nearly all prisons and poor-houses.[11]

By 1815, a further social development was sufficiently clear for the
contemporary surgeon-apothecary, R.M. Kerrison, to be able to point
to 'the middle order of society', who paid their taxes and supported
their families 'by their industry in various trades, and by a commerce in
articles formerly unknown':

> One effect of this augmentation of the middle orders of the com-
> munity was a proportionate increase of sickness, amongst people,
> who were unable to procure medical aid, by seeing physicians, as
> often as their situation required professional care, and, the Members
> of the Royal College of Physicians, having made no diminution in
> their accustomed fee, to meet the actual wants of persons in this
> class of society, they were compelled to resort to others for advice.

By concentrating his practice on the urban middle orders, the medical practitioner could see more patients in less time and charge modestly. Kerrison continued:

> It was convenient for the Physician to limit his practice to the opulent (who likewise increased in number with the advancing prosperity of the kingdom) and to continue taking large fees. It became expedient, therefore, that the Royal College of Physicians should permit others to give advice to those, who could not afford to pay fees to themselves; and the Apothecaries, thus resorted to, found it conducive to their interest, to make themselves as well qualified as possible for the required and assumed task.[12]

Apothecaries can be seen, therefore, responding to the rise of population, to social change within the population and to an increasing middle-class demand for their services. A guild of some antiquity (its dissociation from grocers dated only from 1617) which controlled competition by the traditional means of a system of apprenticeship and licensing was face-to-face with contemporary pressures and new challenges. The jurisdiction of the Apothecaries' Company to license was confined to its own members and to an area within seven miles of London.

So the situation might have remained, a cosy division of the spoils between the College of Physicians and Society of Apothecaries, had there not been other sources of medical practitioners which did not restrict admission in anything like the same way as they did. These other sources were the Scottish medical schools with their professional education which provided the growing and evolving market with precisely the type of general practitioner it sought, to the discomfiture of both the College and the Society.

The college was the first to feel the Scottish assertiveness as early as 1767.[13] The trouble faced by the college, which included action in the courts, physical assault on college buildings and staff, and the disruption of committee meetings, was prompted by the licentiates' views that the grounds of admission to a fellowship were too narrow; that they, as licentiates, were as much members of the college as were the fellows, and that, therefore, they had the right to address the college's comitia (assembly); and that equally they had the right, with the fellows, to elect the college's censors. By 1767 there had developed a situation in which there were more licentiates than fellows, and the licentiates formed themselves into the Society of Collegiate Physicians.

In the first half of the eighteenth century only seven licentiates admitted to the college had been Scottish graduates compared with 30 from foreign universities, 19 who had no medical degree, and three from Cambridge. In the period 1751-75, no less than 53 were Scottish graduates, one each came from Oxford and Cambridge, 31 from foreign universities and only four had no medical degree. Of the 25 Scottish graduates admitted between 1761 and 1765, 17 were admitted in 1765, just two years before the troubles started.[14] At the first meeting of the Society of Collegiate Physicians in January 1767, 31 licentiates attended, of whom 21 were Scottish graduates, and they took four out of the five elected posts in the Society. In the assault on the college building in May 1767, 21 licentiates took part of whom 14 were Scottish graduates.

That Scottish medical education and the sheer incomprehension of it on the part of a traditional social élite lay at the heart of the college dispute is borne out by contemporary illustrations. Licentiates are portrayed carrying two banners, one saying 'Pro Collegiis Scotiae' and the other 'Delenda est Oxonia Delenda est Cantabria'. The fellows are portrayed facing licentiates in Scottish dress and mouthing anti-Scottish sentiments.[15] The tension between the two groups was stirred up by the Scots-trained who felt that they had qualified as general practitioners, that they had had a systematic medical education, and that the Scottish universities granted degrees to people who before or after the award had considerable experience of 'inferior' medical practice as surgeons or apothecaries. A number of them also had experience in midwifery.[16] The Royal Commission of Inquiry into the Scottish Universities (1826 and 1830) was told by the Dean of the Edinburgh Medical Faculty:

At present a great proportion of our graduates, who settle in England and Ireland, and almost the whole of those who settle in Scotland, and all of our graduates who enter the Army or Navy, or the East India Company's service (who form a large proportion of our graduates in the first instance), all these act as general practitioners in the early part of their lives. We conceive that they are better qualified for the general practice of medicine than those persons who have the degree of surgeon or apothecary only.

He was supported by a professorial colleague with the words, 'I know the title conferred by our University is that of Physician; but, at the same time, throughout England and Scotland generally . . . persons practise . . . upon our degree as general practitioners.' Even as late as the 1830s, Dr John Sims, physician to the St Marylebone Infirmary who had taken his MD from Edinburgh in 1818, could tell the Select Committee on Medical Education:

> Most of the practitioners of Edinburgh, I believe, when they first set out, are general practitioners; perhaps excluding midwifery: they practise medicine, surgery, and pharmacy: they are commonly, I believe, fellows of the College of Surgeons, having, at the same time, taken a degree; and they employ themselves for a number of years in practising the various branches of medicine; and when they choose, they confine themselves to medicine more exclusively.[17]

It is clear that the College of Physicians were trying to exclude those who had infringed the traditional social status and aura of physicians which was underpinned by manner rather than professional education. The Scots-trained had, on the other hand, indulged in manual arts and their education did not conform socially: they were not gentleman-physicians. The Royal College was, in 1767, trying to stop the rise of the general practitioner.[18] The fellows saw little place for the new type of practitioner that Scottish graduates represented because it demeaned their concept of what a physician was.

The trouble from 1767 within the Royal College of Physicians represents the first challenge to the traditional medical hierarchy and to the division of both the responsibilities and the spoils of medical care between the College and the Apothecaries' Society. The battle over the Apothecaries' Act 1815 was the second challenge. The intervening years had seen significant social and economic change which led to the battle over rights and status shifting from the realm of the physician in the fashionable areas of practice to the realm of the apothecary in the growing areas of population. The period witnessed growing competition and growing sensitivity to standards: for the apothecaries, competition came from chemists, druggists, uneducated apothecaries and also from the Scots-trained. The sensitivity to standards came from the middle-class patients and from the Scots-trained who had been professionally educated; but it was not confined to them. Between c. 1793 and 1815 a succession of forward-looking apothecaries' groups, sometimes including members of other sections of the medical profession, came together to suggest legislation and to lobby for the raising of standards by prohibiting the unqualified from practice and by establishing a superintending body to regulate and control the profession throughout the country.[19] Such groups were The General Pharmaceutical Association of Great Britain, founded in 1793, the Associated Faculty (1806) and the Association of Apothecaries and Surgeon-Apothecaries (1812). In the end there was legislation, but of a different kind from what they had envisaged.

The Apothecaries Act 1815 was highly restrictive, which satisfied the Royal College of Physicians. They had failed in 1804-06 to take complete control over the medical profession in England and so were quite content with an Act that legislated to control apothecaries, that invested powers in the Apothecaries' Society, and which reiterated that provision of the Society's craft guild charter of 1617 subjecting the Society to the College. The Act had nearly two dozen provisions,[20] but the two most consequential were the right given to the Apothecaries' Society to enter and inspect any apothecary's shop throughout England and Wales — a major extension of power and authority beyond London —and the insistence on a five-year apprenticeship prior to being allowed even to sit the examination for an apothecary's licence. It was the retention of the apprenticeship provision that maintained the craft guild character of the Apothecaries' Society and ran counter to the frequent attempts from the late eighteenth century to elevate the status of the general practitioner. Instead, he was now to remain under the control of a wholesale pharmaceutical trading company and indirectly under the Royal College of Physicians which, for some considerable time, had sought to depress the status of general practitioner. In the passage of the Apothecaries' Act 1815 and its aftermath general practitioners, whether Scots-trained or those who had evolved from English social change in the later eighteenth century, found that the Apothecaries' Society was concerned to entrench and extend traditional rights that had arisen in the different social and economic circumstances of the early seventeenth century rather than respond to the conditions of the early nineteenth century.[21]

The Apothecaries' Act did not define the functions and duties of an apothecary or what constituted his practice. Consequently, the Society, which actively sought to enforce the new legal provisions, left the courts to do the defining. A succession of judgments in the early 1830s laid down that the penalties of the Act were to be visited upon anyone who coupled advice to patients with making-up and selling medicines that were consequent upon that advice; secondly, defined that an apothecary was one who made up and prepared medicines, irrespective of the prescriber; and thirdly defined an apothecary as 'one who professes to judge of internal disease by its symptoms and applies himself to cure that disease by medicine'.[22] The effect of the legal judgment was aptly summarised in 1833 by *The Companion to the Newspaper:*

> The consequence is . . . that over all England the medical practi-
> tioners are also apothecaries, within the meaning of this Act. The
> exceptions are to be found only in the metropolis, and a few of our
> other largest towns. But even in the metropolis, probably nine-
> tenths of the practice is in the hands of persons who dispense drugs
> as well as advice and attendance. Now, by this act, all these persons,
> constituting as they do all but the entire medical profession through-
> out England, must, in the first place, be Licentiates of the Apothe-
> caries' Company.

The point had already been made some years before by John Thomson
in evidence to the Scottish University Commission:

> Though the Act apparently only confers on the Company the exclu-
> sive privilege of licensing Apothecaries, it is well known, that, under
> this denomination are included nine-tenths of the country Practi-
> tioners in England. It is only in large towns, if even in them, that the
> different departments of the Physician, Surgeon, and Apothecary can
> be kept separate. In other places, it is absolutely necessary for every
> Practitioner to dispense drugs, so that the Act really confers on the
> Apothecaries' Company a monopoly of licensing all the general
> practitioners in England and Wales.

Consequently, the Commissioners themselves had to report the humiliating conclusion that the 'result of the operation of this statute is to
exclude the whole Graduates of the Scotch Universities from practising
in England unless they have served the requisite apprenticeship.'[23]

In the enforcement of the Act it becomes clear that the chief victims
were the Scots-trained, just as they had seemed to be in 1767 at the
hands of the fellows of the Royal College of Physicians. It was not only
that their degrees were questioned or that they were disbarred from
practising as general practitioners in England, but they were actually
taken to court. In 1833 a Bill was introduced in Parliament to exempt
the Scots-trained from the penal clauses of the Act, and before it was
withdrawn a number of petitions were presented, including those signed
by numerous Scottish graduates in northern English towns. These petitions show not merely their grievances, and the social and professional
tension, but where, by the 1830s, the Scots-trained had taken their
medical 'Scotch knowledge'. An examination of the reports from the

Select Committee on Public Petitions 1833 shows, however, that there were twice as many petitions in support of the 1815 Act and against the exemption as there were in favour. All the parties in Scotland with a vested interest in exempting the Scots-trained from the Act's provisions were obviously to be found petitioning — all the universities except St Andrews, their students, the Edinburgh Royal Colleges, the Glasgow faculty of physicians and surgeons, and practitioners in such Scottish towns as Perth, Paisley and Renfrew. Petitions from English towns testified to the divisions between their medical practitioners: Liverpool, Leeds, Hull and Manchester each submitted two petitions, one for the Bill to exempt, one for the existing Act. The petition for exemption invariably made it clear that all its signatories had prosecuted medical studies in a Scottish university implicitly indicating the type of English town to which the Scots-trained doctor had gone to pursue his career. No petition for exemption came from south of Yorkshire.

One northern English town which submitted only one petition, and that in opposition to the 1815 Act, was Scarborough. Whereas the Perth petition made the fairly obvious points that the Scottish degrees were renowned, the courses more comprehensive, the examinations strict and searching, and that the Scots-trained did not wish to be put on 'the same footing with ignorant pretenders and quacks',[24] the Scarborough petition was blatantly nationalistic:

> your honourable House will thus perceive that the *London* Apothecaries' Society, practising medicine more as a trade than a liberal profession, secure to themselves the services of their apprentices, for five years, principally for their own benefit, with the *Edinburgh* School, aiming at laying in its pupils the foundation of a systematic and enlightened knowledge of their profession, requires only three years' apprenticeship; . . .
>
> That your petitioners also complain of the necessity of paying fees, and of taking out the Apothecaries' licence at all, as their education embraces pharmacy as well as the other branches of the profession; besides, your Petitioners are led to doubt the competency of a Society of *London* Apothecaries to examine an *Edinburgh* graduate or licentiate, as (for what is known of them either collectively or individually, as respects medical science or literature,) this body had been more remarkable for its silence than for its literary performances or scientific discoveries, and was nothing more than a trading company till raised into importance by the Act of 1815. On

the other hand, your Petitioners have emanated from a medical school which, since its first rise under the tutorage of Monroe, Whytt, and Cullen, has been under the auspices of a long line of distinguished men, and there is no department of the medical sciences but has been improved or illustrated by an *Edinburgh* graduate or licentiate.

What dignity or propriety is that in a Society as much allied to commerce as to medicine, thus dictating the mode of education of the whole practitioners of *England* according to its own narrow views? And what a singular anomaly does it present in professional matters, where the least celebrated medical corporation in the Empire is vested with powers over those at least as distinguished as any; that an *Edinburgh* graduate or licentiate, who is all over the world respected as a well-educated practitioner, is considered as an unqualified person by a trading *London* Corporation; and further should be liable to prosecutions, penalties, &c. for practising his profession, while *St John Long*, and a horde of imposters and quacks, are flourishing undisturbed within call of the shop of the Worshipful Apothecaries Society![25]

Scottish sensitivity was also evident in three petitions, those of the Edinburgh Royal College of Surgeons, medical practitioners in Liverpool, the Glasgow Faculty of Physicians and Surgeons and the medical practitioners of Hull and vicinity, who all quoted the articles of the Treaty of Union (1707) which provided that all the subjects of Great Britain should enjoy a communication of privileges and advantages.[26]

Individual petitions made points unique to themselves. The Edinburgh Royal College of Surgeons observed that

The avowed purpose of this Act was to protect the public from ignorant pretenders and quacks, but it has also the effect of enabling the Apothecaries' Company to interrupt in the exercise of their profession as general medical practitioners, persons whose education and professional attainments, as ascertained by examination, fully qualify them for its duties, and whose qualifications are in fact superior to those required by the Apothecaries Company in their licentiates.[27]

Medical practitioners in Manchester greatly resented the fact that

A chemist and druggist who has received *no* medical education whatever, can prescribe, dispense, and compound medicines with impunity; whereas a Scotch Medical Practitioner, who has studied for four years, and been examined upon medicine, surgery, and pharmacy, is precluded from prescribing for any medical case, and is subject to a fine of £20 for compounding a single pill, draught, or mixture.[28]

Physicians and surgeons practising in Aberdeen fixed on the apprenticeship requirement: the time spent in an apprenticeship, they felt, could be much more profitably used in acquiring general knowledge, and they quoted the Report of the Scottish University Commissioners which stated that an apprenticeship, rather than advancing a young man's training, served rather more the interests of those already practising by giving them inexpensive assistants.[29]

Glasgow University's senate stressed the actual nature of the work now undertaken by medical men in England and Wales, they were 'neither purely and strictly Physicians nor Surgeons, but general practitioners, acting in both capacities, and furnishing medicines to their patients.'[30] The distinctive points made by the Edinburgh Royal College of Physicians were that a 'knowledge of the structure and functions of the human body, and of the nature and right treatment of disease, is of far more difficult acquisition than skill in compounding drugs', and the educational courses available in the cities of Edinburgh and Glasgow were more likely to produce accomplished men than any scheme produced by the Apothecaries' Company. The effects of the Act had been the most restrictive and oppressive, whereas Parliament should be encouraging free competition and the enlarging of professional knowledge. They wanted their own fellows and licentiates free 'to apply themselves to the cure of human malady, unfettered by any restrictions other than such as shall be proved essential to the public welfare.[31]

For all that they were in a minority and that the measure to exempt those with Scottish qualifications from the provisions of the Apothecaries' Act was withdrawn, it is clear that the Act gravely disadvantaged many who had sought careers in England. Numerous sources, directories and various kinds of histories testify to the ubiquity of the medical practitioner with a Scottish education all over England in the first half of the nineteenth century. Kerrison, for instance, in his pamphlet on the Apothecaries' Bill, happened to note in passing that in the market towns of his own Lincolnshire (Horncastle, Spilsby, Alford and Tattershall) there were five physicians, all of them graduates of Scotland.[32] The Scots-educated doctor seeking a career in England had faced pressure from established medical authorities, certainly since the Scottish medical schools had been producing graduates in any numbers. In the first instance, it was the College of Physicians as evidenced by the 1767-71 incidents, and in the second place, it was the Company of Apothecaries who so assiduously enforced the provisions of the Apothecaries' Act. The character of the Scots-educated as general practitioners was the main cause of the challenge to both these established interests. By the post-1815 period the sensitivity of the apothecaries had been heightened by the degree to which the population rise, urbanisation and the emergence of the new 'middling orders' had proceeded, all of which developments were changing the nature and the volume of the available work, and which coincided with the dramatic increase in the number of Scottish graduates. It will be recalled that whereas Edinburgh and Glasgow produced 27 and two medical graduates in 1777 and 1776, respectively, the numbers in 1820 were 121 and 16.

If the established bodies were sensitive to the challenge, however, it is also clear that the 'Scots' were no less sensitive to the response evoked by their qualifications, as was evidenced by the content of their petitions in 1833. In the case of the English who had gone to Scotland for their education that sensitivity was heightened by the fact that they were invariably religious Dissenters with all the civil disabilities that they thereby incurred until the end of the 1820s. It is reasonable, therefore, to interpret the contribution the 'Scots' frequently made to urban culture and social action as prompted by the social and professional difficulties they faced. By taking an active part in such spheres, they assisted and strengthened their claims to that recognition which was often denied to them on the grounds of their medical practice and social affiliations. 'Scotch knowledge' had reinforced marginality in their profession but it also gave them the means to counter it socially.

II

The argument is indebted to the work of social historians of science who, often using particular sociological approaches, have in the last decade or so cogently demonstrated the case that the pursuit of science was used by marginal groups to legitimise and integrate themselves socially.[33] The achievement of these historians will be highlighted here by drawing together the part played in such provincial organisations as literary and philosophical societies, Mechanics' Institutes and Statistical Societies by Scots-educated doctors. Many towns into which they went from the later eighteenth century already had a tradition of scientific culture fostered by associations of other professional men, manufacturers and merchants. The social composition of a town and its economy could shape its approach to science. Hence in Newcastle upon Tyne, with large-scale industry, religious dissent was a powerful determinant: 'the religious quest passed naturally into intellectual inquiry, the attempt to understand and to improve the physical environment was seen to be a religious duty. The kingdom was recognizably coming on earth, even as it was in heaven.'[34] In Bristol, a waning commercial centre, science was, on the other hand, pursued by the Anglican social élite to maintain their domination.[35] Birmingham's 500 trade categories meant that science culture was diffused.[36]

Science culture was continually evolving and a disparate range of factors came to enhance the appreciation of it. The sheer utility of science for manufacturing enterprises was an obvious factor. Another factor was the greater or lesser alienation from traditional literary and classical culture of many in the urban middle classes. The Scots-trained doctors exemplify the point, but it was by no means confined to them: their useful knowledge contrasted with the ornamental learning of the London physicians, Anglican and Oxbridge-trained. They felt much more at home with science. There could also be a political cutting-edge to the situation: urban middle classes who were ardent advocates of parliamentary reform and the removal of Dissenters' civil disabilities were frequently also leading members of scientific organisations to which they pointedly admitted on merit rather than rank, thus associating science with an openness to talent. Equally, science was directed to their social inferiors: Mechanics' Institutes were devised to dissuade artisans and operatives from drunkenness and irreligion. Social control was to be achieved by inculcating acceptance of the natural order of things through natural science and political economy, which had important places in the curriculum, and by encouraging objectivity through the teaching of physical science.[37] Absorption of both lessons would, it was hoped, deflect the respectable working man from being misled into social disturbance by popular radicals. In the Manchester Literary and Philosophical Society a not dissimilar line had led to natural philosophy being purveyed to the young sons of businessmen as a rational amusement in place of drink or gambling or the brothel. Yet another factor at work in enhancing science culture was the social motive to distinguish oneself from the stereotypical early Victorian self-made man and his flagrant philistinism.[38] The Scottish-trained medical practitioner was often to work out his professional predicament as a member of the scientific community in a burgeoning English town. The factors which furthered science were an intimate part of the wider social history of time and place. To that social history, the 'Scot' had much to contribute as well as to receive; he was frequently to be found in a key promotional position in the array of scientific institutions that arose.

The contribution can be illustrated by detailing what 'Scots' did in particular towns, considering first Manchester. Here the activity of the 'Scottish' physicians and surgeons was characteristically broad, encompassing public health, statistics, the literary and philosophical society, medical and artisanal education and hospital construction and organisation. Most of those concerned had been at Edinburgh, a few at Glasgow: they were attracted to Manchester by the opportunities for practice, for teaching and for public-health work. Some had experience of the arts as well as the medical education of Edinburgh and Glasgow and had been in Edinburgh when the university's reputation had been at its highest. Scottish scientific institutions functioned as models for what the medicals sought to establish in Manchester: the Manchester medical school, for instance, may have been partly modelled on Edinburgh which was deliberately inspected by the founder, Thomas Turner in 1820; the Manchester Mechanics' Institute imitated three features of the Edinburgh School of Arts (founded 1821), concentrating power in the patrons' hands, confining teaching to the application of science to practical arts, and awarding prizes and certificates for proficiency. The founder of the Manchester Literary and Philosophical Society had boarded with Principal Robertson's sister while a student at Edinburgh and became friendly with Robertson and Hume.[39] It should also be noted that many of the 'Scots' were also members of Manchester's well-known Unitarian chapel in Cross Street.

It was not novel, by the later eighteenth century, for the Scots-trained to be prominent in Manchester's medical and scientific life. Charles White, who had studied at Edinburgh in the late 1740s or early 1750s, founded both the Manchester Infirmary and the Lying-in Hospital (St Mary's Hospital) and had originated lectures to medical students in Manchester. He and Samuel Kay (MD, Edinburgh 1731) were a surgeon and physician, respectively, in the Infirmary from 1752 until 1782 (Kay) and 1790 (White).[40] Consequently, the way had been paved for the careers of two outstanding figures in the history of Manchester's social and medical history, Thomas Percival and John Ferriar. Percival was a Dissenter, a student of Warrington Academy, who went north to Edinburgh to study in 1761. Ferriar, on the other hand, was a Roxburghshire man who, after taking his Edinburgh MD in 1781, went south, first to Stockton-on-Tees and then, in 1785, to Manchester remaining there till his death in 1815. Percival began by practising in Warrington before moving to Manchester in 1767. He wrote volumes of medical and philosophical essays in the late 1760s and early 1770s, and from then until the 1790s, he wrote also about the rules governing conduct in hospitals which led to his celebrated work, *Medical Ethics, or a Code of Institutes and Precepts adapted to the Professional Conduct of Physicians and Surgeons* (1803).[41] In about 1770, Percival made his 'Proposals for the establishment of more accurate and comprehensive Bills of Mortality in Manchester', one of those not uncommon instances at the time where quantification was called upon to promote particular public health reforms. He wanted quarterly tables of christenings, marriages and burials, including the stillborn; tables of christenings that specified the child's sex; tables of death, giving the age and marital status of the deceased so that relative comparisons could be made of the expectation of life between the two sexes; the ages of the dead to the nearest five years, except for the under fives, a list of diseases by which all had died; and the number dying of each disease in the different stages of life, age and season of the year. All these particulars were to be certificated by an apothecary or physician. Percival's object was to be able 'to ascertain with tolerable precision the increase or decrease of certain diseases; the comparative healthiness of different situations, climates, and seasons; and the influence of particular trades and manufactures on longevity.'[42]

Attention to Carlisle can here be interposed since about a decade later John Heysham began his invaluable record of mortality there. He had been born in Lancaster and after studying medicine in Edinburgh and Holland settled in Carlisle in 1778 to practise. In 1780, he produced 'a very careful and accurate' population survey; in 1787, he corrected the survey undertaken by the constables of Carlisle which resulted in the population being shown to have grown by 1000 which, as Heysham remarked, should have given pleasure to all those who wished Carlisle well. From 1779 to 1787, Heysham kept a careful record of mortality for Carlisle and its suburbs, noting the incidence of death, the age and sex of the deceased, marital status and cause of death. Thereafter, he continued to keep statistics until 1813, becoming convinced that mortality was declining, that the labouring classes were living better, that despite incidents of scarcity and unemployment in the years c. 1798-1813, cleanliness was more prevalent and the standard of living improved, probably leading to the decline in deaths due to typhus fever. Heysham had opened a public dispensary in Carlisle in 1782, and was its first physician, treating 11,382 patients up to 1796. He considered that Carlisle had also improved its mortality rate by the practice of inoculation to eliminate smallpox, which began in 1755 and which was especially carried out in the 1780s, and by the practice of vaccination in the first 14 years of the nineteenth century.[43]

The connection between statistical records and public health was to reappear in a more organised form in Manchester with the Manchester Statistical Society in 1833. Before that, however, the Scots-trained medicals had been prominent in founding the Manchester Literary and Philosophical society in 1781. Thirteen out of its 24 founders were medical, including Percival, and they read 23 of the first 55 papers.[44] Prior to the foundation of the Lit. and Phil. it was apparently common for Manchester medical men to discuss and argue about their cases in public, through the newspapers or printed pamphlets circulated even among laymen, and upon its foundation the tradition was continued there as it constituted a forum for so many medical members.[45] In his time Ferriar too was a leading member of the Lit. and Phil., being secretary and vice-president. Another institution which Percival helped to found was the short-lived College of Arts and Sciences, designed to educate young men after they left school and before they went into business. It offered lectures on belles-lettres, science, anatomy and physiology.[46] In 1792 another more professional development was suggested by Ferriar, namely the establishment of fever hospitals. He requested the Committee of Police to supervise lodging-houses, notorious for their capacity to harbour and spread infection, and to disinfect those houses where fever was found. In 1796 his suggestion led to the foundation of the Manchester Board of Health and the opening of a 'House of Recovery' (fever hospital) in the grounds of the Infirmary.[47] Ferriar had proposed these developments as a direct result of his practice among the poor which had given him considerable experience of infectious fevers. They were rife from 1789 and he began to write several papers on the subject. Ferriar and others undertook treatment in the Manchester Infirmary of home patients from the most unhealthy districts in the town. He became much concerned about social conditions, tried to draw attention to them, and pointed out how they threatened not only the poor but also the wealthier classes.[48]

In 1791 Ferriar addressed the Manchester Committee of Police about protecting the townspeople from fever epidemics. Lodging-houses were seen as the sources of fostering and spreading infection, because new lodgers would be given a bed from which the corpse of a fever victim had only recently been removed. Ferriar wanted lodging-houses licensed by the civil magistrates and prosecuted if the number of lodgers for which they were licensed was exceeded. He wanted the houses inspected regularly by persons especially appointed for the task and with the power to remove uninfected inhabitants to a clean fever house, and to use all necessary methods to fumigate the house, con-taminated clothes and bedding. A nurse was to be appointed to visit the sick who had no one caring for them. Ferriar did not at this time consider it politic to go as far as to suggest the establishment of fever wards as he thought he had probably already pushed the committee too far.[49] He had, as a result of the epidemic fever of 1789-90, advocated the abolition of the poorest lodging-houses and the erection of large barrack-type lodgings so that labourers migrating to the town could be kept healthy and given the opportunity to exercise after work rather than go to the alehouse.[50]

In 1792 he first suggested publicly the opening of fever wards in various parts of the town to which infectious cases could be moved from lodging houses. The suggestion was made in one of the volumes of his *Medical Histories and Reflections* which gave his distinctively rea-soned account of the epidemic fever of 1789-90. The book attacked the management of cotton mills and the living conditions of the cotton operatives which encouraged the spread of infection, such as the system of shift-work for child apprentices by which periods in bed in the factory premises were interspersed with periods at the loom. The conse-quent sharing of beds, in addition to the inadequate ventilation, dirty floors and machinery, the lack of control over the coming and going of the sick, and the lack of disinfection, all were conducive to contagion.[51] In 1794, there was a typhus outbreak at a time when poverty and the decline of trade were great and large numbers of workmen were in the army. The disease spread from Manchester to Ashton-under-Lyne and there was a move to form a Board of Health. Ferriar advocated fever wards and the appointment of a large and influential committee: four small houses were set aside to accommodate 25 patients and part of an adjoining piece of land was enclosed by a wall and used for washing and airing the patients' clothes.[52] In May 1796, the House of Recovery was opened and its success, and the reduction in expense of burying paupers that resulted, led to another opening in 1804. Ferriar also planned a fever ward for Stockport, and suggested the provision of baths for the poor not only to keep them clean but because a cold douche would harden their constitution and brace them against illness.[53] In 1796, too, Percival drew the attention of the Board of Health to the operatives' working conditions in the cotton mills and, perhaps surprisingly for Manchester which was to be regarded as the capital of *laissez-faire*, he proposed an 'application for Parliamentary aid (if other methods appear not likely to effect the purpose) to establish a general system of laws, for the wise, humane, and *equal* government of all such works'.[54] He pointed out the insanitary condition of many cotton mills which spread disease, the lack of ventilation which damaged the health of employees working in a hot and polluted atmosphere, and the damage done to constitutions by day- and nightworking. Children suffered worse from nightwork and he believed, too, that children's earnings encouraged their parents to idleness. He was typical of his age, in combining a physical with a moral observation. He proceeded to deplore children's being debarred from educational opportunities and moral and religious instruction.[55]

Other Scots-trained medicals may not have had quite the impact of Percival and Ferriar but they followed their approaches. Visiting the Infirmary patients in their homes, for instance, was a noted practice of John Cowling (MD, Edinburgh 1768) and George Bell (MD, Edinburgh 1777). With Percival and others, Cowling investigated and reported on a malignant fever which originally broke out in Redcliffe cotton mills in 1784.[56] Bell had moved to Manchester from Berwick in 1781, and in 1783 proposed that a collection of medicinal plants should be grown in the Infirmary garden to supply the apothecary's shop, to make medicinal plants better known to students, and to stimulate generally the study of medicine.[57] The study of medicine was also the interest of Thomas White who gave anatomical lectures.[58] William Henry, who studied in Edinburgh in 1775 and 1776 and who was a physician to the Manchester Infirmary between 1808 and 1817, was noted for his chemical researches on gases absorbed by water, coal gas and on the means of preventing cholera coming into the country.[59] Samuel Bardsley, who studied *inter alia* at Edinburgh and who worked in Doncaster before he moved to Manchester, was involved in a range of social action, like so many medicals in the town, namely the Infirmary, being an honorary physician between 1790 and 1823, the Lit. and Phil. (he was one of the secretaries) and a supporter of the Board of Health.[60] Henry Dewar, physician to the Infirmary from the date of his graduation from Edinburgh in 1804 until 1808, had been an army surgeon and he moved back to Edinburgh, but not before he had spoken to the Lit. and Phil. and had written on the fire and choke damp of coal mines.[61] William Winstanley (MD, Edinburgh 1806) gave evidence to a Parliamentary Select Committee on the effects of excessive hours of labour on the health of young children in cotton factories.[62] Of 55 honorary physicians and surgeons to the Infirmary between 1752 and 1830, no less than 21 were 'Scots', and they invariably had connections with the Lit. and Phil., and with a variety of social questions in which their interest had been whetted by their professional experience.

Another Edinburgh-trained doctor who was for a few years in Manchester but whose name is associated more with an aid to synonymy than with science culture is Peter Mark Roget. He had come to study at Edinburgh through the world of intellectual connection to which he was admitted by his uncle, the lawyer Sir Samuel Romilly. Romilly's own circle included such familiars of the European salons as Etienne Dumont, Mme. de Staël and Benjamin Franklin who knew well the Edinburgh philosophers, particularly Stewart. When Roget wanted to study medicine, it was clear to his family's intimates that there was only one place to go, and once there, the Stewarts well looked after him and his family. His uncle's circle also touched the Bowood of Shelburne/Lansdowne to whom Roget was personal physician for a while, and whose son, Henry Petty, Lord Lansdowne, was to act as a patron to Roget. Romilly also introduced his nephew to John Philips, an early and enlightened Manchester mill-owner to whom Roget acted as tutor on a Grand Tour. By 1804, Roget had collected an Edinburgh MD (1798), toured Europe, attended Lord Lansdowne's household professionally, and was seeking a post as physician at the Manchester Infirmary of whose Board of Trustees Philips was chairman.

Roget's assessment of Manchester at the time is of some interest:

> The number of physicians at Manchester bears certainly a less proportion to the population than in most other towns. For 100,000 inhabitants, six or seven physicians seems scarcely an adequate number. The prodigious and sudden influx of inhabitants during the short interval of peace may in some measure account for this under proportion; and the great reputation of Dr Percival and Dr Ferriar may have deterred such as were ambitious of advancing rapidly into extensive practice.[63]

Roget worked closely with Ferriar in the attack on fevers in Manchester through the Board of Health writing 'Advice to the Poor', which was distributed to them. He also gave courses of medical lectures for students in the rooms of the Lit. and Phil. covering physiology and comparative anatomy. Roget represents in himself the interconnections of the Scottish Enlightenment, the intellectual, dissenting and aristocratic worlds beyond Edinburgh which it touched, and various aspects of early nineteenth-century English social history, He was even Grey's private secretary for a short while.

James Phillips Kay-Shuttleworth (1804-77) is another noted figure of the nineteenth century who connects Edinburgh first with Manchester and then with the world beyond both. Kay (he acquired the -Shuttleworth when he married an heiress) came from Rochdale, his father was a cotton-spinner and manufacturer, and he was a Dissenter. In 1824 he went to study medicine at Edinburgh, graduating as an MD in 1827. It is valid to recall his experience as a student because it had a bearing on his later interests and career. It was in Edinburgh that he first became aware of the social conditions of the poor: in only his second year he was a medical assistant in the New Town Dispensary and he later worked in the Old Town Dispensary covering areas of the town where some of the worst distress were to be found such as the Cowgate and the Canongate. He frequently assisted William Pulteney Alison whom he forever afterwards hero-worshipped. By 1826 he was dealing with a severe outbreak of fever which required the appropriation by the town council of Queensberry House in the Canongate for patients where 300 beds were filled:

> I necessarily became familiar with the foulest slums in which this wretched population seemed to be continually perishing. Their habits, wants and sufferings were constantly before my eyes. I came to know how almost useless were the resources of my art to contend with the consequences of formidable social evils. It was clearly something outside scientific skill, or charity, which was needed for the cure of this social disease. This thought was burned into me by daily experience.[64]

Kay also assisted in the clinical ward of the Royal Infirmary, and for a year was resident clerk of the medical wards.

By 1829 he was physician of the Ardwick and Ancoats Dispensary in Manchester which opened that year. He was again impressed by the living and working conditions of working people: he saw mill discipline to be as strict as that of a military battalion and the long hours of work as a restraint on the people. The origins of disease were the diet, water supply and sewage. Zymotic diseases spread and killed children:

> The vitiated and dusty air of the mills, this excessive heat, and the

greatness of the change to the cold air of a stormy winter night occasioned pulmonary disease. The work of the mothers of families in the mills and the imperfect nursing of children in their absence, combined with these previous described causes, destroyed one half the children before they were five years of age.[65]

In one of his books, Kay noted the timetable of those working in cotton factories: they rose at 5 a.m., worked between 6 and 8 in the morning before breakfasting between 8 and 9, work then resumed between 9 and noon when there was an hour's break for dinner, after which work continued from 2 p.m. until 7 p.m. or later. Another Scottish doctor, John Roberton (1797-1876), who was trained in Glasgow and made his name as an expert on hospital construction and convalescent homes, has left a vivid account of early morning in Manchester in a letter to Mrs Edwin Chadwick, written in 1845. While it begins by evoking pity for Manchester doctors, it soon becomes clear that others are in greater need:

Here our patients lie scattered over the wide suburbs, and often the family doctor mingles in the crowd of mill-people as they leave at night and greets them again in the early morning as they congregate to their toils without his having meanwhile pressed his pillow. By the way it is a curious sight – the swarming streets at a quarter past 5 of a cold stormy winter morning. Who but this poor drudge sees it? Most educated people who live on the spot don't know that the labourers, men, women and children, rise at five, be the weather fine or foul, and hasten at the sound of the bell to their work. It is quite a different thing this assembling in the early morning from the 'dismission of hands' at the dinner hour or in the evening when there is little but life and hilarity. At this hour one sees them all very grave if not serious, trotting along, great numbers in clogs which make an amazing clattering; many of the youngsters only half awake cowering in the cold – the lads ever and anon shrugging up a shoulder as if to put a little warmth in the part by exercise, and the girls drawing close round the throat a mother's old grey cloke or pull as often a canvas cotton-bag worn shawl ways. The grown women are commonly hurrying in the rear detained probably a little by household duties, and the men, very many of them, with a short pipe in the mouth. One thing is very striking, the absolute silence of the tongue – the heels alone speak and this loud enough! The sight makes one think of the primal cure 'by the sweat of thy brow &c.'.

Some of the thriftless ones dive into the recesses of the gin-palace to taste the fire-water, while the more sober in numbers smaller by far assemble round the sassafras tea-stand which a tidy man has erected at the corner of a street, with the flowing charcoal underneath, to buy a warm cup of the beverage which neither cheers nor inebriates. When will our rulers permit the Almighty to give the poor a cup of good coffee or tea out of the plenty of both which he has provided? Meanwhile the man in the belfry, whose summoning note has been some time pealing, strikes with double force and rapidity in tosses as expressive of impatience as can well be imagined, responsive to which is the more noisy and rapid clatter of the clogs and it is well for our meditative doctor if just at this crisis he escapes being pushed into the Kennel by the rapid approach of some half-sleeping lad who having enjoyed his bed five minutes beyond the time is now running for it with might and main. Seriously, this congregating at so early an hour, of such countless crowds of all ages and both sexes is an interesting sight: it shews the habitual self-denial, steady industry and dutiful obedience to the allotment of providence – for which these poor people do not get the credit they deserve. But there is One whose eyes sleep not who notes in His book what pampered, luxurious mortals despise or overlook.[66]

Roberton's perception was not unlike that of Kay-Shuttleworth. He was writing some 14 years after Kay had been made secretary of the Manchester and District Board of Health to meet the threat of cholera. Kay's noted book, *The Moral and Physical Condition of the Working Classes employed in the Cotton Manufacture in Manchester* (1832) describes what he saw when he visited his district at the time of the outbreak. He was physician of Knot Mill Cholera Hospital, a cotton factory stripped of machinery and supplied with iron bedding. He was interested in the nature of contagion and how it was spread, so in the book he considered sanitary conditions, the ill-regulated and unhealthy condition of factories, excessive hours of labour especially for women and children, the discomfort of homes that led to intemperance, the Corn Laws and poor fiscal legislation that led to the increased cost of the necessaries of life, and the ignorance and 'barbarism' of large numbers of working people. He was concerned with the great infant mortality, the ill-effects of the Poor Laws, their administration and the abuse of charity. He saw that all these problems could not be resolved by the physician but there required to be an increase of intelligence and virtue on the part of the people. Education and religion had to influence

them and there had to be certain changes in central and local government.[67]

It is well known that the effectiveness and response of most of the
medical profession to the cholera outbreak of 1831-32 was found
wanting. They were working against a background of social and scientific ignorance. The middle class associated the disease with the lower
orders' poverty and alleged improvidence and it was commonly believed
that cholera was a visitation of Divine Providence. The profession itself
was unable to produce or accept a scientifically adequate account of
cholera because it conflicted with its traditions. Thomas Aitchison
Latta (MD Edinburgh 1819) in Leith faced immense difficulties in con-
vincing his brethren of the value of saline injections because they lacked
knowledge of the cholera bacillus and adhered stubbornly to the
miasmatic theory.[68] In Manchester, despite the best of intentions, the
Board of Health failed.[69] Cholera was a specific way in which the
rivalries of different medical groups manifested themselves. The outbreak also challenged the profession precisely at the time when its
members in the growing urban centres were trying to impress with their
abilities the middle classes, who were so great a potential clientele, and
thus gain that status denied them by their social background, their
religion and their unfashionable place of education.

The pressure of the epidemic brought out all the underlying
tensions: physicians were most reluctant to give general practitioners
authority in local institutions such as Boards of Health. In addition,
members of the profession who were aware of scientific developments
and who believed that they might be able to cure cholera by innovative
means, knew that if they tried they risked the whole enterprise to win
social recognition because the laity were reluctant to be weaned off
traditional remedies and were highly suspicious of the new. Hence
saline injection, croton oil and cauterisation made little headway. The
epidemic broke out after a generation or two of doctors had been
working to gain social recognition through Lit. and Phils., the founding
of hospitals and dispensaries, the establishment of Mechanics' Institutes
and other such means. The part played by doctors in the outbreak was
well remembered in 1833 when the amendment to the Apothecaries'
Act was before Parliament. The timing could not have been worse and
the medicals were put fully to the test. When authorities in London
overcame their reluctance to recognise expertise in the provinces, the
provincial ruling élites appointed to the local Boards of Health those
doctors with whom they were intimate. The practitioners who were as a
consequence excluded did not enter protests for fear of antagonising

precisely those middle classes who constituted their clientele. While cooperation on local Boards promoted recognition of the medicals by ruling groups in much the same way as cooperation in the various ventures of science culture had done, a heavy price was not infrequently to be paid. In Sunderland, to take but one instance, shipowners did not want their vessels quarantined and so expected the doctors to cooperate by concealing the outbreak of cholera.[70] Medical judgement could be subordinated to social connection. Members of the profession in the provinces, the Scots-trained especially, clearly faced numerous constraints and predicaments.

Kay-Shuttleworth, for instance, achieved little that was of immediate practical consequence in the cholera outbreak; indeed he twice failed to be appointed a physician to the Manchester Infirmary. He was, however, prompted to write his books, *Moral and Physical Condition* (1832) and *Defects in the Constitution of Dispensaries* (1834) and to assist in founding the Manchester Statistical Society which fitted more into the tradition of provincial cultural organisations. The house-to-house visitation which enabled him to write the book in 1832 with such authority, encouraged the foundation of the society in September 1833, because statistics promoted the very knowledge that could help avoid moral and physical evils. The brothers, Samuel and William Rathbone Greg, who had also been to Edinburgh University, and Benjamin Heywood, a former Glasgow student who, in 1824, had founded the Manchester Mechanics' Institute, were, with Kay-Shuttleworth, among the first 13 members.[71] The society undertook surveys to assess social improvement and the extent of education not only in Manchester but in all the cotton hamlets and the principal cities of the North of England, such as Liverpool, Sheffield and Leeds as well as the Derbyshire lead mining districts.

Kay-Shuttleworth's survey work began to interest him in the wider reform movement and his coming to know Nassau Senior through the Manchester Statistical Society caused him to be offered the post of Assistant Poor Law Commissioner for the counties of Norfolk and Suffolk. There, increasingly forsaking his medical practice, he broadened his experience by seeing the problems of the rural poor. He was then put in charge of a metropolitan district which included Middlesex and Surrey, writing his *Prevalence of Certain Causes of Fever in the Metropolis* (1838) and developing his earlier forays into education by starting, prior to 1839, a pioneer teaching-training scheme at Norwood, a Poor Law Guardians' children's home.[72] The 'teacher-trainers' came from Scotland. During his time in Manchester Kay-Shuttleworth maintained contact with other doctors who had studied for medical degrees in Edinburgh, endeavouring to found a North of England Medical Association and writing to fellow alumni in different cities. He also used such contacts to collect comparative information on, for example, the conditions of the Irish in various northern towns.[73]

In 1839, while remaining an Assistant Poor Law Commissioner, he took on the duties of secretary to the Privy Council's Committee on Education on which his fellow Edinburgh alumni Lord John Russell and Lord Lansdowne were prominent, illustrating once more an Edinburgh network. His lasting achievement here included the creation of the education inspectorate,[74] a programme of school-building, and the formulation of the minutes of 1846 which established the pupil-teacher system of teacher training. He became entangled in the denominational wrangling that dominated his time at the Privy Council's Committee, and critical allegations that he used the Committee for his own purposes led to his technical demotion in 1847 to assistant secretary. Lansdowne wrote to explain what was to happen to him because he was 'both a personal and political friend'.[75] His writings on education, which were many, consistently pursued the same line as appeared in a 'Sketch of Education Legislation needed for England' sent in 1839 to Lord John Russell: 'The ignorance of the lower classes in any state encourages superstition, impairs industry, and corrupts the manners of the people; but a well-instructed, industrious and religious working class is one of the most fruitful sources of prosperity in peace and security in war.'[76] He had stated the same objective more publicly in his *Report on the Training of Pauper Children* (1838): 'The great object to be kept in view in regulating any school for the instruction of the children of the labouring class is the rearing of hardy and intelligent working men, whose character and habits shall afford the largest amount of security to the property and order of the community', and he stressed that children should know the connection between property and the value of labour.[77] In a later edition of another work originally published also in 1839 he again took the orthodox line of political economy, which, as will be seen later, had permeated *Edinburgh Review* articles of the 1820s:

> Now the sole effectual means of preventing the tremendous evils with which the anarchical spirit of the manufacturing population threatens the country, is by giving the working people a good secular education, to enable them to understand the true causes which determine their physical condition, and regulate the distribution of

wealth among the several classes of society.[78]

On the basis of the science culture and the medical life of Manchester, Kay-Shuttleworth began to paint on an even bigger canvas.

An Edinburgh professor did not neglect to visit Manchester where alumni became so involved. William Pulteney Alison, the Dean of the medical faculty who had defended the position of the Scots-trained before the Royal Commission of 1826 and 1830 and who himself was to write a key work on the poor and urban health in Scotland, went to survey a workhouse in the city around 1840. An account of his visit was contained in Roberton's letter to Mrs Chadwick, and began with a defence of Alison's views:

> For my part, having served my apprenticeship in Glasgow and received my professional training in the wynds and closes of that city my heart is entirely with Alison; and now I think that success will at length crown his noble self-denying efforts. Alas! I admire but cannot imitate that admirable man. He has the strength of a horse, and, having no children to provide for and superintend, makes the wretched his family and is really an ornament of human nature. Some years ago when he was in Manchester I accompanied him in a visit to a workhouse and was greatly struck by his kind and courteous manner towards the old ladies of the wards, to whom he spoke with hat in hand and treated them in all respects as if they had been dowagers. They were not slow in recognizing a friend in him, as appeared by their brightening up and bustling about in a pleasant and (with them) unwonted state of excitement. In the children's wards his tender inquiries of the lame and sick children, concerning their parents and other particulars of their history, was well worthy of notice. I well remember remarking the same trait of character in his behaviour to the sick in the wards of Edinbro' Infirmary, and more particularly when prescribing for the poor wretches (such wretches as I never elsewhere saw and hope never again to see) in the outpatients' consulting-room of the Institution.[79]

The life and work of the Scots-trained in Sheffield was of a piece with those of their colleagues in Manchester, revolving round numerous socio-cultural organisations and a concern for public health. As in Manchester, certain names stand out — Arnold Knight (MD, Edinburgh 1811), G.C. Holland (MD, Edinburgh 1827), Corden Thompson (MD, Edinburgh 1820), William Younge (MD, Edinburgh 1786) and Charles

Favell (MD, Edinburgh 1827). They were but part of the membership of an array of voluntary associations to which medical personnel in Sheffield belonged. It has been shown that whereas from the 1820s to the 1840s there were 120 medical men in Sheffield, 43 can be singled out as considerably involved in the voluntary associations ('considerably involved' has been defined as meaning that they were founders or first subscribers on committees for more than a year or holding posts that carried real duties, and/or contributors to activities that required effort such as the delivery of papers). The 43 ranged over 29 voluntary associations of any consequence, and had 193 distinct connections, that is each association averaged seven of the 43 in influential posts, so that 22 were involved in the Lit. and Phil., and 18 in the Mechanics' Institute. For instance, in 1825, half of the 30 physicians and surgeons in Sheffield were involved in the Lit. and Phil. and in 1833, 23 out of 44 were active in the new Mechanics' Institute.[80] The associations included, in addition, a school of anatomy and medicine (from 1828), the Physical Club (1830s), the Society for Bettering the Condition of the Poor and the Medical Institution (both 1820s-1840s) and a number of others.[81]

An account of the Scots-trained individuals' work can be given against the institutional background. Arnold Knight was a founder and first president of the Sheffield Lit. and Phil. in December 1822. He read medical papers to that body on the anatomy and physiology of the ear and on digestion. He was interested in a number of local health problems (he was a physician to the Infirmary and a founder, too, of the Dispensary in 1832) one of which was dry grinding. Whereas the knife grinders' wheels ran in water, forks were ground dry and flying particles of stone and grit went into the lungs. Although Knight even suggested in another paper to the Lit and Phil. in 1833 that dry grinding was work to which criminals might be applied, he did otherwise combine with others to raise support for dry grinding inventions such as a magnetic filter for the waste. Because the Sheffield Medical and Surgical Society was a body that specialised in encouraging papers on problems relevant to the Sheffield trades, in 1820 it, too, heard a lecture from Knight on the problem of grinders' asthma (the wet grinders contracted it from the steam wheels they used). In 1828 he was investigating the practicality of instituting medical demonstrations and lectures in the town, and in 1832, he was a founder of the Mechanics' Institute. His contribution to Sheffield's life was recognised by a knighthood in 1841, though two years later he left for Liverpool.[82]

George Calvert Holland, born in Sheffield in 1801 and self-made (his father was an artisan), studied in Paris as well as Edinburgh where he was president of two student societies. He was a medical author of some national repute (his two-volume *Enquiry into the Principles and Practice of Medicine* was published in the early 1830s), but locally he was active in the Lit. and Phil. and the Mechanics' Institute, presiding over both. He surveyed local working conditions in his paper to the Lit. and Phil. in 1838, 'Introductory Remarks to an Inquiry into the Social, Intellectual and Moral Condition of the Working Class', which was later published, as was his account in 1841 of the area and the health of its inhabitants, 'The Vital Statistics of Sheffield'. In 1842 his detailed *Mortality of Grinders* appeared, and in 1843 he lectured to the Lit. and Phil. on 'An Inquiry into the Condition of the Cutlery Manufacture in Sheffield' which, with his other works, combined to have a powerful social effect. By their activity in the Sheffield Political Union both Holland and Knight moved from the field of professional expertise to that of radical politics.[83] Corden Thompson rivalled Knight's early moves to promote medical education in Sheffield and opened the School of Anatomy and Medicine in 1828. One of his papers, in 1834, was to the Physical Club on 'An Historical View of the Application of the Magnet to Medical Purposes'.[84] William Younge, a physician to the Infirmary, was particularly active in explaining to local industrialists just how important infirmaries were to a local community in order to win their support.[85] Charles Favell was an associate of Knight's in developing medical education in the town, opening the Sheffield Medical Institution in 1829. In 1845 he became president of the Provincial Medical and Surgical Association.[86]

Derby shows a similar pattern of activity, involvement and motivation, and there[87] Thomas Bent (MD, Edinburgh 1807) and Francis Fox (MD, Edinburgh 1818) are readily identifiable as Scots-trained. In Taunton, the prime mover of the local medical institution for the use of the poorer inhabitants was Malachi Blake, an Edinburgh MD of 1793. Sanitary reform in Sunderland was promoted by Joseph Brown (MD, Edinburgh 1819) who became mayor. Francis Cooper, who studied in Edinburgh, became Medical Officer of Health in Southampton in 1850. George Cuming (MD, Edinburgh 1802) formed and managed the Infirmary and General Dispensary in Denbigh; and elsewhere in Wales and the West, William Kay (MD, 1827) wrote the sanitary report on Bristol and Clifton in 1842, before becoming Medical Officer of Health in Merthyr Tydfil. John Sutherland, who studied in Edinburgh from 1823 prior to taking his MD in 1831, founded the Liverpool *Health of Towns' Advocate* in 1844, edited the *Journal of Public Health and Monthly Record of Sanitary Improvement* and became an inspector under the first General Board of Health in 1848. These are but a fraction of the names that can be culled from an immense variety of reference works and local histories to indicate the ubiquity of the Scots-trained and the character of their activity in the provinces in the early nineteenth century. If the interpretative framework of some social historians of science and their explanation of the use made of voluntary associations that promoted science culture are accepted, it can be seen that the associations and the public health interest they encouraged were a means of enhancing the social acceptability of former Scottish students.

III

For all the activity in the provinces, however, London was by no means bare of Scots-trained medicals any more than it was of politicians and political economists. Just as the non-medicals showed a degree of clannishness and created focal points such as dining clubs, so too did the medicals. The most blatant instance was the Edinburgh Club, founded in 1800 specifically for medical men in London who had studied in Edinburgh. It met monthly in members' houses to discuss medical topics. Its leading spirits were Alexander Marcet (MD, 1797) a physician at Guy's, and John Yelloly (MD, 1796) a physician at the London, who were both contemporaries of George Birkbeck and Peter Mark Roget. Birkbeck was an associate of Brougham's and Roget worked from his arrival in London in 1809 for a charity sponsored by Francis Horner and others which ran the capital's Northern Dispensary, so the 'political Scots' and the 'medical Scots' were not unaware of each other. Indeed the scientist Sir Joseph Banks held 'conversaziones' in his town residence on Sunday evenings in 1812-13, attended by a dozen Edinburgh professors or students, half those present: they included Marcet, Brougham, Petty, Leonard Horner, Birkbeck, Dugald Stewart and John Playfair.[88]

Roget, Marcet and Yelloly, who all lived near each other, promoted the Medical and Chirurgical Society from 1805 to bring the physicians and surgeons of the capital together. Up to 1809 when there were 23 members, about ten were 'Scots', up to 1811 when a further seven members joined 2-3 were 'Scots', and up to 1822 when there were 57 new members, 19 were 'Scots', making a total of 32 'Scots' out of 80.[89]

Roget threw himself wholeheartedly into the Society as its secretary but yet found time, in addition to his medical practice, to undertake other activities that 'Scots' medicals commonly undertook in the early nineteenth century: he lectured at the Royal Institution, wrote, at Dugald Stewart's instigation, for the *Encyclopaedia Britannica*, tried to investigate the epidemic that broke out in the Millbank Penitentiary in the early 1820s, and undertook an official study of the London water supply. Marcet was somewhat less typical in his activities, but maintained his interest in Edinburgh and in friends from his Edinburgh days, staying with Sydney Smith in Yorkshire on his way to the Scottish capital and writing to Roget when he arrived there:

> If our friends were as much improved as the town itself within the last twenty-five years, this would be a delightful world indeed! But while the old houses are all, more or less, looking cleaner and in better repair, with new and magnificent mansions rising on all sides, the men, alas, decay and pass away. Playfair is gone. Sir James Hall is all but gone (so far as his mind is concerned). Gregory is gone. Hope is what he ever was. Rutherford is no more. Stewart is but a noble wreck – etc. Yet the students are animated by the same spirit which was kept up this university for half a century – and in the absence of more illustrious teachers, they still continue to cast on this falling school some degree of lustre.[90]

The foundation of Mechanics' Institutes and a university in London were collaborative ventures of a different kind from the Medico-Chirurgical Society in which medical and non-medical 'Scots' were prominent. Birkbeck is a key figure in the developments: in 1807 he was appointed physician at the General Dispensary in Aldersgate Street where he not only treated out-patients but the Dispensary also arranged for him to make domiciliary visits. His partner was Henry Clutterbuck, an MD of Glasgow who had studied in Edinburgh and who developed a medical school from the Dispensary. Birkbeck was, of course, aware of mechanics' education in that he had been party to establishing the Andersonian Institution in Glasgow and with Brougham, his old associate in the Academy of Physics, he responded to attempts from within the capital to bring the movement to London. In 1823, Birkbeck founded the London Mechanics' Institution which in 1866 became the Birkbeck Literary and Scientific Institution and in 1907 Birkbeck College. In 1825, he was prominent among those who established Mechanics' Institutes at Spitalfields, Hackney, Deptford, Rotherhithe and Bermondsey, Hammersmith and Chiswick. The efforts of Birkbeck, 'Scots' and others led to some five more being in existence in the capital before the end of 1825. Brougham wrote a pamphlet, *Practical Observations upon the Education of the People* urging employers to assist. In 1824 McCulloch wrote to Napier about the impact of the Institutes:

> I was the other night at the Mechanics' Institution, and met there with Brougham. There were about 800 persons present, and I never saw a more orderly and attentive audience. There are about 1,500 workmen subscribers, at the rate of a guinea a year each. The applications for admission are necessarily numerous.[91]

The *Edinburgh Review* lent the cause of mechanics' education enormous support by means of regular articles on the subject in the 1820s.

In his article 'The New Plan of Education for England', Brougham pointed out how Hume and Smith were not opposed to government intervention in all matters of public concern because there were some areas such as the Navigation Acts where it was necessary. So it was with the education of youth which Smith had specifically instanced as a legitimate expense of the sovereign, and he had quoted the example of the Scottish parish school which brought education to the poor whereas for so long, in England, it had been provided only for the rich.[92] Brougham followed this up some four years later in 'Scientific Education of the People', where he alluded to the same point that Dugald Stewart had made about the value of books and the provision of libraries in the neighbourhood of manufactories being conducive to the encouragement of sober habits among working men. He pointed to the value of cheap publications (the *Mechanics' Magazine* and *The Chemist* were two), and the provision of lectures in manufacturing towns. This was the basis for his detailed exposition of what Birkbeck in the Andersonian and Leonard Horner's Edinburgh School of Arts (1821) had achieved, and he argued the spread to other places of Scottish efforts in the field of working men's education such as the Haddington School of Arts.[93] His philosophical justification for the Mechanics' Institutes came in another article later in the year which continued the 'Scottish' approach. He argued in the face of those who saw the education of working men as a danger that a more likely threat to public order was ignorance:

> knowledge begets prudence. The savage is proverbially thoughtless

and improvident; and in the exact proportion as he becomes civilized, he acquires the habit of looking forward and regarding the more remote as well as the immediate consequences of his actions.

So, too, with men who come to take a delight in learning. They

are not likely to engage in scenes which would at once change their whole existence, and for something they can have no distinct idea of. It is upon calculation, as well as by taste, that they have become sober; but the same calculation is far more against any proceedings, which would involve the country in confusion, by rashly changing the established order of things. In truth there is more fear of such men bearing too much, than being too desirous of sudden revolutions.

Working men encouraged to pursue knowledge would

generally be the friends, and the effectual friends of improvement in all our institutions; but they will never be found to aid measures of rash and sudden innovation, by which the peace of society is endangered. The possession of knowledge, . . . must produce the same effect upon the working classes that the possession of wealth does upon the rich; it gives them a direct *interest* in the peace and good order of the community, and renders them solicitous to avoid whatever may disturb it.[94]

In 1827, John Ramsay McCulloch, in an article on the rise of the cotton manufacturing industry and its present and future state, was critical of the Irish in the new industrial towns simply because they lacked property and connections, and were ignorant; hence, they were immoral and profligate. On the other hand, bringing working people into towns meant that they could assemble to educate themselves and sharpen their intelligence. He quoted Millar's *Historical View* in which the political sensitivity of towns and their awareness of even a single injustice was pointed out. 'Nine-tenths of the evils that afflict the mass of society', observed McCulloch, 'have their source in ignorance; and when it has been shown that the intelligence of any class of people has increased, it is next to certain that their condition in other respects must at the same time have improved.' He believed that industrial unrest would disappear if the manufacturing population became intelligent. To aid the process, he advocated the instruction of the working people in

> the principles that must determine their condition in life. The poor
> ought to be taught, that they are in great measure the architects of
> their own fortune; that what others can do for them is trifling
> indeed, compared with what they can do for themselves; that they
> are infinitely more interested in the preservation of public tran-
> quillity than any other class of society; that mechanical inventions
> and discoveries are always supremely advantageous to them; and that
> their real interests can only be effectually promoted by their
> displaying greater prudence and forethought. Such subjects ought to
> form a prominent part of every well digested system of public in-
> struction. And if they were clearly explained and enforced with that
> earnestness which their vast importance requires, we should have the
> best attainable security for the maintainance of public tranquillity,
> and the well-being and comfort of the community.

Manufactures also increased the numbers of middle-class people who, in
McCulloch's opinion, were another factor in ensuring social stability.
He quoted Malthus on the middle class as 'that body on which the
liberty, public spirit, and good government of every country must
always depend'.[95]

In 1827, too, Brougham was stressing the importance of political
economy in the syllabus of Mechanics' Institutes, and its part in promoting social harmony in times of economic crisis:

> I can hardly imagine . . . a greater service being rendered to the men,
> than expounding to them the true principles and mutual relations of
> population and wages; and both they and their masters will assuredly
> experience the effects of the prevailing ignorance upon such
> questions, as soon as any interruption shall happen in the com-
> mercial prosperity of the country, if indeed the present course of
> things, daily tending to lower wages as well as profits, and set the
> two classes in opposition to each other, shall not of itself bring on a
> crisis. To allow, or rather to induce the people to take part in those
> discussions, is therefore not merely safe, but most wholesome for
> the community . . . It is highly useful to the community that the
> true principles of the constitution, ecclesiastical and civil, should be
> well understood by every man who lives under it. The great interests
> of civil and religious liberty are mightily promoted by such whole-
> some instruction; but the good order of society gains to the full as

much by it. The peace of the country, and the stability of the government, could both more effectually be secured by the universal diffusion of this kind of knowledge.[96]

The numbing and disabling effects of the division of labour as perceived, for instance, by John Millar may be recalled here:

[Working-men] become, like machines, actuated by a regular weight, and performing certain movements with great celerity and exactness, but of small compass, and unfitted for any other use. In the intervals of their work, they can draw but little improvement from the society of companions, bred to similar employments, with whom, if they have much intercourse, they are most likely to seek amusement in drinking and dissipation.

Yet, in the advanced stage of society which harboured the division of labour, the communication of reading, writing and other accomplishments to the lower orders were also possible. It was not in the interests of the learned classes to inflict hurt on the ignorant classes but rather to cultivate their minds and in so doing compensate them for their sacrifices to the general prosperity. It was also important to inculcate social virtues of honesty, conscientiousness and aversion to disorder. Maintaining ignorance provided only temporary security and so new kinds of educational seminaries were required for the working people.[97] It is possible to see a relationship between the orderly evolution of society as perceived by the literati of the Scottish Enlightenment and the arguments for Mechanics' Institutes advanced by their students, although the literati would doubtless have disowned the crudity of approach.

The success of the Mechanics' Institutes was one of the reasons for the campaign to establish a university in London. As Brougham put it:

When the working classes are become scientific, their Superiors, ... to continue their betters, must learn a little more than they do now. Accordingly we expect most confidently the greatest increase in the education of the higher and middle classes, and the greatest improvement in their virtues, from the new Institution.

Jeffrey was even more candid:

We allude now to the rapid and remarkable progress which the lower orders are making in [political economy] and in all other branches of knowledge. . . . Of all the derangements that can well take place in a civilised community, one of the most embarrassing and discreditable would be that which arose from the working classes becoming *more intelligent* than their employers. It would end undoubtedly, as it ought to end — in a mutual exchange of property and conditions — but could not fail, in the meantime, to give rise to great an unseemly disorders. To avoid this, however, there seems to be nothing left to the richer classes but to endeavour to maintain their intellectual superiority by improving their understandings, and especially by making themselves thoroughly acquainted with those branches of knowledge on which they and their immediate dependents are most likely to come into direct collision.[98]

The establishment of a university in London was one of those ventures where the 'Scots' cooperated with other groups which had a definable cohesion, such as the Benthamites and the Unitarians. The aim of the university was to provide for Dissenters and for the growing middling orders. From the beginning, Scottish influence was perceptible. An early promoter was Thomas Campbell, the poet, a friend and student of Dugald Stewart, and an intimate of Holland House, who in a preliminary elaboration of the scheme noted that one effect of the institution would be to bring to the capital men like his former professor who would 'chase vulgarity from the character, habits, and pursuits, and from the very idioms and utterance of the vulgar wealthy'.[99] Of the 24 members of the university's first council, six were former students of Stewart — Birkbeck, Brougham, Landsdowne, Mackintosh, Mill and Russell. The education committee which devised the courses and curricula of the new institution included all these, except Russell, and also Campbell, Leonard Horner and Dudley. The work of the committee resulted in key features of the Scottish university system being adopted in London: a wide range of subjects of study, the lecture system, non-resident students, the facility for taking single courses, the absence of religious tests, the class-fee system of professorial remuneration, and the 'democratic' character of the student body.[100]

The original professoriate was drawn predominantly from two sources, Edinburgh and Cambridge, with the former supplying more than the latter. J. R.McCulloch was appointed Professor of Political Economy and John Hoppus Professor of Logic and Mental Philosophy. Hoppus had been a student of Stewart but had none of his eloquence.

He did, however, imitate his mentor in taking in lodgers (one of whom was Walter Bagehot), in his interest in Bacon (he published a book on *Novum Organum* in 1829) and in his following in his lecture courses, Dugald Stewart's plan and content.[101] As might be expected, the bulk of the 'Scottish' professors were in the medical school: they were Robert Grant, Professor of Comparative Anatomy and Zoology; Charles Bell, discoverer of the distinction between the sensory and the motor nerves, who was made Professor of Surgery; Anthony Todd Thomson, Professor of Materia Medica 1828-49 and of Medical Jurisprudence from 1830 (he was also the founder of the Chelsea, Brompton and Belgrave Dispensary); John Conolly, who was appointed Professor of the Nature and Treatment of Diseases; John Elliotson, holder of the Chair of the Principles and Practice of Medicine; Robert Liston, of the Chair of Clinical Surgery; William Sharpey, Professor of Anatomy and Physiology from 1836; and Robert Carswell, Professor of Morbid Anatomy, 1828-40. Well might Jeffrey parody Adam Smith when he pointed out the division of labour inherent in medical education:

> To finish a Doctor, in short, in our improved academical manu-factury, he must pass through as many hands as A PIN. He is first drawn out and cut over by the Professor of Anatomy — the head is then made by the Professor of the Theory of Medicine, and put on by the Professor of the Practice — he is next silvered over by the Professors of Botany and Chemistry — pointed by the Professors of Surgery — burnished up by the Professor of the Art of Obstetrical — and finally papered and labelled by the Professor of *Materia Medica*.[102]

Leonard Horner (1785-1864) was made warden of the university in 1827 and had rather grand ideas about the part he expected to play in the administration of the institution, including authority over the pro-fessors. He not only had founded the Edinburgh School of Arts in 1821 but had helped Henry Cockburn found the Edinburgh Academy in 1823 and was, on the basis of his time as a student at Edinburgh University, intimate with many of those involved in the London Univer-sity project. He was keenly interested in geology, being made an FRS in 1813, and was a prominent member of the Geological Society. His daughter married Charles Lyell. He was one of the first factory inspectors in 1833, remaining in post until 1858, and serving on the Children's Employment Commission (1841-43). He and James Kay-Shuttleworth were Edinburgh alumni chosen to be among the first officials of two administrative innovations in the 1830s, the Factory Inspectorate and the Poor Law Commission. As warden of London University, he was personally a disaster because of his domineering style and his self-regard. In 1830-31 he was engaged in a long battle with the professors over his powers, which was intensified because of the university's financial difficulties and, to the detriment of the institution, the entire dispute was conducted in public.[103] In the quarrel, Birkbeck took the side of the professors against his old associate.[104] James Mill wrote to Macvey Napier making clear on which side of the divided Edinburgh camp he was:

> The warden (though personally far more sinned against than sinning) is the grand source of difficulty; for in the state of hostile feeling among them [the professors] it is vain to expect that the machine will work well — and there is the less hope of it, that it is the rooted opinion of the warden, that there is but one cure for all the evil, and that is giving plenty of power to him. Brougham with sincere friendship for him, did not conceal from me his wish and his hope, that his friends would prevail upon him to resign . . . And yet I should dislike to give any appearance of victory to those professors who have carried on a disreputable war against him; and in this respect differ from him radically — that he has the interest of the University deeply at heart — they have shown that they had not.[105]

Guy's Hospital was the other London centre to which former Edinburgh students in particular flocked to practise. They included Richard Bright and Thomas Addison, both of whom gave their names to a disease, and Thomas Hodgkin (MD, 1823) who founded the Guy's Society for Clinical Reports. Others who were physicians at Guy's, in addition to Alexander Marcet, were James Laird and William Back (MD, 1808). James Blundell (MD, 1813) was Guy's Lecturer in Obstetrics, Physicians at other London hospitals included James Hope (MD, 1825) at St George's, and Thomas Bradley (MD, 1791) at the Westminster. Those involved in teaching in London were James Moncrieff Arnott, a co-founder with Charles Bell of the Middlesex Hospital Medical School, Thomas Watson, Professor of Forensic Medicine at the Middlesex and King's, and Robert Ferguson, Professor of Midwifery at King's.

Though London is the concern here, and while the connection between Scots-trained doctors and medical education in the capital has been noted, they also made a contribution to medical education elsewhere. The provision of lectures in Manchester and Sheffield was one level of operation. More thorough was the work of John Haviland at Cambridge. He had studied at Edinburgh between 1807 and 1809, became Professor of Anatomy at Cambridge in 1814, and Regius Professor of Physic there in 1817. He was the first professor of both subjects to give a regular course of lectures at Cambridge. He lengthened and systematised the courses of medical study (two terms of lectures from him were a requirement for the degree), instituted broad and rigorous examinations (after 1827 every Cambridge medical student, unless licensed by the Royal College of Physicians, had to undergo the MB examination), and he ensured that lectures on anatomy, chemistry and botany were given regularly in the university.[106]

In the field of public health, the investigations and treatises of Kay-Shuttleworth were matched by those of his fellow Edinburgh alumnus Thomas Southwood Smith (1788-1861). He had graduated MD in 1816 after four sessions of study, but while the university's matriculation albums do not indicate that he took other than medical courses, it may well be that he attended moral philosophy lectures. Dr James Wardrop gave the following evidence to the Select Committee on Medical Education in 1834:

It is a common thing for a man at Edinburgh to attend the philosophical classes, towards the termination of his medical studies. I attended the classes of natural philosophy and moral philosophy, after I had attended the medical classes for three years; and that is by no means an uncommon practice with medical students at Edinburgh.[107]

Certainly in 1827 Southwood Smith was a serious candidate for the Chair of Philosophy at London University that was ultimately to go to John Hoppus. Despite the institution's avowed intent to provide education for Dissenters, the Unitarian Southwood Smith was still too heterodox. In 1830, he published his *Treatise on Fever* which, like the treatises of Kay-Shuttleworth, stressed the effects of the phyisical environment on health. In 1833, he was appointed physician to the Central Board of Factory Inspectors, and between 1835 and 1837, he published his two volume *Philosophy of Health*. By 1838, he was working with Arnott and Kay-Shuttleworth investigating fever cases (he himself suffered from typhus three times in his life), wrote reports on which Chadwick drew for his *Report on the Sanitary Condition of . . . Great*

Britain (1842) and served with Chadwick on the Royal Commission on London. Between 1841 and 1843, Southwood Smith also served on the Children's Employment Commission and revealed a flair for propaganda by the illustrations he had caused to be drawn for the report. He was active, with the Earl of Shaftesbury, in the Society for the Improvement of the Conditions of the Labouring Classes (1844) which aimed at providing model dwellings. In the same year, he was on the committee of the Health of Towns Association, from 1848 to 1849 he was Chief Medical Inspector of the General Board of Health and a commissioner for the General Board of Health from 1849 to 1854. He was another of the Alison school of social medicine, some of whom had a national impact and some whose impact was more local.

IV

A distinctive area of medical practice in which Edinburgh alumni particularly figured prominently was that of mental health. Indeed, it was even argued by Alison before the Royal Commission of 1826 and 1830 that as many students found careers in this area of medical practice, a specific Chair should be founded in the university to profess the subject.[108] Here, distinct connections are perceptible between medical and philosophical approaches in Edinburgh and subsequent work in both Scotland and England.

There were two ways in which former Edinburgh students contributed to aspects of mental health, first as 'Commissioners in Lunacy' in the metropolis of London, and secondly, as specialists in various localities. Before the Gordon-Ashley Act 1828, the care of the mentally ill in London was under the surveillance of five London FRCPs. The unsatisfactory nature of the arrangement led to the legislation of 1828 which replaced them by 15 'Metropolitan Commissioners in Lunacy'. In 1842, they inspected provincial asylums in England and Wales, reported on their state in 1844, and thereby paved the way for the legislation of 1845 which established new 'Commissioners in Lunacy' for both countries. Four of the first metropolitan commissioners had studied and/or taken their medical qualifications in Edinburgh – Thomas Drever (MD, 1798), John Robert Hume (MD, 1803), H.H. Southey (MD, 1806) and Thomas Turner, who were all appointed in 1829. Others who served subsequently were Cornwallis Hewett, a Cambridge graduate who had studied in Edinburgh in 1809, and Edward James Seymour who had studied there between 1816 and 1818.

Seymour was a metropolitan commissioner from 1831 to 1839, and Hewett from 1840 to 1841. Seymour believed in better out-patient facilities and in treating patients in the community as soon as possible because of the ill-effects that confinement caused.

A number of Scots-trained took up posts as physicians in local asylums, for example Henry Reeve (MD, 1803) in Norfolk and Norwich. The context of psychiatric treatment from the eighteenth century was much influenced by the apostles of a more humane approach – Philippe Pinel (1745-1826) at the Bicêtre and Jean Esquirol (1771-1840) in France, Andrew Duncan, Senior and Alexander Morison in Scotland, the Tuke family in York. Duncan had founded the Royal Edinburgh Hospital for Mental and Nervous Disorders at Morningside where he planned to implement Pinel's methods. Morison (MD, 1799 with a thesis on hydroencephalitis) was a student of Duncan's and he failed in earnest endeavours to have a Chair established in Edinburgh, but in 1823 he began a course of nine private lectures, which continued for 30 years and were the first course on mental diseases to be given in Britain.

John Conolly (MD, Edinburgh 1821 with a dissertation on the state of the mind in insanity and melancholia) was one of those 'Scots' who took the Duncan and Morison causes south. His dissertation had made the point, little appreciated at the time, that to cure the sick mind the healthy mind had to be understood. He was active in the Royal Medical Society as a student and after graduation, spent nine years first as a general practitioner in Chichester and then in Stratford-upon-Avon. When a smallpox epidemic broke out in Chichester because of the low rate of vaccination, specially among the poorer inhabitants, Conolly wrote *An Address to parents, on the present state of vaccination in this country* (1822) to encourage immunisation. In Stratford, he twice became mayor and initiated several social and sanitary improvements including the establishment of a public dispensary (later the Stratford-upon-Avon Hospital) which offered, among other services, free vaccination.[109] From 1827 to 1831 he was Professor of the Nature and Treatment of Diseases in the new London University. He was said to have been appointed to the post through Brougham's influence.[110] As professor there, he suggested the establishment of a dispensary, supported by students' fees, where he could give them clinical instruction.[111] He maintained his interest in mental health, writing his *An Inquiry concerning the Indications of Insanity with suggestions for the better protection and care of the Insane* in 1830 and offering to lecture on the subject, but the college council, reflecting the contemporary prejudice against the subject perhaps, rejected his offer. In 1831, he returned to practise in Warwick until 1839, being visiting physician to the Warwickshire lunatic asylums. The implementation of his ideas began in 1839 when he became resident physician at the Middlesex County Asylum, Hanwell where he remained until 1843.

Hanwell was the largest asylum in the country and there Conolly introduced the non-restraint methods on a large scale, opening up his work to the inspection of his profession and the public, thus propagandising effectively. British and overseas physicians and medical superintendents of asylums frequently came to visit. Even Samuel Tuke was impressed when he visited in 1841: 'From the zeal, talents and integrity of Dr Conolly, we shall doubtless learn in the most satisfactory manner, the further results of this large and most satisfactory experiment.' He even recommended that his son Daniel, a medical student at St Bartholomew's attend Conolly's clinical demonstrations at Hanwell.[112] In 1842, Conolly gave the first formal course of psychiatric clinical instruction in England when the magistrates of Middlesex allowed him to admit selected pupils from the London medical schools to his demonstrations. They were designed to illustrate the various forms of insanity and he went beyond the Tukes in not merely practising non-restraint, but explaining the humane and scientific theory behind it.[113] He was an advocate of clinical teaching schools being attached to asylums, and of local health services which would provide both in-patient and domiciliary treatment. When he had been a student in Edinburgh, Conolly had been aware that Dugald Stewart encouraged the study of abnormal psychology in his lectures and writings on the human mind. His admiration of Stewart was, however, at a distance; he wished to make the philosopher's acquaintance and pestered a friend in the arts faculty, who did know Stewart, about his conversation and habits but the matter-of-fact friend could only ever reply, 'Ech! he just talks awa.' '[114]

James Cowles Prichard (1786-1848; MD, Edinburgh 1808) was appointed a Commissioner in Lunacy under the legislation of 1845 and died in post. He is an appropriate figure with whom to conclude because his life and interests display many of the facets which it has been the concern of this study to highlight. In his personal history, he is typical of one group of Edinburgh medical students: a Quaker from Bristol whose father was in the iron trade, he decided to study medicine at Edinburgh because it was a means of taking his particular intellectual interests further while suffering no impediment on grounds of religion.[115] He attended and was deeply impressed by Dugald Stewart's lectures, was active in student societies, wrote his MD thesis, *Varieties of Human Kind*, on a topic which proved to be the foundation of part of his life's work and which was first published in 1813 as *Researches into the Physical History of Man* and went through several editions. On leaving Edinburgh, he followed what will now be recognised as a familiar path: he became a licentiate of the London Royal College of Physicians, established with another a 'Medical Institution on the Quay', opened a dispensary offering free medical services to the poor, was physician to St Peter's Hospital, gave medical lectures, had a long association with Clifton Infirmary, became a physician to Bristol Infirmary in 1816, was a leading member of the Bristol Institution and the Lit. and Phil., and took a leading part in the foundation of Bristol College (1829) and the Bristol branch of the Provincial Medical and Surgical Association (1833). He was a proponent of public-health reform, writing the report on the fever outbreak in Bristol in 1817 with suggestions for future prevention, collected case histories from his mental health practice and collecting other statistical information.[116] By the 1820s he was prominent in the cultural life of Bristol, his home was almost a salon and he was forsaking part of his roots. He had turned from the Society of Friends to Evangelical Anglicanism. Like so many others with his background, recognition was accompanied by conformity. He remained in Bristol until his appointment as a Commissioner in Lunacy, when he moved to London. He died from complications following the contraction of a fever while on his inspector's duties.

Intellectually, too, typical traits of so many educated in Scotland in the later eighteenth century can be seen in a magnified form in Prichard. His interests lay in psychology and anthropology. In psychology, while there were areas where he diverged from the Scots, he was none the less indebted to Dugald Stewart who was cited frequently in his writings: he accepted Stewart's terms in describing the powers of the mind, was powerfully convinced of the doctrine of common sense (though he did not use the term) and it has been suggested that the term 'moral insanity', original to him, though it was later discarded, was defining the disease of the moral sense. In anthropology he rejects or, at best, ignores the Scottish thinkers: for instance he was not concerned with the progress but the origin of political systems. Topics such as the origin of ranks or of language or the evolution of religion he either accepted without question, or disregarded or spurned. What the Scots accepted — the unity of man — was, on the other hand, the central concern of Prichard's inquiries. The other main divide was in their respective religious assumptions: the Scots were not as bound to Scripture as was Prichard, who endeavoured to fill in gaps that existed in the Bible. However, his mind was by no means closed to difficulties which arose from a literal acceptance of Scripture: he was prepared to abandon his chronology of man which adhered to the short timescale implied in the Bible, but this was only because his prime belief, that all men descend from one primitive stock, could not be reconciled with it. Religion stimulated his inquiry, but the inquiry itself in due course developed a momentum of its own. While his Evangelicalism can, therefore, explain his anthropological stance it must also have been reinforced by the conditions of his time, the aftermath of the French Revolution and its impact on England. He wished to reinforce traditional faith in the wake of infidelity and scepticism and his own increasing social acceptance would have done nothing to weaken his resolve. While, on the one hand, he clearly owed much to his imbibing of 'Scotch knowledge', like so many others, he responded to the developing circumstances of early nineteenth-century England in which he made his career.

Notes

1. R.S. Porter, 'Science, Provincial Culture and Public Opinion in Enlightenment England', *The British Journal for Eighteenth-Century Studies*, III (1980), p. 27. See also Roy Porter, 'The Enlightenment in England', *The Enlightenment in National Context*, ed. Roy Porter and Mikulas Teich, (Cambridge University Press, 1981), pp. 7-12, 15-17.

2. Porter, 'Science, Provincial Culture', p. 27.

3. Ibid., III, pp. 26, 32.

4. Ibid., III, p. 30.

5. See Chapter 2.

6. *Edinburgh Evidence*, p. 530. The two professors to whom McGrigor was referring were John Thomson, who had been a staff-surgeon at the Battle of Waterloo and who gave free class tickets to substantial numbers of the half-pay medical officers in the years immediately after the Napoleonic Wars; and George Ballingall who wrote a book on the construction of hospitals and had served in India and the Far East as well as Europe. Elsewhere it has been shown how, in the late eighteenth century, the Scottish medical practitioners had played a notable part in reforming the military medical services by, for example, introducing preventive medical practices, developing small regimental hospitals in preference to large general hospitals and requiring military experience for promotion. Military disasters at the time served to convince the authorities of the need for an efficient disciplined fighting force which, the research has alleged, echoed the emphasis on order, cleanliness and sobriety in the hygiene and preventive medicine taught at Edinburgh. This information is drawn from a report of a paper by Rosalie Stott, 'The Scottish Dimension of Enlightenment Medicine: the Political Economy of Health', given to the annual conference of the Society

for the Social History of Medicine (1979) when the theme was 'Medicine and the Enlightenment'. The report, by C.J. Crawford and L.J. Jordanova is in *The British Journal for Eighteenth-Century Studies*, II (1979), pp. 238-9.

7. *Edinburgh Evidence*, p. 307.

8. Charles Singer and S.W.F. Holloway, 'Early Medical Education in England in Relation to the Pre-History of London University', *Medical History*, IV, (1960), p. 6.

9. Major Greenwood, *Some British Pioneers of Social Medicine* (London, 1948), p. 15.

10. Robert Masters Kerrison, *Observations and Reflections on the Bill now in progress through the House of Commons, for 'better regulating the medical profession as far as regards apothecaries'*, . . . , n.p. 1815, p. 315 n; and Edward Barlow, MD, *Observations on Medical Reform: illustrating the present condition of medical science, education and practice throughout Great Britain and Ireland; and proposing such alterations therein, as appear most likely to succeed in remedying the several evils, which abound in this profession, and which have, at length, become subjects of universal complaint* (Dublin, 1807), p. 77. Dr Barlow was, incidentally, an Edinburgh MD (1803?), and practised in Bath.

11. Quoted in Bernice Hamilton, 'The Medical Professions in the Eighteenth Century', *The Economic History Review*, 2nd series, IV (1951), p. 166 n.

12. Kerrison, pp. 324, 325.

13. See Ivan Waddington, 'The Struggle to Reform the Royal College of Physicians, 1767-1771: a sociological analysis', *Medical History*, XVII (1973), pp. 107-26, from which I have drawn subsequent information.

14. Ibid., XVII, pp. 113-14.

15. Ibid., XVII, p. 114.

16. Ibid., XVII, p. 119.

17. William Pulteney Alison and Robert Christison, in *Edinburgh Evidence*, pp. 194, 291; *Report from the Select Committee on Medical Education: with the Minutes of Evidence and Appendix* (1834). Part I: *Royal College of Physicians, London*, p. 135.

18. Waddington, p. 123.

19. The story is told in detail in S.W.F. Holloway, 'The Apothecaries' Act, 1815: A Reinterpretation', *Medical History*, X (1966), pp. 107-29, 221-36. As will become evident, I have here followed the cogent line pursued in the two parts of the article.

20. Given in ibid., X, pp. 124-5.

21. Ibid., X, pp. 127-8.

22. Ibid., X, p. 222.

23. *The Companion to the Newspaper* is quoted in ibid., X, p. 223; John Thomson's quotation comes from *Edinburgh Evidence*, pp. 471-72; the Commissioners' conclusion is to be found in *Report made to His Majesty by a Royal Commission of Inquiry into the State of the Universities of Scotland, October 7th 1831*, pp. 66-7.

24. *Reports from the Select Committee on Public Petitions* (1833), p. 1217.

25. Ibid., p. 251.

26. Ibid., pp. 341, 603, 645, 1125.

27. Ibid., pp. 340-1.

28. Ibid., p. 698.

29. Ibid., pp. 826-7.

30. Ibid., p. 1052.

31. Ibid., p. 1286.

32. Kerrison, p. 326 n.

33. See, for example, the various articles of Ian Inkster, e.g. 'The Social Context of an Educational Movement: a revisionist approach to the English Mechanics'

Institutes 1820-1850', *Oxford Review of Education*, II (1976), pp. 277-307; 'Aspects of the history of science and science culture in Britain, 1780-1850 and beyond', *Metropolis and Province: Science in British Culture 1780-1850*, ed. Ian Inkster and Jack Morrell (Hutchinson, 1983), pp. 11-54; and 'Marginal Men: Aspects of the Social Role of the Medical Community in Sheffield 1790-1850', *Health Care and Popular Medicine in Nineteenth Century England*, ed. J. Woodward and David Richards (Croom Helm, 1977), pp. 128-63. See also Arnold Thackray, 'Natural Knowledge in Cultural Context: the Manchester Model', *American Historical Review*, LXXIX (1974), pp. 672-709; Steven Shapin and Arnold Thackray, 'Prosopography as a Research Tool in History of Science: the British scientific community 1700-1900', *History of Science*, XII (1974), pp. 1-28, esp. Part II, pp. 4-11.

34. Derek Orange, 'Rational Dissent and Provincial Science; William Turner and the Newcastle Literary and Philosophical Society', *Metropolis and Province*, p. 225.

35. Michael Neve, 'Science in a Commercial City: Bristol 1820-1860', ibid., pp. 179-204.

36. Inkster, 'Aspects of the history of science', ibid., pp. 29-30.

37. Steven Shapin and Barry Barnes, 'Science, Nature and Control: Interpreting Mechanics' Institutes', *Social Studies of Science*, VII (1977), pp. 52-3, 56.

38. Shapin and Thackray, p. 10.

39. J.B. Morrell, 'Science in Manchester and the University of Edinburgh, 1760-1840', *Artisan to Graduate: Essays to Commemorate the Foundation in 1824 of the Manchester Mechanics' Institution, now in 1974 the University of Manchester Institute of Science and Technology*, ed. D.S.L. Cardwell (Manchester University Press, 1974), pp. 39-40, 43, 50.

40. E.M. Brockbank, *Sketches of the Lives and Work of the Honorary Medical Staff of the Manchester Infirmary from its foundation in 1752 to 1830, when it became the Royal Infirmary* (Manchester University Press, 1904), pp. 27, 22.

41. Ibid., pp. 85, 87-8.

42. Ibid., pp. 91-2.

43. W.A. Armstrong, 'The Trend of Morality in Carlisle between the 1780's and the 1840's: a Demographic Contribution to Standard of Living Debate', *Economic History Review*, XXXIV (1981), pp. 98, 104-5.

44. Brockbank, p. 94.

45. Ibid., pp. 95-6.

46. Ibid., p. 94.

47. Ibid. pp. 96-7.

48. Ibid., pp. 128-31.

49. Ibid., pp. 131-2.

50. Ibid., p. 136.

51. Ibid., pp. 132-3, 135.

52. Ibid., pp. 137-9.

53. Ibid., pp. 143-4.

54. Quoted ibid., p. 97.

55. Ibid., pp. 97-8.

56. Ibid., pp. 110, 118.

57. Ibid., pp. 115-16.

58. Ibid., p. 125.

59. Ibid., pp. 235-7.

60. Ibid., pp. 164-5.

61. Ibid., pp. 214-15.

62. Ibid., pp. 241-2.

63. Quoted in D.L. Emblen, *Peter Mark Roget: The Word and the Man* (Long-

man, 1970), p. 90.

64. 'The Autobiography of Sir James Kay-Shuttleworth', ed. B.C. Bloomfield, *Education Libraries Bulletin*, Suppl. 7 (1964), pp. 4-5.

65. Ibid., p. 8.

66. John Roberton to Rachel Dawson Kennedy (Mrs Edwin Chadwick), 14 February 1845, University College, London, Library mss.

67. 'Autobiography', pp. 9, 11-12.

68. R.J. Morris, *Cholera* (Croom Helm, 1976), esp. Ch. 8.

69. E.P. Hennock, 'Urban Sanitary Reform a Generation before Chadwick', *Economic History Review*, X (1957), pp. 113-20.

70. Michael Durey, 'Medical Élites, the General Practitioner and Patient Power in Britain during the Cholera Outbreak of 1831-1832', *Metropolis and Province*, pp. 257-78, esp. pp. 257, 259, 260-1, 263-5, 267, 269.

71. M.J. Cullen, *The Statistical Movement in Early Victorian Britain: The Foundations of Empirical Social Research* (Harvester Press, 1975), Ch. 8.

72. 'Autobiography', pp. 13-32.

73. e.g. Letter from John Conolly in Warwick, 17 January 1834 and two letters from W.H. Duncan in Liverpool, 18 January 1834 and 27 August 1834, Kay-Shuttleworth Papers, John Rylands Library, Manchester.

74. See Nancy Ball, *Her Majesty's Inspectorate 1839-1849* (Edinburgh and London, 1963). This study places Kay-Shuttleworth's work in the Education Committee in some perspective.

75. Letter from Lord Lansdowne, 16 December 1842 (1847?), Kay-Shuttleworth Papers, John Rylands Library, Manchester.

76. Paper dated 11 October 1839, ibid.

77. J. Phillips Kay, Esq., MD, *Report on the Training of Pauper Children* (1838), pp. 7-8.

78. James Phillips Kay-Shuttleworth, *Preface to the eleventh edition of a pamphlet entitled 'Recent measures for the promotion of education in England; being a reply to the remarks on that pamphlet contained in the charge of the Bishop of Exeter delivered at his triennial visitation in August, September and October, 1839*, pp. v-vi.

79. Roberton to Mrs Chadwick, 14 February 1845, University College, London, Library mss.

80. Inkster, 'Marginal Men', pp. 147-8.

81. They are all listed ibid., p. 153.

82. William Smith Porter, *Sheffield Literary and Philosophical Society: A Centenary Retrospect 1822-1922* (Sheffield, 1922), pp. 9, 16, 50; Inkster, 'Marginal Men', pp. 141, 144.

83. Ibid., pp. 138, 144-6; idem., 'The Development of a Scientific Community in Sheffied, 1790-1850: a network of people and interests', *Transactions of the Hunter Archaeological Society*, X (1971), p. 114.

84. Inkster, 'Marginal Men', pp. 141-2; and 'The Development of a Scientific Community', p. 106.

85. W.S. Porter, p. 24; Inkster, 'Marginal Men', p. 140.

86. Ibid., pp.142, 150.

87. Ibid., p. 150.

88. Emblen, pp. 107;, 109.

89. I have calculated these figures from the lists given in Emblen, pp. 312-13, notes 16, 17, 25. The figures are not exact: the names that can be checked in the directory of Edinburgh medical graduates are included as are those with Scottish names, unless it is known that they went nowhere near North Britain for their education.

90. Alexander Marcet to Peter Mark Roget, 28 July 1822, quoted in Emblen,

p. 159 from Royal College of Physicians, London, mss.

91. McCulloch to Napier, 2 May 1824, *Correspondence of Macvey Napier*, p. 40.

92. Henry Brougham, 'The New Plan of Education for England', *Edinburgh Review*, XXXIV (1820), pp. 222-4.

93. Henry Brougham, 'Scientific Education of the People', *Edinburgh Review*, XLI (1824), pp. 99, 101, 104, 107, 116-17.

94. Henry Brougham, Supposed Dangers of Knowledge', *Edinburgh Review*, XLIII (1825), pp. 243-5.

95. J.R. McCulloch, 'Rise, Progress, Present State and Prospects of the British Cotton Manufacture', *Edinburgh Review*, XLVI (1827), pp. 36-9.

96. Henry Brougham, 'Society for the Diffusion of Useful Knowledge', *Edinburgh Review*, XLVI (1827), pp. 234-5.

97. Millar, *Historical View*, IV, pp. 146-60, with the quote from p. 146.

98. Henry Brougham, 'High Church Opinions on Popular Education', *Edinburgh Review*, XLII (1825), p. 223; Francis Jeffrey, 'Political Economy', *Edinburgh Review*, XLIII (1825), p. 11.

99. Thomas Campbell, 'Suggestions Respecting the Plan of an University in London', *The New Monthly Magazine and Literary Journal*, XIII (1825), p. 416.

100. H. Hale Bellot, *University College, London, 1826-1926* (University of London Press, 1929), p. 8.

101. Ibid., pp. 109-11, quoting a manuscript on the department of philosophy in the college library.

102. Jeffrey, 'Political Economy', p. 21.

103. For a full account, see Bellot, pp. 195-209.

104. Thomas Kelly, *George Birkbeck: Pioneer of Adult Education* (Liverpool University Press, 1957), p. 159.

105. Alexander Bain, *James Mill: A Biography* (London, 1882), pp. 353-4.

106. *Gentlemen's Magazine*, new series, XXXV (1851), p. 206.

107. *Report from the Select Committee on Medical Education*, p. 174.

108. *Edinburgh Evidence*, p. 216.

109. Richard Hunter and Ida Macalpine, 'An Anonymous Publication on Vaccination by John Conolly (1794-1866)', *Journal of the History of Medicine*, XIV (1959), pp. 312-13, 315-16.

110. Henry Maudsley, 'Memoir of the late John Conolly M.D.', *Journal of Mental Science*, XII (1866), p. 165.

111. John Conolly, *An Inquiry concerning the Indications of Insanity with suggestions for the better protection and care of the Insane* [1830], reprinted with an introduction by Richard Hunter and Ida Macalpine (London, 1964), p. 26.

112. Samuel Tuke, *Description of the Retreat: an Institution near York for Insane Persons of the Society of Friends* [1813], reprinted with an introduction by Richard Hunter and Ida Macalpine (London, 1964), p. 23.

113. Conolly, pp. 1, 23.

114. Maudsley, p. 163.

115. I am much indebted in the subsequent account to the introductory essay by G.W. Stocking Jr, editor of James Cowles Prichard, *Researches into the Physical History of Man* (University of Chicago Press, 1973), pp. ix-cix. Another interesting argument about the impact of Dugald Stewart's psychological ideas and the pedagogic methods of Scottish universities in the Age of Enlightenment on Robert Owen is to be found in David Hamilton, 'Robert Owen and Education: A Reassessment', *Scottish Culture and Scottish Education 1800-1980*, ed. Walter M. Humes and Hamish M. Paterson (John Donald, 1983), pp. 9-24.

116. I have little doubt that the pattern of career and interests, represented here by the case of Prichard, was repeated by numerous other 'Scots' in English towns in addition to Manchester, Sheffield and Bristol, and not discussed in detail in this study.

6 CONCLUSION

Others have observed that it was in the 1760s that Scotland's acceptance of 'Britishness' became apparent. The association of Scotland with England in the Seven Years' War, and the part played by Scottish regiments, contributed to the development of a British consciousness. The American, French Revolutionary and Napoleonic Wars served to reinforce the cause, and the development of the Empire in the nineteenth century provided Scots with an additional British arena in which to play crucial roles as soldiers, administrators, commercial and businessmen. The era of economic growth was obviously an additional spur to the growth of a British consciousness as Scotland's mining, shipbuilding and heavy engineering industries became an integral part of the industrial economy. By the mid-nineteenth century, it verged on the eccentric to campaign for Scottish independence.

The assimilation of Scotland into the new Britain did not occur without comment. Bute was subject to abuse from the early 1760s that made the most of his Scottishness. John Wilkes' attacks, significantly, were published in the *North Briton*, a parody of Bute's own *The Briton*. The 1760s also witnessed the caricaturing of protesting 'Scottish' licentiates of the London Royal College of Physicians. No wonder there was some marked movement of Scottish aristocracy in that decade from the political stage of London to the improvement of their estates at home. In the early nineteenth century, it was Cobbett who reviled the 'Scotch feelosophers', while in the mid-nineteenth century, Dickens' caricature of a hard facts schoolmaster rejoiced in the name of McChoakumchild. Such is the background to the groups of men who have been the subject of this study.

That the Scots were an emigrant people is also familiar. Much more has been written about the connections between Scotland and North America in the later eighteenth and the *ante-bellum* period of the nineteenth century than about the connections with England.[1] Two themes in the American connection, chosen out of the many to which scholars have pointed, are the educational debt of America to Scotland and the influence of Scottish commonsense philosophy. England, too, was a common destination for emigré Scots as well as a source of many who sought, for varied reasons, an education in Scotland only to return home. England, too, as has been seen, found these 'Scots' prominent in a number of educational developments in urban areas and found a distinct use either for commonsense philosophy or for off-shoots of it at a time when war, social disturbance and the consequences of economic growth were being felt simultaneously. As in America, commonsense philosophy, in the hands of a generation that came after its progenitors, acted as a conservative force – in politics, economics, medical social work, even anthropology.

As Scotland's people, economy, political fortunes and social experience came to share in those of England, to blend with them, so too distinctive Scottish influences came to be merged with those that England had herself generated. The lessons of the Scottish Enlightenment (to use shorthand for what was described in the first two chapters) concerted with what increasingly came to be the dominant outlook of the age. A number of groups were endeavouring to achieve similar ends: political reform was advocated by different schools of political thought and by religious bodies; so was social reform which was also urged by those with medical perception and statistical skills; so was education where a variety of impulses, some intellectual, some openly social and political in inspiration, informed developments. The so-called Victorian ethic was effectively espoused by those schooled in political economy and Evangelical religion. Individual reformers could be educated in Scotland, have a medical qualification, keep statistics conscientiously, be Unitarian in religion or a Benthamite by equal conviction. Motivation was indeed multifaceted. The present study has sought to highlight the distinctive influence of 'Scotch knowledge', and to show how, frequently in concert with others, it flowed into the stream of English historical development by means of familiarity, patronage and a shared social predicament.

A new era dawned after mid-century: not only did the generations who had brought 'Scotch knowledge' to the south die out but there were marked alterations in the social and political conditions that had made areas of English life susceptible to it and associated movements. In particular, English philosophy and science of the later nineteenth century challenged the traditional religious assumptions and revealed the limitations of the philosophic, scientific and medical approaches of the Scottish Enlightenment even in the forms in which the students had modified them.

Note

1. See for instance, Andrew Hook, *Scotland and America: A Study of Cultural Relations 1750-1835* (Blackie, 1975); Andrew D. Hook, 'Scotland and America Revisted', *Scotland, Europe and the American Revolution*, ed. Owen Dudley Edwards and George Shepperson (E.U.S.P.D., 1976), pp. 83-8; C. Duncan Rice, 'Scottish Enlightenment, American Revolution and Atlantic Reform', *Scotland, Europe and the American Revolution*, pp. 75-82; Douglas Sloan, *The Scottish Enlightenment and the American College Ideal* (New York, 1971).

LIST OF WORKS CITED

I Manuscripts, Special Library Holdings etc.

British Library of Political and Economic Science: Horner Collection of manuscript correspondence and papers. 8 vols.

Edinburgh University Library: Dugald Stewart mss. Dc. 6. 111 ff 3-4, 11; Letters of Dugald and Helen d'Arcy Stewart, Dc. 1. 100^2;

College Minutes II (1790-1811);

List of Medical Students I (1783-90) and II (1791-95).

Citation is made by kind permission of Edinburgh University Library.

National Library of Scotland: 755 Correspondence Book of the Academy of Physics;

948 Album containing autograph letters of celebrities: Francis Horner to Thomas Logan of Dunglass;

2521 Single Letters: Lord Holland to Dugald Stewart;

3943 Letters of the Robertsons, 1745-88: Dugald Stewart to William Robertson;

5319 Dugald Stewart to Baron de Gerando;

Citation is made by kind permission of the Trustees of the National Library of Scotland.

John Rylands Library, Manchester: Kay-Shuttleworth Papers.

Citation is made by kind permission of the John Rylands University Library of Manchester.

Scottish Record Office: Henry Home Drummond's Opinions, Abercairny Papers, GD 24/1032.

Citation is made by kind permission of the Keeper of the Records of Scotland.

University College, London, Library: John Roberton to Rachel Dawson Kennedy (Mrs Edwin Chadwick).

Citation is made by kind permission of University College, London, Library.

II Parliamentary Papers

Evidence, Oral and Documentary, taken and received by the Commissioners appointed by His Majesty George IV. July 23rd, 1826; and re-

appointed by His Majesty William IV, October 12th, 1830; for visiting the UNIVERSITIES OF SCOTLAND, 4 vols (1837).
Report from the Select Committee on Medical Education: with the Minutes of Evidence and Appendix (1834).
Report from the Select Committee on Public Petitions (1833).
Report made to His Majesty by a Royal Commission of Inquiry into the State of the Universities of Scotland (7 October 1831).

III Unpublished Dissertations

Chitnis, Anand C., *The Edinburgh Professoriate 1790-1826 and the University's Contribution to Nineteenth Century British Society*, Ph.D. University of Edinburgh (1968).
Jarrett, J. Derek, *The Bowood Circle 1780-1793: its ideas and its influence*, B. Litt. University of Oxford (1956).

IV Edinburgh Review Articles
Author attributions taken from *The Wellesley Index to Victorian Periodicals 1824-1900*, ed. Walter E. Houghton, I (Toronto, 1966).

Brougham, Henry, 'The New Plan of Education for England', XXXIV (1820), pp. 214-54.
Brougham, Henry, 'High Church Opinions on Popular Education', XLII (1825), pp. 206-223.
Brougham, Henry, 'Scientific Education of the People', XLI (1824), pp. 96-122.
Brougham, Henry, 'Society for the Diffusion of Useful Knowledge', XLVI (1827), pp. 225-44.
Brougham, Henry, 'Supposed Dangers of Knowledge', XLIII (1825), pp. 242-8.
Horner, Francis, 'Lord King on Bank Restrictions', II (1803), pp. 401-21.
Horner, Francis, 'Thornton on the Paper Credit of Great Britain', I (1802), pp. 172-201.
Jeffrey, Francis, 'Cobbett's Political Register', X (1807), pp. 386-421.
Jeffrey, Francis, 'Craig's *Life of Millar*', IX (1806), pp. 83-92.
Jeffrey, Francis 'The Dangers of the Country', X (1807), pp. 1-27.
Jeffrey, Francis, 'Leckie on the British Government',XX (1812),

pp. 315-46.

Jeffrey, Francis, 'Millar's View of the English Government', III (1803), pp. 154-81.

Jeffrey, Francis, 'Parliamentary Reform', XIV (1809), pp. 277-306.

Jeffrey, Francis and Brougham, Henry, 'Parliamentary Reform', XVII (1811), pp. 253-90.

Jeffrey, Francis, 'Political Economy', XLIII (1825), pp. 1-23.

Jeffrey, Francis, 'The State of the Parties', XV (1810), pp. 504-21.

Jeffrey, Francis, 'Stewart's Life of Dr Reid', III (1804), pp. 269-87.

Lorimer, James, 'Letters and Discoveries of Sir Charles Bell', CXXXV (1872), pp. 394-429.

Mackintosh, James, 'Parliamentary Reform', XXXIV (1820), pp. 461-501.

Mackintosh, James, 'Universal Suffrage', XXXI (1818), pp. 165-203.

McCulloch, J.R. 'Rise, Progress, Present State, and Prospects of the British Cotton Manufacture', XLVI (1827), pp. 1-39.

V Printed Works

Some Account of my Life and Writings: an Autobiography by the late Archibald Alison, ed. Lady Jane Alison, 2 vols. (Edinburgh and London, 1833).

Armstrong, W.A., 'The Trend of Mortality in Carlisle between the 1780's and the 1840's: a Demographic Contribution to Standard of Living Debate', *Economic History Review*, XXXIV (1981), pp. 94-114.

Bagehot, Walter, *Literary Studies*, ed. R.H. Hutton, 2 vols. 2nd edn (Longmans, 1879).

Bain, Alexander, *James Mill: A Biography* (London, 1882).

Ball, Nancy, *Her Majesty's Inspectorate 1839-1849* (Edinburgh and London, 1963).

Barlow, Edward, *Observations on Medical Reform: illustrating the present condition of medical science, education and practice throughout Great Britain and Ireland; and proposing such alterations therein, as appear most likely to succeed in remedying the several evils, which abound in this profession, and which have, at length, become subjects of universal complaint* (Dublin, 1807).

Bell, Alan, *Sydney Smith* (Clarendon Press, 1980).

Brockbank, E.M., *Sketches of the Life and Work of the Honorary Medical Staff of the Manchester Infirmary from its foundation in 1752 to 1830, when it became the Royal Infirmary* (Manchester

University Press, 1904).

The Life and Times of Henry, Lord Brougham, written by himself, 3 vols. (Blackwood, 1871).

Campbell, Thomas, 'Suggestions Respecting the Plan of an University in London', *The New Monthly Magazine and Literary Journal*, XIII (1825), pp. 404-19.

Cantor, G.N., 'The Academy of Physics at Edinburgh 1797-1800', *Social Studies of Science*, V (1975), pp. 109-34.

Chitnis, Anand C., 'Provost Drummond and the Origins of Edinburgh Medicine', *The Origins and Nature of the Scottish Enlightenment*, ed. R.H. Campbell and A.S. Skinner (John Donald, 1982), pp. 86-97.

Chitnis, Anand, *The Scottish Enlightenment: A Social History* (Croom Helm, 1976).

Chitnis, Anand C., 'The University of Edinburgh's Natural History Museum and the Huttonian-Wernerian Debate', *Annals of Science*, XXVI (1970), pp. 85-94.

Cockburn, Henry, *Life of Lord Jeffrey with a selection from his correspondence*, 2 vols. (Edinburgh, 1852).

Cockburn, Henry, *Memorials of his Time* (Edinburgh, 1856).

Connell, Brian, *Portrait of a Whig Peer, compiled from the papers of the second Viscount Palmerston 1739-1802* (André Deutsch, 1957).

Conolly, John, *An Inquiry concerning the Indications of Insanity with suggestions for the better protection and care of the Insane* [1830] reprinted with an introduction by Richard Hunter and Ida Macalpine (London, 1964).

Crawford, C.J. and Jordanova, L.J., 'Medicine and the Enlightenment', *The British Journal for Eighteenth-Century Studies*, II (1979), pp. 238-9.

The Life of Sir Robert Christison, Bart., ed. by his son, 2 vols. (Edinburgh and London, 1885).

Cullen, M.J., *The Statistical Movement in Early Victorian Britain: The Foundations of Empirical Social Research* (Harvester Press, 1975).

The Life and Letters of Charles Darwin, including an autobiographical chapter, ed. Francis Darwin, 3 vols. (London, 1887).

Dickson, W.K. *The History of the Speculative Society 1764-1904* (Edinburgh, 1905).

Letters to 'Ivy' from the first Earl of Dudley, ed. S.H. Romilly (London, 1905).

Letters of the Earl of Dudley to the Bishop of Llandaff (London, 1840).

Durey, Michael, 'Medical Élites, the General Practitioner and Patient Power in Britain during the Cholera Outbreak of 1831-1832', *Metropolis and Province: Science in British Culture 1780-1880*, ed. Ian Inkster and J.B.Morrell (Hutchison, 1983), pp. 257-78.

Edinburgh Annual Register for 1817, X (Edinburgh, 1821).

Life and Letters of Sir Gilbert Elliot, First Earl of Minto, from 1751-1806, ed. Nina, Countess of Minto, 3 vols. (London, 1874).

Emblen, D., *Peter Mark Roget: The Word and the Man* (Longman, 1970).

Ferguson, Adam, *An Essay on the History of Civil Society 1767*, ed. Duncan Forbes (Edinburgh University Press, 1966).

Ferguson, Alex., *The Honourable Henry Erskine Lord Advocate for Scotland with notices of certain of his kinsfolk and of his time compiled from family papers and other sources of information* (Blackwood, 1882).

Fetter, F.W., 'The Authorship of Economic Articles in the *Edinburgh Review* 1802-1847', *Journal of Political Economy*, LXI (1953), pp. 233-59.

Finlayson, C.P., 'Records of Scientific and Medical Societies preserved in the University Library, Edinburgh', *The Bibliotheck: A Journal of Bibliographical Notes and Queries mainly of Scottish Interest*, I (1958), pp. 14-19.

Greenwood, Major, *Some British Pioneers of Social Medicine* (London, 1948).

Hale Bellot, H., *University College, London, 1826-1926* (University of London Press, 1929).

Halévy, Elie, *England in 1815*, trans. E.I. Watkin and D.A. Barker (Ernest Benn, 1961).

Halévy, Elie, *The Growth of Philosophic Radicalism*, trans. M. Morris (London, 1952).

Hamilton, Bernice, 'The Medical Professions in the Eighteenth Century', *The Economic History Review*, 2nd series, IV (1951), pp. 141-69.

Hamilton, David, 'Robert Owen and Education: a Reassessment', *Scottish Culture and Scottish Education 1800-1980*, ed. Walter M. Humes and Hamish M. Paterson (John Donald, 1983), pp. 9-24.

Hans, Nicholas, *New Trends in Education in the Eighteenth Century* (Routledge & Kegan Paul, 1966).

Harvey, A.D., *Britain in The Early Nineteenth Century* (Batsford, 1978).

'John Haviland', *Gentleman's Magazine*, new series, XXXV (1851),

p. 206.

Hennock, E.P., 'Urban Sanitary Reform a Generation before Chadwick', *Economic History Review*, X (1957), pp. 113-20.

Heron, Robert, *Observations made on a Journey through the Western Counties of Scotland, in the Autumn of 1792*, 2 vols. (Perth, 1792).

Hollander, Jacob H., 'Adam Smith 1776-1926', *Journal of Political Economy*, XXXV (1927), pp. 153-97.

Holloway, S.W.F., 'The Apothecaries' Act, 1815: a Reinterpretation', *Medical History*, X (1966), pp. 107-29, 221-36.

Hook, Andrew, *Scotland and America: A Study of Cultural Relations 1750-1835* (Blackie, 1975).

Hook, Andrew D., 'Scotland and America Revistited', *Scotland, Europe and the American Revolution*, ed. Owen Dudley Edwards and George Shepperson (E.U.S.P.B., 1976).

Horn, D.B., *A Short History of the University of Edinburgh 1556-1889* (Edinburgh University Press, 1967)

The Economic Writings of Francis Horner in the Edinburgh Review 1802-1806, ed. Frank Whitson Fetter (L S E, 1957)

Memoirs and Correspondence of Francis Horner, M.P., ed. Leonard Horner, 2 vols., (London, 1843).

Hume, David, *Essays, Moral, Political and Literary*, ed. T.H. Green and T.H. Grose, 2 vols. (Longman, Green, 1874).

Hunter, Richard and Macalpine, Ida, 'An Anonymous Publication on Vaccination by John Conolly (1794-1866)', *Journal of the History of Medicine*, XIV (1959), pp. 311-19.

Ignatieff, Michael, 'John Millar and Individualism', *Wealth and Virtue: The Shaping of Political Economy in the Scottish Enlightenment,* ed. Istvan Hont and Michael Ignatieff (Cambridge University Press, 1983), pp. 317-43.

Ilchester, Earl of, *Chronicles of Holland House 1820-1900* (London, 1937).

Ilchester, Earl of, *The Home of the Hollands 1605-1820* (London, 1937).

Inkster, Ian, 'Aspects of the History of Science and Science Culture in Britain, 1780-1850 and Beyond', *Metropolis and Province* (see Durey above), pp. 11-54.

t of a Scientific Community in Shef-
people and interests', *Transactions of*
, X (1971), pp. 99-131.
Aspects of the Social Role of the

Medical Community in Sheffield 1790-1850', *Health Care and Popular Medicine in Nineteenth Century England*, ed. J. Woodward and David Richards (Croom Helm, 1977), pp. 128-63.

Inkster, Ian, 'The Social Context of an Educational Movement: a revisionist approach to the English Mechanics' Institutes 1820-1850', *Oxford Review of Education*, II (1976), pp. 277-307.

'Biography of the late Professor Jameson', *The Monthly Journal of Medical Science*, XVIII (January-June 1854), pp. 572-75.

Jarrett, J. Derek, *Britain 1688-1815* (London, 1965).

Jones, Peter, 'The Polite Academy and the Presbyterians, 1720-1770', *New Perspectives on the Politics and Culture of Early Modern Scotland*, ed. John Dwyer, Roger A. Mason and Alexander Murdoch (John Donald, n.d. [1982]), pp. 156-77.

Jones, Peter, 'The Scottish Professoriate and the Polite Academy, 1720-1746', *Wealth and Virtue* (see Ignatieff above), pp. 89-117.

Kay, J. Phillips, *Report on the Training of Pauper Children* (1838).

'The Autobiography of Sir James Kay-Shuttleworth', ed. B.C. Bloomfield, *Education Libraries Bulletin*, Suppl. 7, 1964.

Kay-Shuttleworth, James Phillips, *Preface to the eleventh edition of a pamphlet entitled "Recent measures for the promotion of education in England; being a reply to the remarks on that pamphlet contained in the charge of the Bishop of Exeter delivered at his triennial visitation in August, September and October, 1839.*

Kelly, Thomas, *George Birkbeck: Pioneer of Adult Education* (Liverpool University Press, 1957).

Kerrison, Robert Masters, *Observations and Reflections on the Bill now in progress through the House of Commons, for 'better regulating the Medical profession as far as regards apothecaries'*, . . . , n.p. (1815).

Lehmann, William C., *John Millar of Glasgow 1735-1801: His Life and Thought and his Contributions to Sociological Analysis* (Cambridge University Press, 1960).

Lyell K.M., *Memoir of Leonard Horner*, 2 vols. (London, 1890).

Anecdotes and Egotisms of Henry Mackenzie, ed. H.W. Thompson and Humphrey Milford (London, 1927).

Memoirs of the Life of the Rt. Hon. Sir James Mackintosh, ed. R.J. Mackintosh, 2 vols. (London, 1835).

The Miscellaneous Works of the Rt. Hon. Sir James Mackintosh, ed. R.J. Mackintosh (London, 1851).

Maudsley, Henry, 'Memoir of the late John Conolly M.D.', *Journal of Mental Science*, XII (1866), pp. 151-74.

Dissertations by Eminent Members of the Royal Medical Society (Edinburgh, 1892).

General List of the Members of the Medical Society of Edinburgh (Edinburgh, 1887).

Lord Melbourne's Papers, ed. Lloyd C. Sanders (Longman, 1889).

James Mill: Selected Economic Writings, introd. and ed. Donald N. Winch (Edinburgh and London, 1966).

Millar, John, *An Historical View of the English Government from the Settlement of the Saxons in Britain to the Revolution in 1688*, 4 vols. (London, 1803).

Mitchell, Leslie, *Holland House* (Duckworth, 1980).

Morgan, E. Victor, *The Theory and Practice of Central Banking 1797-1913*, Cambridge University Press, 1943).

Morrell, J.B., 'Science in Manchester and the University of Edinburgh, 1760-1840', *Artisan to Graduate: essays to commemorate the foundation in 1824 of the Manchester Mechanics' Institution, now in 1974 the University of Manchester Institute of Science and Technology*, ed. D.S.L. Cardwell (Manchester University Press, 1974), pp. 39-54.

Morris, R.J., *Cholera* (Croom Helm, 1976).

Napier, Macvey,'Stewart's *Philosophical Essays', Quarterly Review*, VI (1811), pp. 1-37.

Selections from the Correspondence of Macvey Napier, ed. Macvey Napier, (London 1877).

Neve, Michael, 'Science in a Commercial City: Bristol 1820-1860', *Metropolis and Province* (see Durey above), pp. 179-204.

Nomina Eorum qui Gradum Medicinae Doctoris in Academia Jacobi Sexti Scotorum Regis quae Edinburgi est adepti sunt 1705-1845 (Edinburgh, 1846).

Orange, Derek, 'Rational Dissent and Provincial Science: William Turner and the Newcastle Literary and Philosophy Society', *Metropolis and Province* (see Durey above), pp. 205-30.

Parker, Irene, *Dissenting Academies in England: Their Rise and Progress and their place among the Educational Systems of the Country*, (Cambridge University Press, 1914).

Porter, Roy, *English Society in the Eighteenth Century* (Penguin, 1982).

Porter, Roy, 'The Enlightenment in England', *The Enlightenment in National Contest*, ed. Roy Porter and Mikulas Teich, (Cambridge University Press, 1981), pp. 1-18.

Porter, Roy, *The Making of Geology: Earth Science in Britain 1660-*

1815 (Cambridge University Press, 1977).

Porter, R.S., 'Science, Provincial Culture and Public Opinion in Enlightenment England', *The British Journal for Eighteenth Century Studies*, II (1980), pp. 20-46.

Porter, William Smith, *Sheffield Literary and Philosophical Society: A Centenary Retrospect 1822-1922* (Sheffield, 1922).

Prichard, James Cowles, *Researches into the Physical History of Man*, introd. and ed. G.W. Stocking Jr (University of Chicago Press, 1973).

Rendall, Jane, *The Origins of the Scottish Enlightenment* (Macmillan Press, 1978).

Rice, C. Duncan, 'Scottish Enlightenment, American Revolution and Atlantic Reform', *Scotland Europe and the American Revolution* (see Hook, Andrew D. above), pp. 75-82.

Robertson, William, *Works*, 12 vols. (London, 1812).

Robertson, William, *Works*, 8 vols. (London, 1825).

Memoirs of the Life of Sir Samuel Romilly, written by himself, with a selection from his correspondence, ed. by his sons, 3 vols. (London, 1840).

Russell, John Earl, *Recollections and Suggestions 1813-1873*, 2nd edn (London, 1875).

Sanders, Lloyd C., *The Holland House Circle,* 2nd edn (Methuen, 1908).

Shapin, Steven and Barnes, Barry, 'Science, Nature and Control: Interpreting Mechanics' Institutes', *Social Studies of Science*, VII (1977), pp. 31-74.

Shapin, Steven and Thackray, Arnold, 'Prosopography as a Research Tool in History of Science: the British scientific community 1700-1900', *History of Science*, XII (1974), pp. 1-28.

Simon, Brian, *Studies in the History of Education 1780-1870* (Lawrence & Wishart, 1960)

Singer, Charles and Holloway, S.W.F., 'Early Medical Education in England in Relation to the Pre-History of London University', *Medical History*, IV (1960), pp. 1-17.

Sloan, Douglas, *The Scottish Enlightenment and the American College Ideal* (New York, 1971).

Smith, Adam, *An Inquiry into the Nature and Causes of the Wealth of Nations*, ed. R.H. Campbell, A.S. Skinner and W.B. Todd, 2 vols., (Clarendon Press, 1975).

The Correspondence of Adam Smith, ed. E.C. Mossner and I.S. Ross (Clarendon Press, 1977).

Smith, Adam, *Lectures on Jurisprudence*, ed. R.L. Meek, D.D. Raphael and P.G. Stein (Clarendon Press, 1978).

The Letters of Sydney Smith, ed. Nowell C. Smith, 2 vols. (Oxford University Press, 1953).

A General List of the Members of the Speculative Society (Edinburgh, 1814).

History of the Speculative Society of Edinburgh from its Institution in 1764 (Edinburgh, 1845).

Collected Works of Dugald Stewart, ed. Sir William Hamilton, 11 vols. (Constable, Edinburgh, 1854-60).

Thackray, Arnold, 'Natural Knowledge in Cultural Context: The Manchester Model', *American Historical Review*, LXXIX (1974), pp. 672-709.

Thomas, William, *The Philosophic Radicals: Nine Studies in Theory and Practice 1817-1841* (Clarendon Press, 1979).

Thomson, John, *An Account of the Life, Lectures and Writings of William Cullen, M.D.*, 2 vols. (Edinburgh, 1832-59).

Tuke, Samuel, *Description of the Retreat: an Institution year York for Insane Persons of the Society of Friends* [1813], reprinted with an introduction by Richard Hunter and Ida Macalpine (London, 1964).

Vassall Fox, Henry Richard [Lord Holland], *Further Memoirs of the Whig Party 1807-1821 with some miscellaneous reminiscences*, ed. Lord Stavordale (London, 1905).

Waddington, Ivan, 'The Struggle to Reform the Royal College of Physicians 1767-1771: a sociological analysis', *Medical History*, XVII (1973), pp. 107-26.

Walpole, Spencer, *The Life of Lord John Russell*, 2 vols., 2nd edn (Longman, 1889).

Welsh, David, *Account of the Life and Writings of Thomas Brown* (London, 1825).

The 'Pope' of Holland House: Selections from the Correspondence of John Whishaw and his Friends 1813-1840, ed. E. Seymour (London, 1906).

Ziegler, Philip, *Melbourne: a Biography of William Lamb, 2nd Viscount Melbourne* (Collins, 1967).

INDEX